Routledge Revivals

Comparative Industrial Relations

First published in 1985, *Comparative Industrial Relations* is a comprehensive introductory text exploring the subject of cross-national comparisons of industrial relations.

The book surveys, integrates and reviews a wealth of literature and research relating to comparative industrial relations structures and procedures. It covers key themes within industrial relations and incorporates material from a wide range of areas, including Western Europe, North America, Japan, and Australia. The considerable variety of differing practices and institutions are highlighted and examined, and extensive analysis and explanation is given to their similarities and differences.

Comparative Industrial Relations provides detailed and varied perspectives on the contemporary state of knowledge within this important field.

Comparative Industrial Relations

An Introduction to Cross-National Perspectives

By R. Bean

Routledge
Taylor & Francis Group
Routledge Revivals

First published in 1985
by Croom Helm Ltd.

This edition first published in 2020 by Routledge
2 Park Square, Milton Park, Abingdon, Oxon, OX14 4RN
and by Routledge
605 Third Avenue, New York, NY 10017

Routledge is an imprint of the Taylor & Francis Group, an informa business

Publisher's Note
The publisher has gone to great lengths to ensure the quality of this reprint but points out that some imperfections in the original copies may be apparent.

Disclaimer
The publisher has made every effort to trace copyright holders and welcomes correspondence from those they have been unable to contact.

A Library of Congress record exists under LCCN: 84022889

ISBN 13: 978-0-367-65075-9 (hbk)
ISBN 13: 978-1-003-12772-7 (ebk)

Comparative Industrial Relations

AN INTRODUCTION TO CROSS–NATIONAL PERSPECTIVES

R. BEAN

CROOM HELM
London & Sydney

Croom Helm Ltd, Provident House, Burrell Row,
Beckenham, Kent BR3 1AT
Croom Helm Australia Pty Ltd, First Floor, 139 King Street,
Sydney, NSW 2001, Australia

British Library Cataloguing in Publication Data

Bean, R.
Comparative industrial relations: an introduction
to cross-national perspectives.
1. Industrial relations
I. Title
331 HD6961

ISBN 0-7099-3251-0
ISBN 0-7099-3281-2 Pbk

CONTENTS

PREFACE

For some time there has been a developing interest in comparative studies as a sub-teaching area within industrial relations in universities and polytechnics together with a considerable expansion in recent years in the number of industrial relations research studies which are avowedly comparative in their orientation – particularly those relating to socio-political influences on the patterns of industrial conflict. Yet there is a notable absence of student texts in this field which are not either dated and/or overly descriptive and factual in the material which they include. Over the past decade the proliferating output of monographs, symposia and journal literature concerned with international and comparative aspects of the subject has been impressive in its volume and breadth, if not always in its depth or quality. A specialised periodical, the *Bulletin of Comparative Labour Relations*, has also appeared on the scene. Moreover, the better studies

> have progressed beyond merely describing country-by-country variations in trade union structure, collective bargaining institutions and public policy frameworks. Attempts are made to provide analytical tools for cross-national comparisons and build theories to account for different patterns of industrial relations. (Slack, 1980, p. 27)

Thus the aim of this book is to present an introduction to the broad domain of comparative industrial relations via a survey and a drawing-together of the recent, more analytic literature, thereby providing some varied (although by no means exhaustive) perspectives on the current state of knowledge in a number of mainstream topics within the field. In consequence, the treatment adopted is both selective – which inevitably involves some arbitrary decisions of inclusion and omission – and thematic. It is organised around a number of central topics rather than being in the form of a side-by-side treatment of a number of individual countries, that is to say, by focusing on issues across national boundaries it adopts what Blanpain (ed.) (1982b) has termed an 'integrated' approach. This avoids a concentration on the domestic minutiae and empirical details of industrial relations practices within particular countries which are both readily available elsewhere (e.g. Blanpain (ed.) 1978; Blum, 1981) and may be of less enduring interest since they can soon become outdated.

The justification for the approach adopted here is that in an attempt to explain systematically the uniformities and diversities encountered in cross-national industrial relations selected countries might usefully be used to provide data for comparative purposes, or as 'ideal types' of particular patterns, but they are not in themselves sufficient. Rather, the focus needs to be directed towards the factors that determine the observed variations, making it necessary to go beyond what Kerr *et al.* (1962) call 'topographical studies describing the lay of the land in the individual countries':

> to go beyond saying that in Nigeria it was this way and in Turkey that [since] looking at one country at a time each situation appeared historically unique and the totality of the detail was almost incomprehensible. (p. 11)

Dunlop (1972, p. 102) has described such detailed, institutional comparisons between countries as tending 'to portray an industrial relations zoo' in which form, rather than substance and purpose, is emphasised.

In any case, selections of country-by-country studies often found in comparative volumes, although they may be individually revealing, are frequently repetitious in content, as well as tending to be preoccupied with the maze of diverse institutional forms and bargaining arrangements. It has also been pointed out (Kassalow, 1969) that many are not genuinely comparative at all since the individual countries could easily stand in their own right as they are largely disconnected, drawing little or nothing from each other, and having little in the way of a common, integrating analytical framework. Shalev regards these sort of studies as displaying what he calls the 'Victorian traveller's approach' since

> Rather like the Victorian gentleman on his 'grand tour' the reader is presented with a diverse selection of exotic ports of call and left to draw his own conclusions about their relevance to each other and to the traveller himself. (Shalev, 1981, p. 242)

In this book it is not the intention, therefore, to examine in great detail the structure and practices of industrial relations in individual countries as such. It is hoped that the format which has been utilised, by concentrating upon analysis and explanation and drawing together an extensive but scattered literature in this field of enquiry, will prove particularly suitable for the needs of undergraduates in departments of economics, sociology, business and management studies.

In writing the book I have incurred a number of debts. Stan Jones and Tony Lane provided useful suggestions, Alan Gladstone and Keith Sisson kindly allowed me to see prior to publication their studies on employers' organisations and the staff of Liverpool University library, particularly the late Mike Jones, were most helpful in obtaining reference material. The text has greatly benefited from the constructive criticisms of the publisher's readers; Peter Sowden of Croom Helm was constantly encouraging from the outset and Vivienne Oakes typed the manuscript most efficiently and uncomplainingly. To all of them I express my thanks.

1 INTRODUCTION: COMPARATIVE APPROACHES

The academic field of industrial relations is typically defined as being the study of the various aspects of job regulation (Bain and Clegg, 1974), with a consequent attendant focus on rule-making in the employment relationship. Alternatively, for those who regard this definition as too restrictive – particularly in its implicit overtones of stability, regularity and mutual accommodation between the parties[1] – the central core of the subject is the 'study of the process of control over work relations' (Hyman, 1975, p. 12). This latter emphasis is intended to highlight the underlying but centrally important issues of control, power and interests together with the generation of conflict, rather than with mechanisms and techniques for its resolution. Such a definition considerably broadens the scope of the subject away from a traditional institutional orientation, towards an examination of wider societal influences which affect the character of relations between workers, employers and their respective collective organisations. The primacy of the power relationship has been stressed by Korpi (1981, p. 190), who maintains that

> of basic importance for understanding the functioning of the industrial relations system is the distribution of power resources between sellers and buyers of manpower and changes in this distribution. The power resources . . . are, on the one hand, the pattern of ownership of capital and of organisation among employers, and on the other hand, union organisation and political power.

Frames of Reference in Industrial Relations

A recent survey of industrial relations research traditions viewed from an international standpoint suggests that studies tend to cluster around two underlying assumptions: first, the 'pluralist–institutionalist' approach, which is especially predominant in Anglo-Saxon countries. Here the discipline is regarded as being of an applied and pragmatic nature and research is empirically oriented, usually with an emphasis on procedural and institutional concerns, towards policy relevance and problem-solving. Second, in contrast in a country, such as Italy, the system of stratification and class structure in society forms an important part of the analysis, which is as much concerned with workers and the working class as with unions and collective bargaining. In class-oriented studies 'politics, political action and the tensions between employers and employees are prominent . . . and less attention is devoted to the actual procedures and practice of industrial relations' (Doeringer, 1981, pp. 10-11). These two assumptions are not mutually exclusive, however, and research formulations in France, Japan and Sweden, for instance, have utilised both.

Closely related to these contrasting emphases regarding the nature and parameters of the subject is the question of devising an appropriate, conceptual framework of analysis in industrial relations, as well as the extent to which this is explicitly grounded in theory. Doeringer distinguishes between three major divisions: a pragmatic approach in which theory plays little or no role although, as Eldridge (1975, p. 7) has reminded us 'the pragmatists in emphasising the need for realistic solutions often carry a good deal of conceptual and theoretical baggage around with them'; secondly, a Marxist approach, stressing class relations and conflict irreconcilability; and, following Dunlop's (1958) seminal work, the highly influential 'systems' model focusing on the rules of industrial relations and their determinants. In Dunlop's conception of an interdependent industrial relations system three principal actors,[2] namely workers, managers – as well as their representative organisations – together with certain state agencies, all interact to establish a network of rules governing their relationship in the workplace, the rules being the output of the system. The actors, however, are subject to pressures and constraints arising from the environmental setting in which they operate, assumed to be given and exogenously determined.[3] This background context within which the rules (both substantive and procedural[4]) are developed impinges upon the relationship between the actors and the nature of the rules which they establish. It consists of technological factors, product and labour market determinants, social influences affecting the ideology of the actors, as well as the political environment which, for Dunlop, consists of power relations in the larger society.

Moreover, a basic premise of Dunlop's prescription for the advancement of knowledge in industrial relations is the need to break away from the restrictive and myopic confines of problem-solving, institutional studies within individual countries – what has been termed an 'ethno-centric' bias – in favour of broader comparisons over the course of time and across countries. He suggests that the systems model is applicable to the study of comparative industrial relations since, although every county displays special or particularistic industrial relations characteristics because of differences in the environmental settings in which they operate, 'the attention to rule-making in industrial relations systems provides a common denominator for the comparative analysis of different forms' (p. 27). It is probably more valid, however, to argue that the main use of his model is as a means of identifying the relevant, strategic variables and ordering empirical data. It gives little guidance as to the individual weightings to be attached to explanatory variables for evaluating between them, or the precise ways in which they interact, and lacks predictive power (Gill, 1969).

Comparative Industrial Relations

As regards the nature of comparative investigation itself within the subject, Sturmthal (1958, p. 77) defines it as 'research dealing with the same (or similar or related) phenomena in different countries'. A further conceptual distinction may be drawn between 'comparative' industrial relations, and 'international' and 'foreign' studies within the field. International, or transnational, studies deal with those institutions and phenomena which cross national boundaries, such as the industrial relations aspects of multinational companies or the international labour movement. In studies of 'foreign' labour movements in countries other than one's own, the selected countries are usually treated separately and comparisons between them are rarely made (Meyers, 1967). This latter category may form the raw material or foundation for comparisons, but such studies are to be regarded as preparatory, rather than being fully comparative, since the questions asked of the data are at best implicit and few analytical statements are drawn from them. Essentially, then, comparative industrial relations is a systematic method of investigation relating to two or more countries which has analytic rather than descriptive implications.

In addition to the need for identifying appropriate bench-marks and a suitable framework of analysis, we may also ask about the rationale for engaging in work within the field of comparative industrial relations. What can be learned by comparing one system with another? Should comparison be undertaken for its own sake simply out of intrinsic interest or intellectual challenge, or should it be directed towards some more closely-defined objective? Comparative studies can lead to a greater understanding of the factors and processes which determine industrial relations phenomena since 'the comparative method leads to questions regarding the reasons for the observed comparisons and contrasts' (Dunlop, 1958, p. vi). The studies can be illuminating largely because, as Banks (1974) puts it, of the way in which they reveal differences between systems which in many other respects are similar, and similarities in systems which otherwise are different. Hence they throw into relief and bring out the significant aspects of the phenomenon in question. As an illustration, he notes that despite the many differences between industrial relations under communist systems in certain countries such as the Soviet Union and Yugoslavia, and those under the capitalist system in Britain, the emergence of the shopfloor representative in the workplace as a crucial role-player is common to all, albeit making representations about different issues. Used in this way the comparative approach can afford a perspective and lead to greater insight into domestic issues by sharpening understanding of the same phenomena in one's own country.

There may also be a desire to utilise comparative studies for practical policy considerations by attempting to derive 'lessons' from overseas experience. Comparative findings might be used for normative, or even polemical, purposes in order to support or oppose certain aspects of a country's domestic industrial relations policy. Recently, for instance, West German trade unions undertook a campaign to secure the legal prohibition of the lockout during industrial disputes. For this they prepared a comparative study to show that the lockout was far more extensively used by German employers than by employers elsewhere (Schregle, 1981). Sometimes a case will be made on the basis of what is known to happen abroad for the actual transfer or importation into a country of particular industrial relations methods or techniques. Efforts were once made to export American-type trade unions and collective bargaining to occupied countries such as Japan in the early post-World War II period.[5] Yet a regression from those principles soon occurred after it became apparent that the orderly industrial relations which were sought were not being achieved (Levine, 1958; Barkin, 1980).

The hazardous nature of any such attempts at interchangeability or piecemeal transplant forms a recurrent theme in the literature, and has become something of a commonplace. Comparative industrial relations is not an 'export–import exercise' (Schregle, 1981) since industrial relations phenomena reflect the characteristic features of the society in which they operate. It follows that because a practice may work well in one country, there is no guarantee that it will continue to do so should it be transferred elsewhere, especially if it conflicts with indigenous traditions and social values. More generally, it has been contended that international comparisons can be a trap:

> 'Look how much better the Lilliputians do it', is a tempting cry, but the more one looks into it the more one finds that the Lilliputians aren't a fair comparison with us: they haven't got our antiquated industries . . . our legal system; and they are less than six inches tall. (Kahn-Freund and Hepple, 1972, p. 1)

There is a need to proceed cautiously regarding the possibility of making out-of-context transfers to different social and economic milieus. As Kahn-Freund (1974) has shown, although transplantation of labour relations rules relating to individual workers – such as legislative protection against unfair dismissal – is relatively straightforward, this is not the case with provisions of a *collective* nature. Collective bargaining institutions and rules cannot be expected to function adequately when wrenched out of their original context and implanted elsewhere, since they are closely linked with the structure and organisation of political and social power in their own environment or habitat.

Numerous studies attest to the validity of this insight within the industrial relations field. In the case of Britain, Wedderburn (1974, p. 31) notes that the failure of the 1971 Industrial Relations Act, many of whose legalistic provisions had US antecedents, 'might serve as a warning against over simple enthusiasm for the translation of developments from other countries into the British framework'. Similarly, for those who are impressed with the low level of industrial conflict characteristic of the Swedish industrial relations system as it traditionally operated, she points to the significance of broader influences. Swedish society has experienced a wide measure of consensus about priorities in respect of general social goals, not only within the industrial relations sphere. As a result,

> this Swedish consensus is a precedent to the development of certain institutional forms rather than a result of them, and it would be useless for Britain to look to the forms rather than to the antecedent substance. (ibid., p. 38)

As well as the case of Sweden, a good deal of interest has also been shown in recent years in certain features of industrial relations in West Germany and Yugoslavia. In regard to the co-determination system in Germany, it is quite possible that the institutional arrangements which appertain under that system may be a model for other countries. In Europe the EEC has already been strongly influenced, *inter alia*, by German and Dutch experience in its attempts to devise a common statute for employee participation within European companies. But it should be remembered that more than institutional factors are involved, since the co-determination system is also 'an expression of specific social and attitudinal characteristics which are not exportable' (Schregle, 1978, p. 97). In the case of the Yugoslavian system of self-management, any notions of possible imitation would need to take account of the specific ideological and socio-political context in which the Yugoslav experiment took place because

> it is extremely doubtful that the overall system . . . can ever be made to work without the kind of total ideological commitment and radical transformation which underlie its operation in socialist Yugoslavia. (Miller, 1978, p. 285)

All this is not to deny the possible relevance of the results of comparative experience as an aid to practitioners and policy-makers who may hope to utilise ideas, approaches or techniques adopted in other countries. But it is necessary to take into account not only the specific features of given industrial relations arrangements but also the environmental context which impinges upon them, and therefore the appropriateness of any transfer to a different context. It is not necessary to adopt a 'systems' theory approach, interrelating the background conditions within a social system, in order to recognise that when some particular aspect of another country's industrial relations is removed from its social, political and cultural surroundings it may then lose its validity and rationale.

In the Japanese setting, for example, it would be wholly inappropriate to conclude that a particular element such as seniority-based wage payments would be desirable as a policy prescription elsewhere, without a prior understanding of how that wage system relates both to the general security of employment in large Japanese firms and, possibly, the cultural assumptions concerning the importance of age in other parts of Japanese society (Dore, 1973). It may also be noted that some US multinational companies attempted, quite unsuccessfully, to introduce into Japan (and other Asian countries) wage systems based on job evaluation and merit rating, as opposed to the more usual Japanese system of seniority and educational qualifications (ILO, 1973).

In the case of many of the former British territories in Africa they had something of a common industrial relations heritage built around an institutional framework in the British mould which was fostered by colonial administrations. Yet here too, it was ultimately found to be totally inadequate for the needs of the countries concerned (Kilby, 1973; Gladstone, 1980).

Theoretical Considerations

In fact, as we have already indicated, there can be little doubt that the most important and overriding purpose of comparative studies is not for any practical policy implications which may be derived. Rather, by exploring the determinants of similarities and differences found between national systems, they can help promote the development of industrial relations as an academic discipline. Investigation which is directed towards international comparisons should prove more illuminating as an aid to systematic explanation than confining observations to a single national system. Does a certain relationship retain its explanatory power for a number of countries rather than just for one – can it stand up to a comparative analysis? Findings which are replicated throughout a number of countries, or which can be shown to vary under specified conditions,[6] become much more powerful since 'an explanatory theory of industrial relations cannot be based upon the narrow range of industrial relations processes observable in one, or even a few, countries' (Walker, 1967, p. 108). Findings based on very limited evidence cannot be regarded as being firmly established and need to be verified by means of additional observations and cases.

By means of a comparative approach, as Galenson (1952, p. v) expresses it, 'hypotheses that grew out of peculiar conditions in one country can . . . be tested against other bodies of experience, and reconciliation sought in differences among the determining factors.' Thus the aim of comparative analysis is to promote wider understanding of, and foster new insights into, industrial relations, either by showing what is unique about any one set of national arrangements or, equally well, reducing what might appear to be acutely specific and distinctive national characteristics by demonstrating their recurrence elsewhere (Rose, 1983).

However, in order to make meaningful comparisons more is needed than merely comparative information, since within any field of study theory is necessary both to provide a framework for the systematic analysis and accumulation of the existing stock of knowledge and to serve as a guide for the selection of research problems. Theoretical studies in this sense might adopt an approach which utilises the findings from a variety of national contexts in order to produce generalisations that attempt 'to distinguish the invariant from the variant, the stable and continuing from the fluctuating and transitory' (Schollhammer, 1973, p. 24). Alternatively, the studies could begin explicitly with *a priori* hypotheses about the relationships between environmental variables and industrial relations arrangements and proceed to test their validity – corroborating, relativising, refining or rejecting them – via an examination of the experience of a number of different countries. With this latter approach there is a measure of agreement, however, that industrial relations theories themselves need to be built up from observed facts rather than from abstract speculation and require to be tested (and possibly modified) in the light of new information. There is thus a reciprocal, feedback relationship between theorising and observation (Clegg and Bain, 1974; Hill and Thurley, 1974).

Whatever the ultimate objectives, the fact remains that a good deal of the *existing* work within the comparative industrial relations field, although often rich and insightful, has not so far been explicitly theoretical in either its purpose or method (Shalev, 1980a). With notable exceptions such as Clegg (1976), many studies present empirically derived information arising from cross-national investigations, often relating to institutions and practices, which is then analysed and interpreted with no direct orientation towards theoretical considerations. Yet, as we shall see, the last few years have witnessed a remarkable upsurge in research in those areas where quantification is possible, such as strike activity and its determinants (see Chapter 6). In comparison with institutionally-oriented studies this kind of work is much more directed towards the specific testing of hypotheses via the use of multivariate, statistical techniques and it can utilise variables from a number of relevant disciplines. Although the quantitative approach raises its own problems of methodology and measurement in attempting to model complex behaviour, it can be useful in sharpening concepts, providing some common ground between different disciplines and isolating the effects of one particular variable whilst allowing for the influence of the others.

Another strategy which has been suggested is to attempt at the outset to ground comparative analysis firmly within the context of explicit and already well-formulated theoretical debate, such as 'convergence' theory (Shalev, 1980a). This particular perspective is based on one of the most influential studies in the comparative labour field in the last two decades, Kerr *et al.*, *Industrialism and Industrial Man* (1962). In this book the integrating strand in the analysis of industrial relations within developed and developing countries is the universal drive towards industrialisation. Their thesis maintains that as technology – seen as the driving-force of change – and industrialisation become more uniformly applied the countries involved will tend, over an extended period, to develop more similar industrial features, including their industrial relations arrangements, practices and 'web of rules'. Nevertheless, it is recognised that industrial relations will continue to reflect elements of diversity as well as uniformity. Significant national differences will reflect, for instance, the nature of the pre-industrial economic and political order whose lingering effects will continue to influence the newly industrialising society, as well as the particular historical periods at which countries began to industrialise. A national industrial relations system which had its formative stages during the past 20 years is more likely to accord a greater role to the state, for instance, than those developed in earlier periods when the government's role as employer and regulator was less pervasive.

In a subsequent postscript (Kerr *et al.*, 1971), the original convergence thesis itself has become somewhat modified away from an emphasis on a trend towards uniformity. The restatement holds that no identical systems will emerge, and that the convergence of industrial societies is towards a range of alternatives rather than to a particular point. It is now recognised that the industrialisation process is complex and that

> there are several marked differences in the way that industrialisation has proceeded country-by-country; that there is no single logic of industrialisation, though there may only be a few paths. (Hill and Thurley, 1974, p. 154)

Comparative studies by Sorge and Warner (1980) in Britain and West Germany also suggest that although factories in different countries may be very similar in terms of their size, technology and products they can, nevertheless, bring forth distinctly dissimilar forms of organisation and industrial relations.

Yet notwithstanding these specific criticisms the notion that one source of difference within cross-national industrial relations may reflect the different stage of development that societies have reached, along some continuum – that the stage of industrialisation affects the character of industrial relations – this provides one possible focus for inter-country studies. It suggests ideas and implications which can be tested by further research. Dore (1973) used this framework in a comparison of the contrasting employment systems in British and Japanese industry; and Kobrin (1976) empirically tested the convergence thesis itself using cross-national research for more than 90 countries and found some support for it. He was able to show a reduction in the variance of some selected indicators of convergence (as measured by the standard deviation) at higher levels of industrialisation.

Historical and Cultural Factors

The exposition of the convergence thesis also points to the fact that countries which are alike in other respects would be expected to develop significant differences in their industrial relations if they had industrialised at different historical periods. In fact, it is clear that the main characteristics of national industrial relations, their dominant and distinctive features, seem to be established at a fairly early stage in the industrial development of a country. Subsequently, in the absence of major dislocations such as war or revolution, the provisions appear to show a good deal of tenacity, retaining many of their early characteristics despite subsequent evolution. Thus the central and distinctive features of 'voluntarism' in Britain, arbitration courts in Australia and Denmark, and the concept of 'exclusive' bargaining representation in the United States emerged early in the formation of those countries' industrial relations (Kerr *et al.*, 1962). Britain, as the first industrialised nation, pioneered the development of many industrial relations institutions and arrangements. In consequence, its contemporary industrial relations scene has been markedly conditioned by values, conventions and traditions that were established in the past. Hyman (1982b, p. 108) reiterates the general point that in industrial relations 'the present must be viewed as historically conditioned and historically contingent, and as incomprehensible except by means of historical understanding.'

In the case of developing countries, different dates of origin may in themselves be expected to lead to quite different features in their industrial relations despite the attainment of a similar stage of economic development. Dunlop has explained that

> A national industrial relations system formulated with labour organisations which are an adjunct to a successful nationalist movement, which has secured independence, may be expected to show some characteristics different from [one] in which national independence antedated the union movements or in which the union movements played a minor role in the nationalist movement. The relations between the labour organisation and the government or the party of independence, and hence the status of these actors . . . may be expected to be quite different in these two types of situations. (Dunlop, 1958, p. 308)

The consequence of all this for a study of comparative industrial relations is that international differences cannot be understood solely in terms of cross-sectional analysis at any one point in time. Instead, longitudinal studies incorporating a time dimension are also required for supplying historical perspective, together with a sharper appreciation of change through time and the conditions which generate it.

Employment relationships have been influenced, not only by the environmental or contextual variables already discussed, but also in some societies by distinctive cultural features. An understanding of industrial relations in the Netherlands, for instance, requires an appreciation of the vertical segregation (or 'pillarised' structure) between religiously defined groupings and non-denominational organisations which for long characterised Dutch society and affected not only unions but also employers. In that country for many years organisation at the social, cultural and political level was founded upon a system of ideological blocs. More generally, Blum (1981) concluded from an examination of 27 countries that the form which industrial relations takes in any one nation does markedly reflect the culture of which it is a part. From a methodological standpoint, however, one problem is that without some analysis of the cultural determinants themselves, and their influence on other variables, this is something of a non-explanation.[7] 'Culture' can be defined in a myriad of ways and often appears to be used not as an independent, or explanatory, variable but as a residual one representing a variety of unspecified influences. Nevertheless, a recent study (Ahiauzu, 1982) emphasises that culture[8] is an important environmental factor which cannot be ignored in cross-national studies of industrial relations. It views the connection between culture and job regulation as occurring through the shaping influence of culture upon the attitudinal characteristics of the actors and, therefore, on their behaviour. Thus, in societies with different cultures objective situations may be interpreted in markedly different ways.

Methodology

In the light of the preceding discussion it is necessary to consider the methodology of comparative industrial relations more fully since it is clear that to be of value the studies need to be appropriately designed and the cases to be compared require careful selection. In terms of the question of what might usefully be compared, *typologies* are very important in comparative analysis. They are a classificatory device in the form of a limited number of recognisable patterns into which industrial relations arrangements can be grouped according to their common elements. Since careful attention needs to be given to the economic, political and social setting when analysing industrial relations in various countries, it is useful to compare countries with broadly similar characteristics in these respects: 'By looking at industrial relations problems within a given grouping one achieves an "automatic", major reduction in the number of background . . . variables' (Kassalow, 1968, p. 103).

Broad groupings of this kind are typically based upon the nature of the political system and the stage of economic development of the countries included, such as the threefold distinction between western market-industrialised societies, communist states and developing Third World countries. In some cases we may wish to compare the categories themselves such as the advanced/underdeveloped dichotomy, in order to illuminate any evolutionary aspects of industrial relations. For other purposes narrower groupings within the market-industrialised category may be more appropriate. For instance, some years ago among writers in the United States an evolutionist theory of trade union development was popular. It was claimed that unions set out by being radical and militant in their outlook, but then went through a 'maturation' process, ultimately becoming pragmatic and less militant. This type of generalisation, however, was based on the assumption that US union development was the norm, and only British, Swedish and German unions were included in the comparison. Other European countries, such as France and Italy, were excluded because no such uniform pattern could be found there (von Beyme, 1980). Therefore, rather than attempting to generate theories which hold good for *all* countries, generalisations may only be possible if 'types' can be established. Yet it remains true that unless the typologies are elaborated beyond a mere classificatory and descriptive labelling of different situations – that is, by attempting to specify the conditions under which each type develops – they remain at only a very preliminary stage of theorising.

Within any given grouping there is a further need to determine the number of countries to be investigated and also the level at which the comparison should proceed. There are strong grounds for limiting the sample size of the investigation because it is not the number of countries *per se* which is usually important, but rather the range of variation which they provide (Walker, 1967). Similarly, a very restricted comparison – perhaps of only two or three cases – permits a more intensive analysis than may be possible with multi-country studies and if the cases are dealt with in a consistent and systematic way minimises 'the danger of lapsing into either vacuous description or superficial comparison' (Shalev, 1980a, p. 40). However, a possible limitation of this approach is that industrial relations variables are themselves frequently clustered into national contexts. Consequently, when the number of countries is small and each very similar, the clustering becomes particularly tight, thereby making it a matter of arbitrary choice to select any one variable for explanatory purposes. In such cases there may be a need to take account of a somewhat larger number of markedly different national contexts in order to make possible a more precise isolation of explanatory variables (Sorge, 1976).

Once the countries to be compared have been selected, much of the analysis often focuses on the national level, in the form of comparative macro studies, which are sometimes extended to include industry-level comparisons. In contrast, relatively few investigations centre on the workplace – although there are exceptions such as Dore (1973), Gallie (1978), Jacobs *et al.* (1978) and Marsh *et al.* (1981). Marsh's study of the engineering industry in Britain and West Germany adopts the standpoint that, whatever the form which industrial relations takes, similar topics for regulation will appear, thus providing a basis for comparison. The structures and activities involved in regulating relations at workplace level, such as wage payment systems, employee hiring and work discipline are then compared, subject-by-subject, for five engineering plants in each country.

It has long been recognised, however, that international comparisons of industrial relations which are confined to the national level may produce misleading results because of the possible dominance of one or more particular industries within a given country. Since there are substantial differences between industrial relations across industries, which may be unrelated to the national context in which they operate, what is really an 'industry' effect could be misinterpreted as being a 'national' effect in a comparative study confined solely to the national level.[9] To overcome this problem and allow for differences in the industry-mix between different countries industrial relations at industry level also need to be taken into account. That is to say, it is useful to examine the double variation of both national *and* industry factors. By comparing similar industries across countries the more industry-specific forces of technical and market contexts are held fairly constant. It is then possible to test for any separate impact of environmental forces appertaining to the national level, in terms of broader social and political influences.

Such an approach was originally utilised by Dunlop (1958) in his examination of available evidence from the coal mining and building industries across a number of countries. He showed the predominant influence in coal mining of the industry factors of a common technology and similar market or budgetary constraints in shaping certain rules in that industry, including those concerned with safety, lay-off procedures and wage structures. The building industry was also found to display common features in many countries. These included highly competitive product markets, with many small-sized enterprises, ease of entry and subcontracting, together with an unstructured labour market typified by short job duration at variable work sites, as well as much self-employment. The special characteristics of the industry itself led to an emphasis on rules designed to regulate the forms of product and labour market competition. However, in both industries other rules, relating to the status of the actors and their organisations, bargaining representation and union security (closed shop) arrangements, were largely influenced by features of the national industrial relations environment within each country.

A similar strategy integrating the national and industry levels has also been adopted by the Geneva-based International Institute for Labour Studies (IILS). Its comparative research programme has been designed so that

> variations between industries in the crucial determinants of industrial relations, and in the relative strength of such determining factors, can be studied against the range of variation provided by international differences. (IILS, 1969)

The differential impact of national and industry environmental forces upon the structure, process and outcomes of industrial relations have been examined empirically for the important metalworking industry across five countries. The findings suggest that, although there is an interacting effect between the two, many of the fundamental characteristics which are shared by all the cross-national systems investigated for that industry are the result of a common response to modern technological development and mechanised factory production. In contrast, it appears that most of the distinguishing features are the result of differences in the national, rather than in the industry, environments (Derber, 1976).

Problems in Comparative Studies

It is apparent from the foregoing discussion that comparative industrial relations is by no means an easy field of study and has considerable inherent problems. It is not only that, as with industrial relations generally, it is multidisciplinary in its dimensions but it reaches across cultures – thereby exacerbating the difficulties of finding appropriate bases for making inter-country comparisons. There can also be problems in ensuring a measure of concept-equivalence across societies, since what are nominally identical practices or institutions may perform varying functions, or have a very different significance. The French use 'participation', for instance, in one sense to mean 'profit sharing', whereas the term is more usually understood in the sense of participation by workers in the management of enterprises (Blanpain, 1974). We also know that in a number of countries labour disputes are brought before so-called 'Labour Courts' for resolution. But in any attempt to compare these institutions on an international basis there are immediate difficulties of terminology in that bodies with the same name may perform different functions. The West German Labour Court, for instance, is empowered to settle labour disputes by means of statutory binding decisions whereas the Irish Labour Court acts only as a conciliation body. In some other countries Labour Court functions are performed by bodies with different names such as Labour or Industrial Tribunals. Schregle's (1981) approach to this basic problem of what is comparable in cross-national studies is to compare the methods and ways in which particular industrial relations *functions* are carried out in various countries, rather than simply comparing institutions and procedures carrying the same designation. Consequently, a comparative study of the settlement of labour disputes through statutory binding decisions would have to omit the Irish Labour Court (despite its name), but include other bodies such as Industrial Tribunals in Britain, Conciliation and Arbitration Boards in Mexico and Labour Tribunals in India.[10]

As well as difficulties arising from terminological variations, Henley (1978) also points to other fundamental issues in this respect. He notes the erroneous conclusions which have been drawn from comparing the functioning of the Kenyan Industrial Court with apparently functionally similar wage-regulating institutions in New Zealand and Australia, in the absence of any consideration of the vast differences in the nature and basis of trade union power as between African countries and industrialised economies. As we have indicated, there can be problems in attempting to extract a single institution or rule from a national industrial relations system in order to compare it with what happens elsewhere since

> Institutions must be considered within the general context of the industrial relations system of which they are an integral part . . . [given that] the point of departure of international comparison cannot be an institution as such but must be the function it carries out. And functions are a reflection of the operation of the industrial relations system in its entirety. (Schregle, 1981, p. 22)

It is also important to try to avoid the tunnel-vision whereby industrial relations arrangements elsewhere are viewed from the particular perspectives and orientations of, say, Anglo-Saxon countries.

Despite the inherent difficulties in comparative work it has been argued that an international perspective has always been implicit to some extent in the study of industrial relations. For many years this was confined mainly to comparative considerations embracing strong ideological overtones, such as factors which have engendered 'the labour problem' (Weber, 1974). Yet, as we have noted, more recent work has adopted a wider focus and a more analytical approach to the subject. It provides a way of helping to dismantle and correct oversimplified explanations where generalisations have been made from particular cases – or even on the basis of a single example – which clearly will not stand up to broader comparative investigation. For instance, one important factor put forward to explain the growth of trade union membership among white-collar workers in Britain has been government policy which created a favourable climate for such union expansion. The more general international implications of this thesis, however, may require modification since in a country like Sweden, which has a very high level of white-collar union density, government action was apparently not a necessary condition for the growth of such unions (Adams, 1974).

The method of enquiry employed in much of the work within the comparative field proceeds at the empirical level[11] and arrives at more general conclusions through a process of inductive reasoning, or more *ad hoc* interpretive insights. Relatively few studies begin with an explicit (*ex-ante*) theory which is then rigorously tested against the data. In large part this is a reflection of the underdeveloped state of industrial relations theory itself to whose improvement, by way of helping more general theory construction, well-designed comparative studies may be expected to contribute. It is thus a field of considerable potential. As Shalev (1981) points out, comparative analysis not only raises substantively interesting and important questions but it also offers a natural and fruitful avenue for the advance of the discipline as a whole.

Plan of the Book

In the remainder of the book we survey and discuss the findings of the literature relating to the comparison of national industrial relations systems and their particular aspects in terms of an analysis of the major actors and their organisations together with their activities and interactions. Chapters 2–4 concern workers' trade unions, employers and managements as well as collective bargaining – in most western countries the most important mechanism for determining wages and employment conditions. There follows in Chapter 5 an examination of the increasing role of the state and its agencies as a regulator within the industrial relations field. Chapter 6 deals with strikes and industrial conflict, an area where more specific hypothesis-testing via quantitative methods is possible. As a result, there has been a recent proliferation of studies seeking to explain international differences in strike activity. Similarly, a good deal of attention has been directed to the important and topical issues of workers' participation in enterprise decision-making, along with 'international' studies concerned with the operation and labour relations implications of multinational corporations. These matters are discussed in Chapters 7 and 8.

The first eight chapters principally concern comparative aspects of industrial relations in advanced, market-type economies in Western Europe, the USA, Japan and Australia although there is some discussion of the role of trade unions in communist countries and of the Yugoslav self-management system. Industrialised countries with a market economy possess at least some basic similarities and common elements of importance which allow comparative examination. Chapter 9, however, relates to the special features within a markedly different environment of industrial relations in Third World, developing countries, where not only is the state the largest single employer and the number of wage-earners a small part of the economically active population, but in addition the trade unions perform a dual role. As well as the traditional function of protecting and furthering their members' interests, they are also expected to play a role in the country's development effort towards economic growth. This duality presents certain inconsistencies which, as we shall see, are not easily reconcilable. A brief overview of comparative industrial relations in Chapter 10 completes the book.

We begin, however, with a discussion of the role and functions of trade unions in comparative perspective, primarily within western industrialised economies.

Notes

1. Ideological overtones are illustrated in a study of Norwegian industrial relations where the 'stable' system in that country is contrasted with the British, which is described as having all the appearance of 'an anarchists' football match' (Balfour, 1972, p. 52).

2. Dunlop wanted a less passive term than 'participants', and therefore used 'actors' in the sense of 'doers' or 'reagents'. Sociologists would regard this conceptualisation as being broadly equivalent to 'role-players'.

3. It can be argued that they are partly endogenous (internally determined) and interact with the industrial relations system, for example the parties' attempts to influence the pace of technological development and control market structure via the exercise of industrial and political power.

4. It is usual to distinguish between 'substantive' rules of industrial relations which deal with wages, hours and working conditions and set the standards of employment, and 'procedural' devices for administering the substantive rules and for the peaceful settlement of industrial disputes.

5. 'We Americans have hoped that we could transplant our industrial relations practices into these countries, but the soil has not been receptive' (Ross and Hartman, 1960, p. 177).

6. Some writers view comparative methodology in the social sciences as a (limited) counterpart to the controlled experiment in the natural sciences, enabling observation of differences made to the phenomenon under investigation by varying circumstances in different countries. (See Porter, 1967.)

7. Compare Marsh and Mannari (1981, p. 458): 'All too often "culture" or "values" are used as explanations when what is needed is better theory.'

8. In his study, culture is conceived as being the historically-developed and learned pattern of beliefs, values and customs of a people.

9. For a discussion of the problems of separating industry and country effects in relation to strikes, see Edwards (1977), pp. 551–70.

10. Similarly, an international comparison of the extent of worker influence on management decision-making would not confine comparison of works councils in, say, West Germany with similar formal institutional schemes for worker participation elsewhere. In the case of Britain it would also investigate the role of shop steward organisation and in the United States the local union.

11. 'Empiricism involves observation, classification and the evaluation of relations between observables' (Marsden, 1982, p. 235). Critics would maintain that observation which is unguided by theory implies that what the empiricist sees depends on where he stands, i.e. his vision is partly obscured by his own preconceptions.

Further Reading

Two major, recent articles on comparative approaches to industrial relations are Shalev (1980a) and Schregle (1981), although the earlier articles by Walker (1967) and Kassalow (1968) for the International Institute for Labour Studies are well worth reading. There is also a useful introduction in the symposium edited by Blanpain (1982b). For a good discussion of the possibility of 'exporting' the industrial relations models of particular countries, see Kassalow (1983).

2 TRADE UNIONS

Trade unions are institutional representatives of worker interests both within the labour market and in the wider society, and they accentuate the collective rather than the individual power-resources of employees. However, as well as basic similarities there are also major differences as between trade union movements in advanced industrialised countries, not only in the extent of their membership density but also in their role and objectives and the structural divisions that characterise them, which require investigation. In some unions the emphasis is more upon representing aspirations of the working class as a whole rather than functioning as collective bargaining agencies merely for their own members. In the case of France, it has been said (Kendall, 1975) that in the past a worker's decision to join a union represented as much a reflex of class consciousness as any intention to organise practically on his own behalf for enhanced conditions and improved job control. Thus,

> it would be a commonplace to historians that the union movements in the United States or in Britain are very different in character from the union movements in France or in Italy, each conditioned by its own historical experience, and each with a distinctive conception of its role within the wider society. (Gallie, 1978, p. 33)

In much of Western Europe a predominant characteristic has been trade union pluralism (and sometimes reluctance to engage in continuous relationships with employers) promoted by ideological, philosophical and religious differences, although in recent years there has been rather less emphasis upon the importance of religious affinity. As a result, the major dividing lines have been less between the craft and industrial unionism dimensions than between, on the one hand, secular and confessional (generally Catholic) unionism, and reform-oriented (mainly socialist) or revolutionary (communist or syndicalist) unionism on the other (Windmüller, 1974). In Italy, for instance, a unique aspect of the trade union movement has been its formal close ties to various political parties (although somewhat weakened in recent years) whereby there were as many union confederations as political persuasions. Also in that country the unions have been financially supported by the political parties (a reversal of the typical relationship found in, say, Britain or Australia) and the normative stance of the Italian movement is that its role is far more comprehensive than simply bargaining for improved wages and work conditions (Guigni, 1981). Similarly in France, a notable feature is the unions' political pluralism, offering a trinity of communist, socialist and radical Catholic organisations in comparison with the relatively unified movements of West Germany and Britain which are not structurally divided on the basis of religion or politics and have only one coordinating organisational centre (the DGB and TUC, respectively). In fact, trade unions may seek to achieve their objectives not only by collective bargaining but also by lobbying the legislature, or by a more fundamental form of political action aimed at transforming society. Moreover, union objectives and orientations are themselves of an extremely diverse nature between different countries and they require further elucidation.

Trade Union Objectives and Methods

In his comparative examination of industrial relations in French and British oil refineries, Gallie (1978) noted the strikingly dissimilar conceptions of the role of unionism and its typical mode of action at plant level. Broadly, the French unions as class-oriented organisations viewing contemporary western society in predominantly Marxist terms, aspired to promote overall, long-term worker interests rather than defend particular and narrow craft or job interests.[1] They interpreted their role as being one of heightening the consciousness and awareness of the workforce, seeking to mould perceptions and mobilise workers ideologically towards a far-reaching structural transformation of what was seen as an exploitative and alienating society. Their strategy for the achievement of this objective 'was essentially one of sustained ideological warfare in the context of steadily escalating action over concrete disputes with management' (ibid., p. 313). Conversely, the British unions conceived their role within the factory as being basically one of continuing representation of workforce interests on narrow bargaining issues, pressing for objectives which were consciously and explicitly desired by the workers themselves. These aims were to be accomplished by means of negotiation backed up by 'a powerful, well-disciplined and cohesive organisation that would represent such a potential threat in the event of conflict that management was unlikely to risk being unduly unreasonable in negotiation' (ibid., p. 313).

In the USA, the particularly distinctive features of unionism which distinguish it from that found in most continental European countries include 'job consciousness and job control,[2] business unionism, an overwhelming emphasis upon economic struggle and collective bargaining, as opposed to broad political reform of the society and the economy' (Kassalow, 1969, p. 6). The important concept of 'business unionism' relates to the securing of pragmatic, job-related goals in the form of improvements in the economic and social conditions of members, rather than concern with social reorganisation. The classic statement of its main features is that of Hoxie (1920, p. 45) who characterised it as being

> essentially trade-conscious, rather than class-conscious . . . It aims chiefly at more, here and now, for the organised workers of the craft or industry [and] accepts as inevitable, if not as just, the existing capitalistic organisation and the wage system . . . It regards unionism mainly as a bargaining institution and seeks its ends chiefly through collective bargaining.

Unlike most European countries where a close association between unions and political parties has been a longstanding phenomenon, US unions have little close and direct connection with political parties and have relied very heavily on collective bargaining rather than political activity as the means of achieving their ends. (The position in Canada, however, is somewhat different since the union movement there – probably because of the different system of government – has developed a broader view of political ideology and has close ties with the New Democratic Party.) In West Germany, on the other hand, there has been greater emphasis by unions upon legislative enactment to further their general objectives since, historically, the unions accepted the republic created after World War I as being 'their' state and consequently pressed for government legislation in the social and labour field (Günter and Leminsky, 1978). And in Sweden, although in the 1930s unions and managements found common ground in their efforts to increase efficiency under capitalism and avoid state intervention in their relationship, since the 1970s the unions have been promoting new socio-political goals. These include successful pressure for the introduction of new co-determination laws limiting employer prerogative, together with measures to socialise the economy by the statutory provision of collectively-owned investment capital, or 'wage-earner funds' (introduced in 1984).

It can be argued, however, that the dichotomy often noted between the more restrictive business union orientation in the United States and European 'welfare' unionism concerned with wider social objectives as well as the terms and conditions of employment of union members, is somewhat overdrawn. In recent years US unions have not been inactive in the political sphere and have actually had a large degree of impact on influencing legislation concerned with broader social and economic issues (Lewin, 1978). Also, although in European countries some union leaders undoubtedly regard trade unions as having a mainly political role to help change the social and economic order, many rank-and-file members appear to view unions differently – as instrumental agencies concerned with matters arising in the employment relationship. Van de Vall (1970) showed that among Dutch unionists the most prevalent motive for taking up membership was to secure individual 'conflict insurance' (i.e. the provision of legal and material assistance in possible disputes with the employer and protection against arbitrary management decisions). Similarly, despite the incessant advocation of the abolition of the private enterprise system by two of the major French unions, a majority of French workers seemed unconvinced, and rejected the legitimacy of the unions' attempt to relate 'industrial' and 'political' issues in shopfloor agitation (Gallie, 1978). Form's (1973) study of car workers at various skill levels across four countries (USA, Italy, Argentina and India) showed that they all rejected political unionism in favour of job-related unionism concerned with raising wages and improving working conditions.

Unlike their western counterparts, trade unions in Soviet bloc Eastern European countries are markedly different kinds of organisation and, although there is some diversity along national lines, they are essentially variants of a single type.[3]

> In the Soviet-type Communist system . . . theoretically the trade unions are an independent organisation, not a Party or state organisation, and no one is allowed to interfere in their activities and to impose decisions upon them . . . Actually, the trade unions are subordinate to the Party and have to ensure the execution of assigned tasks. Consequently, their autonomy is low or, at best, moderate. (Porket, 1978, p. 72)

Although unions sign 'collective agreements' at factory or establishment level, the content is very different from those in western countries, embracing matters such as the fulfilment of state economic plans, the growth of labour productivity, work organisation and the administration of state social insurance and pensions. Trade unions do not have the right to strike[4] nor negotiate wage levels, which are determined by the administrative centre. But they are required to defend their members from management abuses and bureaucratic excess (including dismissal) as well as from infringements of labour laws. (There is evidence, however, of periodic worker revolts directed partly against alleged union ineffectiveness and conniving in management abuses.) At the same time, unions bear responsibility for labour discipline, particularly in preventing labour turnover and encouraging the attainment of production targets and work norms. In short, they have a dual role to perform (Ruble, 1979) in mobilising workers behind production goals, whilst defending those same workers in job-related grievances against unscrupulous administrators and illegitimate managerial practices. Nevertheless, their interest articulation role is very much qualified in practice in the sense that 'unions are asked to act as filters rather than as mouthpieces' (Pravda, 1983), passing on shopfloor grievances to management or higher union bodies.

Soviet experience has also helped to shape the role of labour unions in socialist states elsewhere. Thus in China (despite some important differences) trade unions act as 'transmission belts' to put the Party's view to workers, and encourage production and engage in political and ideological education. Additionally, they oversee safety and sanitation, take part in grievance-handling and execute numerous welfare and cultural responsibilities (Hoffman, 1981; Littler and Lockett, 1983). Since trade unions reflect features of the society in which they have developed, it is scarcely surprising to find sharp contrasts between their role and orientation within the Soviet type communist system compared to that in western countries. In the former the interests of workpeople are to be protected not only by the unions but also by the state and the Party. Official ideology proclaims the unity of individual, group and societal interests and 'Soviet trade union leaders perceive the interests of the assembly-line worker and that of the Soviet state (and through that state, factory management) as identical' (Ruble, 1981, p. 9).

What also requires explanation, however, are the marked variations in union role and purpose (despite common impulses towards unionism) found between trade unions within some western capitalist countries. Although all modern workers' movements have developed strategies comprising both labour market and political components how can we explain within the European context the greater emphasis upon the achievement of radical change in the structure of society by French and Italian unions, whose thrust (certainly up to the late 1960s) has been at least as much ideological and political as industrial, in comparison with West German or British unions? Also, at the other end of the scale, why has US unionism traditionally shown a more restricted interest in the political sphere, regarding collective bargaining as being overwhelmingly its major business?

Explaining Cross-national Differences in Union Character

Kendall (1975) draws a contrast between continental European unions and those not only in the United States but also in Britain, unlike many observers who regard the latter two countries as displaying important similarities. He sees Anglo-American unions as being set apart by an emphasis on wage bargaining, together with their greater organisational unity[5] and financial resources. These differences are in turn related to variations in economic and socio-political conditions which existed during the unions' formative period and in their subsequent historical development. Kendall's explanation concerns the earlier and more vigorous industrialisation process which occurred in Britain and the USA, in comparison with continental Europe, favouring greater popular support for the *laissez-faire* economy and the values which supported it, with a correspondingly reduced role for the state and politics. Equally important, he notes that within these two countries industrialisation proceeded within a context relatively free from the 'trammels of a pre-capitalist past'.

In this latter respect other authors (e.g. Bok and Dunlop, 1970) have pointed out that labour movements in continental Europe developed against the backdrop and carry-over of a feudalistic tradition of an earlier age that denied workers access to economic opportunity or political power, and which engendered a feeling of isolation and oppression. Throughout the nineteenth century, Europe remained predominantly a rural society, particularly in southern and central Europe (including France, Italy, Spain, Belgium and Austria) where great importance attached to the Catholic Church. In feudal conditions, where workers lack citizenship rights and where class privileges and distinctions are deeply entrenched, labour movements tend to be highly politicised in order to help effect a radical change in the social order (Kassalow, 1969; Shalev and Korpi, 1980). Whereas in Britain (and Sweden), the state controlled the Church, feudalism had ended well before it generally disappeared elsewhere in Europe, and manhood suffrage had been extended to large sections of the population – unlike most continental countries where it was attained only at a later date, sometimes not until the early part of the present century. (The demand for universal male suffrage had always been high on the agenda of all the continental labour movements.) Thus in the second half of the nineteenth century the British labour movement, in contrast to its continental counterparts, was an industrial movement without, at that time, the establishment of a political wing. Conversely, 'the simultaneous and combined economic and political struggle of European workers . . . helps account for the more articulated class character of [their] labour movements' (Kassalow, 1982, p. 210) directed against a very visible and expanding bourgeoisie and, in part, a response to a more repressive state apparatus (Geary, 1981).

As for the United States, there was an absence of a feudal past (except in the South) as well as an early attainment of the franchise for white males prior to the rise of the modern labour movement, together with free public education. As Lorwin has observed,

> American unionism has had the inestimable advantage of being born in a land whose social landscape was not cluttered up with the débris of a feudal age. It was easier for workers and their organisations to accept private property and industrial capitalism where economic inequity was not compounded by apparently hopeless social stratification. (Lorwin, 1957, p. 31)

This absence of feudal social and political structure prior to the onset of industrialisation has been held to help account for US 'exceptionalism', in the form of a weakened socialist consciousness and the lack of strong political Party-union ties, although there are undoubtedly other important factors as well, including the scarcity of manpower and ample employment opportunities for skilled workers, which militated against challenge along political and ideological lines; a complex ethnic (immigrant) labour force composition and racial cleavage, which impeded collective action on a class basis; and a political and constitutional structure that discouraged the setting up of third parties (Lipset, 1977).

Although one limitation of Kendall's explanation of European and Anglo-American distinctions is that it takes no account of the substantial differences which exist *within* his two comparison groups (especially those between Britain and the USA) nevertheless it is, as

Shalev (1980a) has shown, a useful approach in linking contextual structure to behaviour as a means of explaining the broad contrasts between the greater economism and internal unity of British and US unionism as compared with politicisation and (outside Britain and Scandinavia) religious/ideological divisions in Western Europe.

The political character of much of the union movement on the European continent also provoked a counter-response by the non-socialist forces in society, particularly the Catholic Church, which proceeded to establish rival workers' organisations. In a religiously-divided country such as the Netherlands, trade unions had been formed in a period of strong Protestant and Catholic religious revival when a socialist trade union movement was regarded as implying a secular view of society. Therefore, new Protestant and Catholic trade unions were organised which rejected both the class war concepts and the optimistic socialist utopianism of the secular unions, with the result that three rival trade union centres were created (Albeda, 1977). In Germany a division into socialist, Liberal and Christian unions remained until the end of the Weimar Republic in 1933. Even outside Europe, in Canada, Catholic unions were set up at the beginning of the twentieth century in order to 'protect' French-Canadian workers from the more suspect ideological influences of American 'international' (actually bi-national) unions which were organising there.

In addition to broad European-American comparisons which have been considered, it is also necessary to explain some of the major variations and country-by-country differences in the characteristics of unionism which exist *within* the European context itself. In particular, the French union movement differs in a number of important respects from other union movements in Western Europe. In that country membership is relatively low, unionism has been characterised by weakness and instability and has failed to achieve a mass base comparable to the union movements in Germany, Britain, Belgium and Scandinavia. Also, it has somewhat different political perspectives in terms of a 'persistent leftism' (Adams, 1983) rather than pragmatic reformism, and is more committed to direct political action than elsewhere. This may be attributable in part to employer attitudes in the form of an extreme hostility to trade unionism (Clegg, 1976). However, an important structural factor by way of explanation again relates to the nature and pace of industrial development. The slow rate of industrial growth in France and relative lag within an industrialising Europe at the formative period of trade unions meant that they consisted of relatively skilled workers employed in comparatively small-scale enterprises. (As late as 1906 a majority of the industrial workforce were in establishments of less than 100 employees.) This helped give French unionism an élitist philosophy, organising a minority of politically conscious and literate workers in contrast with the more solid and comprehensively organised, dues-paying membership of the British model (Kendall, 1975).

Other specific historical conditions and institutions distinct from those found in other Western European countries were also important in accounting for differences in the major characteristics of French trade unions. These include the conservatism of the large rural sector together with that of the nineteenth-century Church which supported an apparently immovable state. 'These factors and the repeated abortive revolutions gave to the French worker a sense of total mistrust in political parties and the political system' (Meyers, 1981, p. 204). The result was the development of strong anarcho-syndicalist tendencies within the labour movement in which the potential for revolutionary political change was seen as residing in the trade unions or *syndicats*, so that 'the workers, schooled by militancy, made irresistible by the all-powerful weapon of the general strike, would take over society themselves, without need of a political party' (Kendall, 1975, p. 17). Although it is true that this philosophy was dominant only in the relatively short period from the turn of the century until World War I, it subsequently left its imprint upon the labour movement and its appeal has not entirely been extinguished. The labour unrest and factory takeovers of 1968, for instance, evinced echoes of earlier syndicalist strategies.

Maurice and Sellier (1979) draw comparisions between what they term the 'charismatic' character of French unionism, appealing to elements of 'emotional commonality' with the accent on class struggle, and the more functional (bureaucratic and professionalised) nature of unions in West Germany. They ascribe the difference to factors such as a more socially homogeneous working class in Germany with less diversification in attitudes, in comparison with France. Also, they note the more marked occupational stability of manual workers in West Germany as a result of the greater prestige of industrial employment,[6] in contrast to France where the employees' aim on achieving promotion or becoming successful is typically to leave the ranks of the working class and become office workers or independent craftsmen. These factors help to explain the emergence in West Germany of a more unified and organisationally disciplined trade union movement which, unlike French unionism, accepts severe restrictions on the use of militancy within the enterprise under the co-determination system. In fact, in contrast to those countries in which trade unions form virtually a single channel of representation for workers (as in Britain), in West Germany a dual system exists. The enterprise is the domain of the works councils (Jacobs *et al.*, 1978) which provide an enterprise-based negotiating partner for management and are restricted by a 'peace obligation', whereas trade unions operate in principle largely outside the workplace (see Chapter 4). We may also note that with the reconstruction of the German trade unions after World War II, following their demise under the Nazi regime, the DGB was founded as a unitary organisation to include members of all occupations and political persuasions. This contributed to a formal union neutrality and 'depoliticisation', although in practice there are strong links with the Social Democrats (Günter and Leminsky, 1978).

As well as the existence of ideological cleavages between unions on political and religious grounds, together with differences of function – as organisations for representation and bargaining, or as a vehicle for mobilising the power resources of the working class – unions also differ as between countries on a structural basis relating to industry or occupational boundaries. These structural differences will now be examined more closely.

Trade Union Structure

Unions may organise according to 'exclusive' principles, dependent upon their market capacities and resultant ability to erect boundaries, or they may recruit upon an 'inclusive' basis. Thus craft unions in pure form are confined to apprentice-served skilled workers and are intended to protect and promote a marketable skill. (Sometimes occupational unions, which are not confined to apprentice-served workers, are seen as a form of craft union.) By contrast, industrial unions cover all workers within a particular industry and general unions are completely inclusive in terms of their recruitment, representing a large number of different industries and occupations. Technology is a major explanation for the establishment of these various types of union. The early experience of industrialisation (prior to mechanisation) in both Britain and the USA and the emergence of skill patterns associated with it saw the rise and consolidation of craft unions. Because of the early onset of modern economic development in these two countries workers' experience with industrial capitalism was slower and the transition period longer than was the case in most of Northern and Central Europe (Kassalow, 1982). As a consequence, forms of craft unions, with an attendant focus on occupational solidarity and ideas of job consciousness, became well entrenched over many decades. Complications were, however, introduced into the overall structural pattern with the later growth of unions of other types, such as big competing general unions and white-collar organisations in Britain along with industrial unions in the USA.

In other countries such as Germany and Scandinavia, although craft unions were also foremost in the early stages of union development, their predominance was more short-lived – with the notable exception of Denmark (Gill, 1984). As far as West Germany is concerned the post-1945 reorganisation of the union movement into just 16 industrial unions made trade union structure in that country the least complex in Europe. In countries where the onset of industrialisation came later (as in Sweden) increasing mechanisation and mass-production techniques, with easily learned and repetitive tasks, did not provide particular occupations with resources to construct powerful unions. Instead, semi-skilled mass-production workers looked to industrial and general union structures (Clegg, 1976). In the case of France, Sellier (1973) has suggested that the tendency towards workers' organisations formed on the basis of craft unionism was hampered by the lack of a manpower surplus as a result of an early decline in birth rates. His argument is that the motivation to form strong craft organisations to control entry to the trades will be greater in conditions of labour surplus which endanger the market position of skilled workers.

Other factors would also appear to be important in explaining the tendency towards organisation along industrial lines. In a country such as Sweden where most manual workers (although not necessarily white-collar employees) are organised in industrial unions this seems to be partly a reflection of prior employer organisation on an industry-wide basis (see Chapter 3). More generally, political influences appear to have been especially important by way of a facilitating role of socialist ideology in broadening the structural form of unions away from concern with narrow and particularistic special interests. A contrast may be drawn in this respect between the highly fragmented union movements in Anglo-Saxon countries where the historical and ideological connection between socialism and trade unionism was much weaker, and the formation of broad, comprehensive interest organisations on the part of the working class by way of the existence of large industrial unions in those European countries such as Sweden, Austria and Germany with a strong socialist tradition (Streeck, 1981). As von Beyme has explained,

> The industry principle was realised best in countries where there was a close co-operation between a big Social Democrat Party and a relatively centralised union movement. Whether there was a direct organisation link between the Party and the unions (Denmark, Norway and Sweden) or only an informal relation (Germany and Austria) was only of secondary importance. (von Beyme, 1980, pp. 32–3)

In France unions have long been organised predominantly along industrial lines. National unions exist in each industry for each of several main confederations (national groupings of trade unions), including the communist-oriented CGT, the socialist CGT–FO and the radical (originally Catholic but now secular) CFDT. These sort of divisions create a markedly different system from the 'multi-unionism' which exists in Britain. Within any given plant French workers have a choice between several unions differentiated on political and ideological grounds rather than by means of any structural principles of organisation. Similarly, Italian unions have never been organised on a craft or occupational basis (apart from a few exceptional cases). They are, nevertheless, complex organisations comprising national, vertical unions which organise all workers of the same branch of the economy (with provincial, regional and local sections), together with horizontal structures aggregating all workers and/or vertical structures within each geographic area. Horizontal linkages have been particularly important in Italy, probably more than in any other European country, as a result of a number of factors. These include

> the late development of Italian industry and the fragmented character of the labour market, the traditionally high level of unemployment, the very political orientation of the Italian labour movement, particularly of CGIL [the major federation] giving great importance to the unity of the working class . . . and to the pursuit of general goals by the unions. (Treu, 1981, p. 114)

In a number of countries including France and Italy, it is also apparent that a good deal of prominence attaches to the central union federations. Kendall (1975, p. 70) notes that 'the competitive, politically-oriented nature of French unionism, the undeveloped character of collective bargaining' endows the national confederations with more power than they otherwise might possess. In Denmark, Sweden and Norway the trade unions work together in similarly long-established federations called the National Organisations (Landsorganisationen, or LO) which exist not only for manual employees but with separate confederations for white-collar and professional workers. Ulman (1974a) attributes this predominance of the central federations in relation to their constituent national unions (in contrast to the position in the United States) to greater governmental intervention in the employment relationship in European countries, since a comparative advantage of the federations lies in political activity in direct dealings with various government bodies (Hartman and Lau, 1980).

The prevalent structural forms of a country's trade union movement have a number of important consequences. A predominance of occupational unions leads to highly fragmented unionism and ideological and religious divisions also make for duplication of union organisation, thereby weakening bargaining potential and often making for difficulties in promoting effective representation of workers in individual establishments. By contrast, the presence of a relatively small number of unions – even if not entirely structured according to the principle of one per industry at least covering large sections of industry – appears to be associated with markedly fewer inter-union jurisdictional disputes. This may be illustrated by the contrast between Britain and the United States, *vis-à-vis* Sweden and West Germany (Windmüller, 1981). A further comparison between railway workers' unions in Britain and West Germany (Seglow *et al.*, 1982) has shown that the cleavages between the three railway unions in Britain, arising from the occupational exclusiveness of the drivers and the separate footplatemen's 'line of promotion' (unlike Germany[7]), has been a notable restraining influence upon the attainment of an integrated approach to pay bargaining to promote the interests of railway workers as a whole.

Outside Europe and the United States, however, the structural features (and consequences) of trade unions in Japan and Australia are of particular interest and will now be considered more fully.

As compared with other advanced economies, a notable feature of the structure of labour organisation in Japan is the prevalence of comprehensive unions at the level of the individual enterprise. Enterprise unions generally group all regular workers, including white-collar staff, who are employed in an undertaking operated by a single management, but they are not 'company' unions and are basically independent of management. In 1978 there were more than 33,000 unions of this kind, some 90 per cent of the total, covering more than 12 million members. Because of the lack of a pervasive craft history, since Japan incorporated advanced mechanisation and new technologies at a comparatively early stage in its development, the unions which were formed were unable to make a sharp separation among job groups a basis for organisation. Indeed, because job distinctions and jurisdictions within largely self-contained, internal labour markets are very weak, and in the absence of an (external) market based wage system, it was probably inevitable that unions would be established on an enterprise basis. Within any given industry,

> Wages and conditions of work varied from firm to firm. The employer sought to establish a paternalistic relationship with his workers and would not tolerate attempts by outsiders (e.g. trade union officials) to participate in negotiations. The workers, for their part, were not conscious of sharing a common interest with the body of employees in the whole industry, and their conditions of employment were hostile to the appearance of any such consciousness. Such attitudes were conducive to the development of enterprise unions rather than occupational or industrial unions. (Allen, 1981, p. 84)

This enterprise form of unionism does not create distinct organisations of craft and professional employees, and is therefore associated with an absence of demarcation problems. Also, because of greater security from the related systems of seniority-based wages and lifetime employment (see Chapter 4) workers are less inclined to resist technological and organisational change or productivity improvements. A further consequence of enterprise-based unions is that, although they permit a high degree of rank-and-file participation in decision-making, they nevertheless fail to organise large proportions of workers in smaller firms where unionism is discouraged by paternalistic employment relationships. As Levine (1981) points out, the decentralisation, exclusiveness and high degree of autonomy of enterprise unions (despite their affiliation to industry-wide federations) sacrifice a high degree of labour movement solidarity and leave them open to at least the possibility of employer influence.

In comparison with the countries so far considered some rather different distinguishing characteristics typify the trade union movement in Australia. Its trade unions have a structural complexity similar to that in Britain as a result of 'the movement's craft origins, the subsequent grafting on of semi-skilled and unskilled employees [and] flirtation with industry unionism' (Cupper and Hearn, 1981, p. 25). However, the development of Australian unions has been markedly and uniquely influenced by the institutional support given to them by the federal arbitration system which has long played a fundamental role in wage-determination and the settlement of disputes (see Chapter 5). Arbitration not only led to centralised wage-fixing and a high degree of centralised decision-making by both employers and unions, as well as inhibiting the development of a strong shop steward movement, it also fostered a fragmented union movement (Lansbury, 1978a). Arbitration bestowed legitimacy upon the early trade unions – they were explicitly recognised and the system depended for its effectiveness upon their participation. Unions became registered, thereby conferring access to an arbitration tribunal, and once registered they were largely protected from the emergence of new, rival organisations.[8] As a result, the system of registration led to the early establishment and subsequent continuation of a large number of small unions and, as a secondary consequence, helped to impede amalgamation and union rationalisation. In 1979 there was a multiplicity of 315, mainly small, unions organising a total union membership of less than 3 million employees. Many Australian unions have therefore lacked the industrial strength to be able to achieve their industrial aims outside the framework of the arbitration system (Martin, 1975).

Having now examined the objectives and formal structural characteristics of trade unions in market-type economies,[9] it is also necessary to consider their more informal organisation at workplace level since, in many Western European countries during the post-World War II period, there has been a notable growth of bargaining at plant level – often outside official union channels – along with a progressive enlargement of its scope (see Chapter 4). This has been one reason for the increasing prominence of work groups at local level often demanding greater autonomy and a more active role in policy formulation than that provided by the official union structure. (In Britain this development may also have accelerated the adoption by firms of multi-divisional forms of organisation, partly as a management control device to raise the level of effective decision-making away from the shopfloor.)

Workplace Organisation

In much of British industry the absence of exclusive bargaining jurisdiction for any one union created a hiatus in the lines of authority and communication between shop stewards and national union organisations. As a result, shop stewards have been more closely tied to their work groups, and in several industries created spontaneous, coordinated organisations at factory level to take advantage of increased bargaining opportunities during a period of high economic activity. These shopfloor pressures presented an important challenge to trade unions to which, as dynamic and changing institutions, they responded in a number of ways including attempts to decentralise wage negotiations (as in certain industries in Britain, and to a more limited extent in West Germany). In West Germany, pressures from the shopfloor movement were also to some extent incorporated by legislation (in 1972) to extend the size and powers accorded to works councils in order to tackle workers' grievances. In Holland, the unions made structural adaptations to their own organisations to meet the needs of the rank and file. They retained their existing, geographically-based, local structures but supplemented them with official plant-based groupings, and union plant representatives became recognised. In this way their organisational structures reflected and incorporated the shifting focus of trade union activity from national, regional and local interests down to the plant (Albeda, 1977).

In Swedish manufacturing industry, workplace bargaining is conducted by the workplace union organisations ('works clubs') which are sub-organisations of the branches of national unions (in contrast to some industries in Britain especially during the 1950s and 1960s workplace unionism is incorporated into the formal union organisation, although the bargaining which it conducts has a somewhat more restricted range of subject matter). Nevertheless, workplace bargaining in Sweden is highly informal and there is evidence, certainly for the metalworking industry, that the works clubs have acted independently of the branches and headquarters of the national union (Korpi, 1978b). The unions have attempted to accommodate work group aspirations by allowing local unions a greater say in employment practices and – via legislation – expanding the role and powers of shop stewards, including the right of safety stewards to order a work stoppage in certain circumstances (Forsebäck, 1980).

There have been even more intensive organisational changes within the Italian union movement during the 1970s together with the development of new structures at plant level. These were designed to reduce the gap between the formal and informal structures of union representation and lessen the distance between shop stewards and unions (Sciarra, 1977). In this respect they show interesting similarities to developments in Britain. Traditionally in Italy the official bargaining structure lay outside the factory and was in the hands of the industry-wide union. The works council, as the representative structure at the plant level, was formally union-independent and had no powers beyond the handling of grievances resulting from the interpretation of the industry agreement. In the post-war period, although the union confederations tried to limit organisation at plant level (as being potentially destructive of class consciousness), the councils became increasingly significant. They were the only source of direct involvement for the rank and file as the channel through which they expressed their demands and discontent. Consequently, new union-based structures ('factory councils') were developed as organisations of the shop stewards, to be directly representative of the rank and file. They are regarded by many employers' associations (although lacking official recognition) as a means of encouraging greater stability in shopfloor relations.

As well as workplace organisation, a further level at which cross-national comparisons may be directed is the 'internal' government of trade unions and the extent of democratic control by their membership, as opposed to oligarchic domination by the leadership, since unions are formally democratic institutions.

Internal Union Democracy

von Beyme (1980) has pointed to the potential influence of union size and pluralistic divisions upon the degree of union democracy. The pressures of bureaucracy are seen as being greater within large, comprehensive unions so that fragmented, ideological unions (as in the Latin countries) do not possess specialised staff resources to the extent of more pragmatically-based general unions, and they therefore leave greater room for local and plant initiatives by the membership. Clegg (1976) maintains that power within unions is concentrated at the level at which bargaining is typically conducted (although this is not the only influence), so that 'industry bargaining concentrates power at the centre [and promotes integrated, bureaucratic union government], whereas bargaining at lower levels disperses it to the regions or branches' (p. 54).

Thus in Sweden, where industry or higher level bargaining predominates, although there are variations as between unions within individual industries, the unions are generally strongly organised and their officials have considerable power. The central union federation (the LO) is also very strong largely because it plays a significant and continuing role in collective bargaining. Conversely, in the United States, where collective bargaining takes place mainly at plant level, union government is also very much decentralised and the branches ('locals') have considerable independence. In Britain the development of informal, workplace-level bargaining and shopfloor activism since the 1950s led to some (although by no means universal) decentralisation of union government in some of the public service unions for instance but, most notably, in the Transport and General Workers Union (TGWU). In the latter union these changes 'were less a surrender of power to the shopfloor than a formal accommodation to the reality of decentralisation which had occurred during the post-war years' (Hyman, 1983, p. 42).

A contrasting perspective, however, which makes little allowance for the effects of collective bargaining arrangements, is the study of democracy in British and US unions by Edelstein and Warner (1975), and that for Mexico by Thompson and Roxborough (1982). The so-called 'structural' approach adopted by these studies concentrates upon the organisational structure of unions rather than focusing upon the activities of their membership. It looks for formal arrangements such as size and frequency of union conventions or conferences, selection and voting methods for the union executives and the existence of intermediate union governing bodies, that is, the devices which can facilitate, when full advantage is taken of them, the development of power bases independent of union leaders. The studies tentatively suggest that such union organisational factors are more important influences in promoting internal democracy than are national, contextual characteristics such as the political and industrial relations systems, or the existence of competing union federations. However, this remains an open question since the research needs to be replicated for a considerably increased range of countries.

In addition to those dimensions of trade union activity which have already been discussed, a further important aspect relates to the significant cross-national variations which exist in the extent of trade union membership. Despite the fact that many advanced western economies have similar characteristics in terms of a high degree of industrialisation, urbanisation and technological development, they nevertheless display markedly different degrees of labour force unionisation. Also, the size of union membership is an important consideration in its own right since it is one of the main indices of the unions' industrial power.[10]

Levels of Trade Union Membership

Some indication of the disparities to be explained is contained in Table 2.1. This shows overall union 'density' (percentage of the number of potential union members) by country, in rank order.

There are, of course, problems with measuring and interpreting trade union membership since in the United States, for example, some professional bodies may not call themselves trade unions although they engage in bargaining activities and in France the only source of such statistics is from the unions themselves (or, indirectly, via the support given to the various unions in elections for enterprise committees). Again, in countries such as West Germany and the Netherlands – despite their fairly low union densities – a higher proportion of workers are covered by the terms of the union-negotiated collective agreements as a result of the legislative provision for the 'extension' of agreements throughout an industry (principally in order to protect employers from the effects of low wage competition). Furthermore, at a disaggregated level corresponding to where collective bargaining is actually conducted in most countries, unions may be well-organised in spite of an overall low average density (e.g. in the USA 70-80 per cent in some areas of employment).

In France the importance and influence of unions are certainly much greater than the low membership figures would imply – in 1975, for instance, a local union section had been established in 46 per cent of all enterprises with more than 50 employees. In the public sector of the economy, Sellier (1978) has shown that the influence of French unions is particularly strong since the high concentration of workers within that sector reduces the costs of organisation, the bureaucratic tendencies of large undertakings encourage trade union membership, and the official role accorded by government to the unions gives them a greater authority than they possess in the private sector. (Indeed, in most countries – with the exception of the USA – trade union density is fairly uniformly high in public employment.) Such qualifications notwithstanding, however, what require explanation are the major inter-country differences in density which are depicted in the table. In particular, we need to explain the contrast between the high

Table 2.1: Trade Union Membership as a % of Non-Agricultural Workers, 1976

Sweden 82-3	West Germany 40
Finland 78	Netherlands 39-40
Belgium 70	Canada 37
Denmark 65	Switzerland 37
Norway 63	USA 28-9[a]
Australia 55	(France 25)
Britain 51-2	

Note: a. Includes membership of some 'employee associations'. If these are excluded the USA figure is of the order of 25 per cent.
Source: B. Martin and E.M. Kassalow (eds) (1980) ***Labour Relations in Advanced Industrial Societies: Issues and Problems***, Carnegie Endowment, Washington, DC, p. 47.

Scandinavian figures (with Sweden having the highest rate of trade union membership in the western world[11]), and the low levels of unionisation found in the United States and France.

Clegg (1976) has put forward a theory of union density for those countries which rely predominantly upon collective bargaining to regulate employment terms. Inter-country divergences 'are explained by variations in the extent and depth of collective bargaining and in support for union [membership] security, either directly from employers or through collective agreements' (p. 27), i.e. the greater the 'depth' of bargaining (in terms of the involvement of local union officers and shop stewards) and union support, the higher the density.

In this approach the high level of unionisation in Sweden is not the result of any cultural propensity on the part of the Swedish population (because of its ethnic homogeneity) to seek objectives by way of interest group organisations – a factor which Adams (1975) notes has sometimes been suggested by way of explanation. Rather, not only does Sweden have the widest coverage of collective bargaining for manual and white-collar employees, along with well-developed workplace organisations, but most importantly member firms of the centralised employers' body support trade union membership and encourage employees to join and remain in the union. As early as 1906, after a period of intense industrial conflict, an agreement was reached (the 'December Compromise') on the membership issue between the union and employer central federations. In return for the unions' consent formally to acknowledge managements' prerogatives of decision-making at plant level, employers would recognise the right of workers to join unions and would not discriminate against them for doing so. Yet employers were not prepared to give similar support to organisations of white-collar and professional employees. Indeed, they vigorously opposed their unionisation. Therefore, the catalyst helping to promote high density among salaried staffs was government support in the form of legislation since 1936 guaranteeing the right of association and negotiation to white-collar as well as manual employees.

In contrast to Sweden, at the bottom end of the union membership table a country with a comparatively low (and declining) overall density is the United States. The explanation cannot be solely the fact of differences in labour force structure (a higher proportion of white-collar employment where unions have generally found greater difficulty in recruitment) since, on an inter-country basis, white-collar unionisation itself is also appreciably lower in the United States than in other comparable countries (von Beyme, 1980). Once again the dimensions of collective bargaining would seem to be important as contributory factors by way of a somewhat narrower extent of bargaining in the USA, as well as employer hostility to trade unionism (especially in the South). Moreover, to achieve recognition within the legalistic and decentralised bargaining system in the United States a union needs to win a majority vote in a ballot, and although perhaps 40 or 45 per cent of the employees in a given enterprise may desire union services the union fails to achieve recognition because of the unwillingness of the majority of their colleagues to opt for unionisation. Consequently, because non-recognised unions are of little benefit to employees, there is less incentive to join. (In European countries with industry-wide or regional agreements it is not uncommon for a union to represent less than a majority of workers within any given enterprise.)

In the case of France, also at the foot of the table, the low level of union membership may be explained partly by the deep-rooted ideological divisions within the fragmented trade union movement but more importantly, according to Clegg, because of the late development and lack of depth of collective bargaining whose regulatory effect has been relatively limited. 'The system is characterised by union pluralism, complexity of the representative institutions at the enterprise level, and freedom to strike at any moment and on any issue' (Delamotte, 1982, p. 327). Not only has there been strong opposition to trade unionism and lack of support for union security at enterprise level by employers (particularly those in small, paternalistic firms) but trade unions have also not regarded the negotiation of agreements and protection of immediate job interests – certainly at plant level – as their central concern. Rather, a contestative stance towards the employer coupled with political action has ranked highly in their strategy. All this has no doubt limited the perceived usefulness of union membership to workers.

Other factors may also have been important in France. The low capitalisation of industry together with its subordinate place to agriculture until fairly recently (and an early development of the service sector of the economy[12]) has tended to limit workers' bargaining power, and diversification made for greater difficulties of organisation. It has also been pointed out by Kendall (1975) that the original 1936 legislation on union rights within the enterprise gave the 'most representative' unions in the plant the right to bargain,[13] which was not necessarily the majority union. This allocation of bargaining rights to minority unions in some cases (thereby institutionalising union pluralism) may also help to explain the chronic weakness of union organisation in France over a long period.

As well as the influence of collective bargaining, a further thesis put forward to help explain more general inter-country membership differences relates to the effects of concentration of capital. Stephens (1979) claims that in the Scandinavian countries, whose industrial structure (in contrast to the United States and, especially, France and Germany) is characterised by a small number of highly concentrated oligopolistic employers, to be able to operate effectively unions must organise a higher proportion of the labour force. Under these conditions it is necessary to organise all employers operating within the same market to preclude the possibility of a wage increase secured at one firm adversely affecting its competitive position, and therefore employment.

Having considered possible explanations for some of the major inter-country differences between the levels of union organisation at a particular point in time it is also useful to examine the related question of the factors which help to explain the year-to-year growth and fluctuations in union membership over the course of time.

Union Growth

Much of the work in this area has been done by economists whose approach is based upon the hypothesis that workers will join unions if the expected benefits and returns from the services which unions can provide – in the form of relative wage gains, taking up grievances, access to specialised information and the like – exceed the expected costs. These costs comprise not simply membership dues but also such factors as the possibility of employer hostility and retaliation (in the form of job loss or victimisation) as a result of taking up membership. Most of the early studies on the causes of union growth related it primarily to the influence of the business cycle and its key components, including employment, industrial production and price changes. It was claimed that union growth was positively correlated with business prosperity, increasing when it was good and falling when it was bad. A notable early study of union growth which employed data relating to changes in general business conditions for France, Germany, England and the USA over the period from the 1890s to the 1930s was that of Davis (1941). He was able to show that fluctuations in union membership appeared to be determined, at least in part, by fluctuations in economic conditions. Nevertheless, he emphasised that 'a mere analysis of economic conditions does not suffice for an adequate understanding of the ups-and-downs of unionism' (p. 627). In addition, he pointed to the influence of union leadership which can have a decisive impact on union menbership growth via the policies and organising techniques which are adopted, and governmental encouragement which may also become a major factor in promoting union growth.

The main contemporary study of union growth which utilises international comparisons is the model derived by Bain and Elsheikh (1976). This is tested against empirical data from four countries – the UK, USA, Sweden and Australia. The general form of the model employs the rate of change of prices (ΔP), the rate of change of wages (ΔW), the level and/or rate of change of unemployment (U or ΔU), together with the (lagged) level of union density (D_{t-1}) as determinants of the proportional rate of change of union membership (ΔT), i.e.

$$\Delta T = f(\underset{(+)}{\Delta P}, \underset{(+)}{\Delta W}, \underset{(-)}{U}, \underset{(-)}{D_{t-1}})$$

with the anticipated positive (+) and negative (–) influences shown in brackets. It is contended that for union growth to take place workers require both a 'propensity' to join a union and the 'opportunity' to become a member. The explanatory variables which are utilised are expected to have an impact on union growth because they affect the opportunity and/or the propensity of workers to join a trade union. Briefly, the rationalisation for their inclusion is as follows. Rising prices are perceived as a threat to living standards, so that the faster prices are increasing the more likely are workers to wish to join a union in order to maintain their standards of living. Also, in so far as price rises are a reflection of business prosperity, they may also favourably affect the opportunity to organise. This is because employers may be more willing to concede worker demands and grant trade union recognition when any resultant higher labour costs can be passed on to their customers in the form of price increases. Secondly, a wage-change variable is included in addition to a price variable since it is hypothesised that workers may seek to unionise not only to defend existing standards of living but also to attempt to improve upon them. 'Hence, when money wages are rising, workers may, rightly or wrongly, credit such rises to unions and hope that by beginning or continuing to support them they will do as well or even better in the future' (Bain and Elsheikh, 1976, p. 64).

A further variable, unemployment, is presumed to influence both the opportunity and the propensity to unionise. In conditions of high unemployment, employers, having relatively increased bargaining strength, may be in a better position and be more willing to oppose trade unionism. At the same time unemployment is likely to reduce the propensity of unorganised workers who are in work to become unionised for fear of antagonising their employer. It may also affect the propensity of workers who become unemployed to remain union members, since the cost of membership becomes relatively more expensive and any collective bargaining advance which the union secures will have little relevance for them. Finally, it is anticipated that union membership growth will also be affected (negatively) by the existing level of union density because of the 'saturation', or upper limit, effect. Union organisation tends to take place first among groups of workers who are the easiest to organise and, as union density rises, the greater the difficulty of increasing membership still further.

Although it might be thought that it would be difficult to capture the phenomenon of union growth across a number of countries on the basis of a single behavioural equation of this kind without making allowances for additional socio-political factors, or resorting to *ad hoc* explanations for individual countries, in fact the model performs surprisingly well. When tested initially for UK data over an 80-year period (1893–1970) all the explanatory variables are statistically significant and have the expected (positive or negative) signs and the model is stable over time, i.e. the same factors explain union growth in various sub-periods. For the entire period it accounts for some 70 per cent of the year-to-year variation in the rate of change of aggregate union membership. However, in attempting to ascertain the applicability of the model to other countries, in order to strengthen confidence in the results, it is recognised that instead of simply applying it to them mechanically, some account needs to be taken of prevailing differences in their industrial relations systems.

Nevertheless, it was found that only one modification to the basic specification of the model was required. Allowance had to be made in the USA and Australia (though not in Sweden) for the impact on union growth of government action. In the United States union membership from the mid-1930s to 1947 was undoubtedly stimulated first by the 1935 Wagner Act and later by the actions of the War Labor Board in promoting collective bargaining and union recognition (see Chapter 5). Therefore, an additional variable is added to the equation to take account of this influence.[14] The results of testing the model over a period from the late 1890s to 1970 are satisfactory for all the variables employed, and the government's impact upon union growth is shown to be highly significant. Also, as we noted earlier, in the case of Australia government arbitration directly promoted the formation and growth of unions. Indeed, in the three decades from the turn of the century when the compulsory arbitration system was introduced the proportion of union members in the workforce increased sevenfold – from 6 per cent in 1900 to 47 per cent by 1927. This was a figure unmatched anywhere else in the world at that time (Martin, 1975).[15] Allowance for this favourable influence from the early introduction of arbitration is included in the equation, and it is further anticipated (correctly) that in the case of Australia the price-change variable will be statistically insignificant in accounting for union growth. The reason is that the arbitration system to a large degree adjusts wages in line with the cost of living thereby reducing the 'threat' effect which rising prices would otherwise pose to workers' living standards.[16]

Similarly for Sweden, three of the four variables are found to be significant – although the results generally for that country are less satisfactory than for the other three. In Sweden, as in the USA and Australia, the government attempted to foster union growth by legislation. The major intention of the 1936 Act, however, was specifically to encourage white-collar unionisation, and Bain and Elsheikh (1976) find no evidence that it had a significant impact upon aggregate union growth. Therefore, in applying the model to Swedish data (as with union growth in Britain) it was not felt necessary to take account of government promotion of unionism. Of the four basic variables utilised, the rate of change of wages is not significant and has the wrong (negative) sign. The authors speculate that this may be because, with a centralised collective bargaining system which is fairly remote from the workers, 'the less conscious they will be of the gains achieved, and hence the less likely they are to be credited to union activity' (p. 109). This explanation is not entirely convincing, however, since it overlooks the important industry and workplace negotiations which also take place. In addition, the model employing Swedish data is not stable over time so that the relationships pre- and post-1939 are significantly different – again it is suggested because of the way in which the Swedish bargaining system became more centralised after 1939.

More generally, we may conclude that the Bain–Elsheikh study provides support from several countries for the effects of economic conditions and the influence of public policy[17] upon union growth. The model does not claim to include *all* the possible determinants of union growth, and because it is concerned with the rate of change (rather than the level) of union membership influences such as the structure of the labour force, which exhibit little annual variation, are excluded. There are, however, a number of valid criticisms which can be made of the study. These include conceptual problems such as the lack of theoretical explanation for the assumed 'credit' effect of money-wage increases to trade unions by potential members and the possibility of a two-way relationship between wage increases and union growth which, unless allowed for, could limit confidence in the results. Furthermore, given that much of trade union growth in the four countries over the post-World War II period has been in the white-collar field there are difficulties in relating aggregate union membership changes to changes in the wages of manual workers only.

Although the authors do not deny the importance of the social and political environment in which unions operate, as well as the effects of economic forces, these influences are dealt with in only a limited way. Little is said about workers' consciousness (awareness and interpretation of their situation), or the social and political impulses towards joining the labour movement which have undoubtedly been important in Western Europe. (At particular historical periods political ideology helped provide a unifying force for labour, instilling a sense of perspective and purpose beyond the mere rectification of current grievances.) In France, for instance, a country not included in the comparison, the bursts of activity and membership growth – interspersed with long periods of relative dormancy – seem to have depended more on political events (as in 1936, 1947, and post-1968) than upon changing economic circumstances (Sellier, 1978).

Summary

This chapter has examined from a comparative standpoint a number of important characteristics of trade unions, mainly in relation to industrialised, market-type economies. In these countries unionisation emphasises the (collective) situation of employees as sellers of labour power, counteracting the bargaining strength of the owners of capital who direct their labour. Beyond such common features, however, it has been shown that there are marked diversities between national labour movements as well as within them, in relation to their goals and objectives (broader or narrower conceptions), structural features, size and membership densities. These differences have multiple causes since trade unions are responses of workers to the varying economic and political features of the environments in which they operate. Ideology has been one major determining factor in the strategic approach adopted by unions. In some continental European countries, where workers were confronted with deep-seated social and political inequities, unions have been markedly political in orientation, seeing themselves as committed and class-oriented agents of social change on behalf of all workers, and not merely union members. By contrast, in the United States (and some would argue in Britain), greater emphasis has been placed upon the attainment of shorter-term economic gains for their own members, although broader considerations of social justice and 'movement' are by no means absent.

The importance of the formative stages of unionism in determining structural features (which are themselves closely related to function and objectives) and in giving direction to subsequent developments has also been emphasised. Thus in countries where industrialisation and the establishment of the trade union movement came somewhat later this facilitated the organisation of industrial rather than craft unions and, in turn, often contributed to a strongly socialist influence over the labour movement. Also in Western European countries social and political impulses towards joining a trade union have been important as well as any individualistic evaluations of the relative economic benefits and costs of membership. This may help to explain why in models of the historical determinants of trade union growth which concentrate solely upon economic variables up to 30 per cent of membership growth typically remains unexplained. Moreover, workers need to be predisposed, or mobilised, to take advantage of the opportune environmental conditions for unionisation which arise. These conditions can include not only economic factors but also government encouragement and the willingness (or otherwise) of employers to recognise and negotiate with them. Employer policies in relation to trade unions, together with the more general role of employers and their organisations in industrial relations, are considered in the next chapter.

Notes

1. 'In France . . . even if an agreement was signed by the unions, it was merely regarded as a temporary embodiment of the existing balance of power, and as a basis from which a new and more ambitious set of demands could immediately be unleashed' (Gallie, 1978, p. 255).

2. 'Job control' includes control over access to the job (via such devices as union insistence upon seniority rights), its security and work content.

3. With the notable exception of the short-lived Solidarity in Poland, the first legal trade union movement to be independent of the Party organisation and state administration. To some extent the freedom of action of Hungarian unions was also enlarged at the end of the 1960s when they became solely the representatives of workers' interests – although in practice it appears that the unions have been reluctant to utilise their greater potential.

4. Nevertheless, Soviet workers are by no means docile: 'Non-sanctioned demonstrations and disturbances occur, ranging from full-scale vodka and food riots in Ukranian and Siberian cities, to a wildcat taxi strike in Leningrad' (Ruble, 1979, p. 24). Some shopfloor power undoubtedly exists, largely because of labour market considerations, e.g. factory directors being reluctant to discharge labour which may be needed for meeting production quota deadlines.

5. Although before the 1955 merger of the two central union organisations, the AFL and CIO, US unions were deeply split over a number of issues, including their political role.

6. Partly because of the long-established, high technical performance of industry, German society gives priority to vocational training (as provided by industry) over theoretical training and general education, and there is also great respect among employers for craft skills and values.

7. In Germany trainee engine-drivers are recruited not from footplate occupations but more broadly from the skilled fitters or mechanics employed in railway workshops.

8. No new union can be registered if its members can 'conveniently belong' to an existing organisation.

9. In (Soviet-type) communist countries trade unions are typically organised according to the 'production principle', i.e. every employee (including the managers) who works in one enterprise or establishment belongs to the same union, which embraces all the workers throughout a single branch of the economy. The number of unions therefore remains small – 25 in the Soviet Union in the early 1970s, 19 in Hungary in 1966 and 23 in Poland in 1976 (Porket, 1978).

10. Industrial power depends significantly upon the extent of union organisation (although it is by no means the only determinant) since, other things remaining equal, the greater the degree of unionisation 'the lower the substitutability of the relevant workforce, the greater its potential solidarity and the greater therefore its strike potential' (Wilkinson and Burkitt, 1973, p. 114). For a broader, theoretical discussion of power relations, see Lukes (1974).

11. In communist states membership is even higher and almost universal, embracing some 90 per cent of the eligible employed population. Special factors are applicable, however. These include pressure upon workers to join, non-Party members wishing to display their loyalty to the regime, and the material advantages which membership confers – in the Soviet Union inexpensive holidays and higher temporary disability and welfare benefits unavailable to non-union workers.

12. In 1954 the percentage of the French labour force employed in the service sector, 38 per cent (and 36 per cent as early as 1938), exceeded that in industry with 35½ per cent – whilst agriculture still employed 26 per cent.

13. Such a provision was necessary since, where unions are divided between several central organisations, it is difficult to grant the same prerogatives to all unions on the same terms.

14. Using the technique of the 'dummy' variable (see Chapter 6).

15. A figure in excess of 52 per cent had been recorded in the German Weimar Republic however in 1920.

16. Yet, at the same time, because ΔW is found to be significant the 'credit' effect still appears to be operative, i.e. the unions will still claim the credit for wage increases which have been secured because they make the case to the Arbitration Tribunals.

17. A more recent study (Smith, 1980), which slightly modifies and re-estimates the Bain and Elsheikh model, suggests that for the UK there may, in fact, also have been a significant effect of government action on union growth after the mid-1960s, and perhaps around the two world wars.

Further Reading

A general introductory survey of trade unions which includes much comparative material is the short book by Jackson (1982). Kendall's (1975) study of the European labour movement provides a detailed treatment, and a shorter analysis of trade union development in the pre-1939 period is contained in Geary (1981). For the USA, Australia and Japan a useful source is the book on trade unions in developed economies edited by Owen Smith (1981), and on France there is an excellent chapter by Meyers in Blum (1981). Cross-national analytical studies of importance are Clegg (1976) and von Beyme (1980), whilst there is a stimulating chapter on diversities within national trade union movements by Cella and Treu in the symposium edited by Blanpain (1982b). A fascinating comparative discussion of the sources of divergence between US and British trade unionism (as well as Canadian and Australian) is Phelps Brown (1983).

3 EMPLOYERS

Employer interests in industrial relations may be promoted by individual firms or undertakings acting singly, by a group of enterprises acting together via an *ad hoc* body, or by a permanent association of employers to represent their collective interests. In the United States, although associations for multi-employer bargaining purposes exist in a number of key areas and industries, there are none with the membership density or authoritative stature possessed by many of their European counterparts (Adams, 1981). In fact, as we shall see, employers in the USA – particularly in the manufacturing sector where enterprise-level bargaining and large corporations predominate – have felt less need for association with other employers for negotiating purposes, while in Britain over the past two decades there has been a trend towards the adoption of company-centred industrial relations policies rather than continued adherence to the norms laid down by an association. This tendency has been especially marked within large establishments in the engineering and chemical industries, although multi-employer bargaining by means of an employers' organisation still remains the predominant pattern in highly competitive industries with low capitalisation and a high ease of entry such as clothing, construction and printing (Sisson, 1984).

It is therefore necessary to consider on a cross-national basis for industrialised market (or mixed) economies the genesis and evolution of employers' associations, external to the firm or enterprise, which have typified collective bargaining arrangements with unions in most Western European countries. Equally, as in the USA and Japan especially, where bargaining is conducted mainly inside the undertaking and employers negotiate separately with union representatives, we shall need to consider aspects of industrial relations management within the individual undertaking itself. Even in these countries, however, although employers' organisations may not be direct bargaining institutions they can still play an important role in industrial relations by helping to achieve a degree of cohesion among employers through their coordinating and advisory functions. In Japan the influential Federation of Employers' Associations (Nikkeiren) draws up wage-bargaining guidelines which are often worked out by bodies where the major undertakings that will apply them are represented.

We shall see that employers are key actors within industrial relations and that they possess a considerable margin for defining their own policies which are not wholly determined in response to the actions of unions, or to economic and political pressures.

Employers' Associations and their Development

Where the main impetus towards collective action on the part of employers related to the regulation of trading and commercial matters what are now called trade associations were set up. If, however, a clear distinction could be established between such economic interests and social and labour policy matters then employers' associations were formed – as in the Nordic countries, and Germany and Switzerland. They would undertake responsibility for all aspects of the employment relationship including trade unions and government legislation relating to labour matters.[1] Sometimes the two functional concerns were closely linked,

> [since] the aim of achieving a strong competitive position in international markets, or at least the concern not to be at a disadvantage in comparison with competitors in other countries was one of the chief arguments advanced by some of the first employers' associations against proposals for social reforms through protective labour and social legislation. (Windmüller, 1984, p. 2)

In France trade associations dealt both with 'economic' and 'social' matters, although, as far as industry-wide relations with trade unions were concerned, organisation among employers remained greatly underdeveloped until well after World War I. At confederal level the central (peak) organisation, the CNPF, also combined the functions both of an employers' and a trade association from the time of its establishment in 1919, as did the Confindustria in Italy. By contrast, the central bodies in Sweden and West Germany (the SAF and BDA) are exclusively employers' associations.

For individual industry organisations a further important consideration in this respect concerns the nature and characteristics of the particular industry itself. In the building industry, not only in France but also in Sweden, West Germany, Italy, as well as in Britain, the main body was (and still is) both an employers' and a trade association since it is not easy to separate the negotiation of wages from matters such as agreed arrangements for contract tendering. Conversely, in the case of the metalworking industry in all these five countries the main body is exclusively an employers' association, since the great diversity and heterogeneous product range of the industry (basic steel, cars, electrical equipment, etc.) precluded representation via a single trade association. Although dual employer structuring may be common in some industries, nevertheless our main concern is more specifically with the origins and development of employers' associations themselves, which will now be delineated.

The historical development of associations concerned with the employment relationship during the late nineteenth and early twentieth centuries may be explained as a negative response on the part of employers to accommodate the external challenges which confronted them on the basis of three broad sets of factors. The objectives were first to counter the rapid growth of trade unionism which was taking place with the acceleration of the industrialisation process. Secondly, to stimulate employer alliances for purposes of market regulation, especially in those industries with competitive product markets as a means of regulating wages and thereby helping to stabilise market conditions. And thirdly the inducement in some countries for employers to federate was as a result of actual or threatened state intervention in the employment relationship, or sometimes because of the growing complexities of the legislative framework under which employers had to operate. Each of these factors will be examined below.

There is no doubt that the early growth of trade unionism was a major influence in establishing the possibility of a cohesive bond between undertakings which otherwise would have been difficult because of their commercial rivalry. Thus in France a quickening movement favouring *patronal* associations in the 1890s was in part a defensive response to a trade union movement which was about to adopt an ideology of radical syndicalism that appeared more threatening. There was also a felt need for mutual protection against the changing nature of strikes, which were becoming organised and coordinated rather than being spontaneous reactions (Oechslin, 1972). A central employers' body in Austria was similarly formed to resist working-class agitation after the ground had been prepared by a manufacturers' strike indemnity association. In Sweden employers' associations were set up as a counter-mobilisation to the growing organisational strength and apparent centralisation of the trade union movement. In particular, the 1902 general strike there accelerated the creation of a central employers' organisation to provide financial assistance to strike-bound firms (Forsebäck, 1980). Further, in the case of Australia, employers' associations were established partly to counter and present a united front against the rapid expansion of trade unions (Ford, 1980). In Britain, also, the intention was 'to establish a countervailing power to the growing effectiveness of unionism' (Yarmie, 1980, p. 212).

The genesis of employers' associations, however, was not only as a response to trade union growth and militancy because to some degree it was, in addition, a reaction to economic pressures. The impetus for employers to associate was particularly marked for those undertakings which operated in highly (and often increasingly) competitive product and factor markets, provided that most of the market could be covered.[2] Association bargaining could prove a means of enhancing market control in labour-intensive industries since wages could be taken out of competition as between employers themselves. Thus in Israel associations were formed on an industry-wide basis which usually coincided with product and labour markets (Shirom and Jacobson, 1975). In the Japanese textile industry, long-standing employers' organisations were equally active in regulating employer competition for labour and in fixing labour standards – even at a time when the supply side of the market was little affected by trade unions (Taira, 1973). It has been argued by Johnston (1962) that in Sweden, however, it was not so much the benefits of having uniform wage levels which were the major attraction of association, rather, it was the negative purpose of employers being able to present a united front to prevent the unions from 'whipsawing' individual firms (see Chapter 4). More generally under association bargaining it has been shown that

> the employer is not only provided with maximum assurance that his competitors will make the same settlement that he does; he is also assured that his competitors will be shut down . . . when he is shut down, so that he need not reckon on a permanent reduction in market share when calculating the costs of a strike. (Ulman, 1974a, p. 104)

These considerations have been used to help explain the prevalence of multi-employer (association) bargaining in non-manufacturing industries in the USA such as trucking, construction and retailing which are characterised by a large number of small- and medium-sized firms operating within highly competitive and often localised markets – conditions which favour common settlements. Where competing firms are small they may wish not only to help regulate competition in the product market by joining together, but also to protect themselves against a marked inequality in bargaining power, since they are too small to be able to deal effectively with the trade unions unaided. Conversely, large establishments may be reluctant to join since they will be more self-sufficient for bargaining purposes and less dependent on the services and support which an association can offer. They may also wish to avoid the possible constraints of association membership if they enjoy lower unit costs as a result of economies of scale or capital intensity so that they can make wage concessions which might jeopardise the existence of smaller enterprises. Therefore, very large firms which have secured a degree of market dominance will often prefer independence or, where they do retain formal employers' association membership, may have 'non-conforming' status whereby they are not required to follow the terms of a national agreement and disputes procedure (such as a number of firms in the Chemical Industries Association in Britain, including ICI and Glaxo).

Yet it can be argued that large size and a high degree of industrial concentration of capital tend to assist the organisation of employers by making agreements between them easier to secure. Ingham (1974) maintains that this was the case in Sweden where strong, centralised employers' associations could develop as a consequence of the domination of a narrow and specialised export market by a small number of large-scale employers who had interests in common. Also in Germany it has been claimed that cartelisation (reflecting the later date, and a particular mode, of industrialisation) gave rise to strongly structured employers' organisations which attained an authority over their members that was never to exist in the smaller diversified and undercapitalised industrial enterprises in France (Maurice and Sellier, 1979). It would appear, therefore, that although large size may well reduce the propensity of firms to organise into associations it can enhance their opportunity to do so should they wish. They could find it easier to come to an agreement to support each other during a lock-out for example, because they would have sufficient financial resources to enable them to survive periods of inactivity. Moreover, given that such firms will wish to attain stable parameters for future planning within the undertaking over extended time-horizons, in order to reduce uncertainty, the need to secure market regulation will not be the only motivation to associate. There may also be a need for more predictable and controlled behaviour on the part of the labour force, particularly in relation to the calling of strikes; that is, a desire for labour, as well as for market, regulation and control. In this respect the associations can try to ensure that disputes are processed in an orderly way (to promote stability) through the imposition of an industry procedure agreement.[3]

In addition to the factors already discussed, the main stimulus to employers' organisation in a number of countries appears to have been less that of a counter to growing union power, or an attempt to achieve market or labour force regulation, and more a response to what was perceived as a threat to common employer interests arising from increasing state intervention. This was true to some extent in France where, by the turn of the century, it was necessary to articulate more forcefully to the government employers' opposition to labour legislation in view of 'the apparent receptivity of lawmakers to demands from Socialists and organised labour for assistance' (Kuisel, 1981, p. 20). It was especially notable in the case of Holland where early employer alliances had been forged for pressure-group purposes with a view to opposing the introduction of new social policies and labour legislation. With the advent of such legislation after World War I the creation of a central employers' association fulfilled the need for an authoritative spokesman to represent employer interests before the legislature. At industry level there was also a demand by individual firms for association services and technical assistance in applying and interpreting the legislation since 'most employers had neither the economic strength nor the managerial skills . . . to cope by themselves – and simultaneously – with the unions and government apparatus' (Windmüller, 1967, p. 49).

In Japan during the 1920s expanding employers' associations also became active in opposing government labour policy. They delayed revisions of the Factory Law which were aimed at strengthening protective measures for workers and they effectively opposed government attempts to grant legal recognition to trade unions at that time (Taira, 1973). At an even earlier date in Australia, the development of employers' associations had been facilitated by government intervention and by the increasing complexity of the legislative, labour-management framework (see Chapter 5). In that country the original intention was to oppose the compulsory arbitration system which employers had regarded as a fundamental challenge to management rights, and subsequently to disseminate information and advice to association members 'in interpreting the maze of awards, classifications and legislation that the system was producing' (Plowman, 1980, p. 253).

It is apparent from these factors that, although it is sometimes assumed (by drawing on the basis of US experience, for instance) that the main driving-force behind the establishment and growth of employers' associations is related to market or 'economic' factors, wider international evidence suggests that a more eclectic explanation is required. Jackson and Sisson (1976, p. 319) have warned against ignoring 'the processes which mediate the effects of economic forces upon actual behaviour.' For one thing, employers' behaviour both in the USA and Sweden was profoundly influenced by what they perceived as the threat posed by unions to their ability to manage. Furthermore, the juxtaposition of particular historical, political events with economic forces often seems to have been decisive in stimulating defensive reactions by employers. In Sweden there was the 1902 general strike for manhood suffrage and in Germany, during a period of anarchist violence, the 1904 Crimmitschau strike had a critical influence on employers and accelerated the trend towards their organisation (Puységur, 1951). Certainly, it was the effects of such rising social tensions and widespread industrial conflict which motivated the giant Siemens company in the electrical engineering industry to join the metalworking employers' association (Homburg, 1983). In France Sellier (1978) has pointed out that the (late) appearance of employers' organisations oriented towards labour rather than commercial interests, in 1919 and again in 1936, corresponded to two periods of social crisis and state intervention towards resolving it. A confederated employers' organisation was set up in 1919 at the behest of the state which wanted a partner for the application of the new law on collective wage agreements.

European-North American Contrasts

The role of political pressures such as these as a major influence upon the development of employers' associations has been emphasised by Adams (1981), who puts forward a theory to account for the broad differences between Western Europe and the USA both in the extent of organisation among employers themselves and in their behaviour towards trade unions. He notes that in Europe employers generally have formed associations and have been willing to accept trade unions, whereas in US industries, especially in manufacturing, employers have pursued more independent policies and their attitude towards unions remains at best, as Thompson and Moore (1975) have shown, one of grudging tolerance, if not of open hostility. Adams maintains that these observed variations may be traced historically to differences in government action.

After the 1880s European unions expanded their membership among the ranks of the unskilled. Many of these worker organisations also embraced a class philosophy, were centralised in structure and had links with Labour or socialist parties. In Germany, for instance, important unions initially grew out of the socialist political movement itself, but they failed to achieve recognition in heavy industry because of employer resistance to the whole idea of joint regulation of employment which was interpreted as a political challenge to employer power and authority. The position in other European countries was similar and, with exceptions such as Sweden and Britain, the unions were unable by their own devices to force employers to seek an accommodation with them.

At the same time, however, in response to the growing political power of labour, governments began to pursue a more conciliatory approach towards the labour movement. Instead of openly siding with employers they instituted a rather more even-handed policy intended to bring labour and management together to regularise their relations. Pressures began to be put on employers to recognise and negotiate with unions. As a result employers came to reappraise their previous strategy of attempting to contain unions by means of active opposition since that was more likely to result in increased government intervention to facilitate recognition. In any case, as has been shown elsewhere, 'total suppression of trade union activity without the help of the state was impossible' (Jackson and Sisson, 1976, p. 311). Thus employers came together for mutual support since labour's (political) goals posed a threat not merely to individual employers but collectively to employers as a class. Moreover, in view of the government's stance, their new associations began to recognise and establish on-going relations with unions on an industry or regional basis – although they continued strongly to oppose a union presence within the enterprise in order to maximise their own control.

By way of contrast, the situation in the USA was quite different. There, the mainstream of the labour movement was content to confine its challenge to employers to the economic sphere and in the absence of any socialist party alliance no serious political challenge was posed. Employers, therefore, had less reason to associate for defensive purposes since although trade unionism did represent a challenge to employers' power to manage 'it was manifest as a threat to specific employers in specific industries at specific times and places rather than as a general threat to employers as a class' (Adams, 1981, p. 286). It is true, however, that for US employers direct control of the workplace was crucial,[4] and many of them fought unionism with every weapon at their command. The difference in their market situation was also important in explaining their opposition to unionism, since US manufacturing employers concentrated upon standardised products sold on price – which had to be kept down (Phelps Brown, 1983).

In industrial relations within the major steel industry the most striking difference between the United States and Britain in the late nineteenth and early twentieth centuries was undoubtedly the behaviour of employers (Holt, 1977). As in other US industries technical change was more extensive and rapid than in Britain so that the importance of introducing technical innovation also helps to explain the greater hostility of US employers to (craft-type) unions. In the US steel industry not only did employers control a rapidly changing technology but the small number of very large firms which existed possessed vast financial resources. Also, employers were uninhibited by political constraints, unlike their counterparts in Britain, a country in which the working class was politically more potent. As a result, US employers were adamant in their determination to resist efforts to unionise their steel mills. In fact, more generally it has been shown that the most important single cause of violence in labour disputes in the USA during the early years of the twentieth century, involving at least 700 deaths and several thousand serious injuries, was the denial of union recognition for purposes of collective bargaining (Taft and Ross, 1979).

In the United States government support for organised labour came at a later date than in Europe (only in the mid-1930s), and even then it still remained open to employers to try to persuade their own workers (short of using overt coercion) not to vote for union bargaining rights (i.e. they still maintained 'an ethical mandate to continue with their belligerent behaviour towards unions' (Adams, 1981, p. 287)). Thus, according to Adams, employers in the USA – unlike those in much of Europe – were not required by government to recognise unions as the legitimate representatives of the working class. Certainly, employers were not propelled into joining associations since by the time they were required by legislation to bargain with unions US manufacturing was itself organised into sufficiently large company units for employers to be self-sufficient and not to require association bargaining (Thomson, 1981). Also, in several European countries legislation had been passed to 'extend' agreements to employers who were not a party to the negotiations (see Chapter 5). This, too, encouraged the growth of employers' associations because non-members would then join in order to have a voice in determining bargaining outcomes which affected them. In the USA such extension provisions were virtually non-existent. Finally, independent single-employer (rather than association) bargaining meant that US firms could still continue to deal with their own employees – even if they were now organised into trade unions – rather than be faced with an external trade union body against which they had fought for so long (Sisson, 1984).

In Western European countries, however, by the time of World War I, well-developed and stable associations of employers had become established both at national (confederal) and at industry levels, with the notable exception of France. Their role and legitimation were further strengthened during the war since governments tended to incorporate the associations in order to assist in war-time economic administration. As Windmüller (1984) has shown, employers' associations were then further consolidated and entrenched during the inter-war period (although there were some marked exceptions[5]) since collective bargaining became institutionalised in this period in many countries. Similarly, in the post-World War II period more interventionist governments wished to deal with authoritative employers' representatives, sometimes with the aim of promoting greater centralisation in collective bargaining. Since association (or multi-employer) bargaining became a major part of the industrial relations systems of these countries the specific collective bargaining role of employers' associations now requires more detailed analysis.

Collective Bargaining via Associations

There is no doubt that the growth and authority of employers' associations has had a major influence both upon the development and the direction of collective bargaining in many countries. In Britain once employers' federations had been established, albeit often in response to trade union expansion and activity, they then proceeded to assume the initiative by redesigning the existing system of industrial relations to their own wishes. This involved the introduction of centralised procedural agreements for dispute settlement and the associations were also a very significant influence upon the adoption of industry-wide agreements on pay and hours (Clegg, 1979). Conversely, where employers' associations remained weak and underdeveloped – as in France up to the inter-war period – collective bargaining played a negligible role in setting the terms and conditions of employment, with the result that legislative provisions assumed relatively greater importance.

In Sweden the reaction of employers to the rise of trade unions was also vital in determining the level at which collective bargaining would be conducted. The fact that employers were organised by industry had a feedback effect on the structure of manual workers' trade unions. Employers demanded that unions bargain with them on an industry-wide basis and their pressure was critical for the eventual securing of the industrial union principle of organisation. In more recent times the functioning of Swedish industrial relations has been as much, if not more, dependent upon the centralisation of power within the employers' confederation as upon the unions' peak organisation. Similarly in the pre-1914 period in Germany the authority of employers' organisations over their members helped the attainment of an earlier recognition of collective bargaining (outside manufacturing industry),[6] in contrast to its much later acceptance in France. The tight organisational structure of employers' associations both in Sweden and West Germany has also helped to make the lock-out (which is rarely used in most other countries) a potent weapon in contemporary industrial relations to be used, on occasion, against the unions.

In addition, the structure of collective bargaining is an important influence upon the role and locus of decision-making within employers' organisations themselves. In West Germany where industry-wide bargaining on a regional basis is the most prevalent, industry-based employers' associations and their regional sub-groupings are the important bodies which carry out the major bargaining activities. In fact, the employers' central confederation (BDA) does not engage in collective bargaining and, although it does provide information and guidance to its affiliates via its collective bargaining coordination committee, its pronouncements on wages take the form of non-binding recommendations. In the building industry in France, Sweden, Britain and West Germany the fact that the respective employers' organisations are essentially federations is also tied up with the structure of collective bargaining, since in most cases the local or regional organisation was – or is – a bargaining agent (Sisson, 1984).

Although the central confederations of employers' associations are usually much less involved in collective bargaining than are the industry associations, nevertheless in a few countries the peak organisations do play a major role. In Sweden the negotiation of economy-wide agreements on wages by the union and employer confederations has reinforced the prominent position of the Swedish Employers' Confederation (SAF). In the Netherlands, as a result of a long history of legislative enactment in socio-economic affairs and close involvement of unions and employers with government in this area the two national employers' confederations (denominational and non-denominational) also carry somewhat greater weight than their member associations. This is a consequence of the fact that 'a central body, like a national federation, is best suited and equipped to represent the employers' view on any proposed legislative or administrative action' (Bomers, 1976, p. 78). In Australia under the compulsory arbitration system, the peak employers' confederation (CAI) makes representations before the wage hearings of the Federal Arbitration Commission; and in Israel the central body represents its member firms before the Labour Courts.

At industry level, multi-employer bargaining under the auspices of employers' associations continues to play an important role in Western European countries such as Germany, France, Sweden and Italy. In the case of Britain, however, and during the last 15 years especially, multi-employer bargaining within manufacturing has declined in favour of single-employer negotiations. (This shift in bargaining level has, as we noted, been most apparent in the engineering and chemical industries.) The reasons for the contrast have recently been investigated by Sisson (1984). His explanation is not, as is often supposed, the fact that in Britain multi-employer agreements failed to determine actual earnings levels in the workplace, or that employers have come to prefer independent negotiations. (Interestingly, in the car industry, although Ford has never belonged to an association in Britain nevertheless in Germany it is an active member of the metalworking employers' association and follows the terms of its negotiated agreements.) Instead, Sisson maintains that the real reason is that in Britain multi-employer bargaining has increasingly been found to be incapable of performing what employers regard as its major function, namely the neutralisation of the workplace from the activities of trade unions. He therefore views multi-employer (association) bargaining as being principally a political institution rather than an economic one – a contention which now requires further examination.

For the important group of metalworking industries in all of the five countries which Sisson investigates, multi-employer bargaining was established by the parties themselves in Britain and Sweden, and by legislative enactment in the other three, but in response to a somewhat differing challenge from the trade unions. In Britain it came from the craft unions which, due to the early date of industrialisation, were already well established in the workplace. The emphasis in agreements was therefore placed upon procedural, rather than substantive, rules designed to uphold the employers' right to manage in the face of attempted unilateral imposition of working rules by craft unions. In continental Europe, however, the union assault came not from workplace-based craft organisations but from centralised and more politicised trade unions. Multi-employer bargaining outside the establishment at regional and industry level – whose detailed substantive agreements were backed by law and left less scope for supplementary bargaining for improved terms – could therefore be a means of continuing to exclude trade unions from the workplace. In Sweden, for instance, a strong employers' confederation enforced managerial prerogatives from the early years of the present century, prerogatives which were also supported by the legal framework until the law was changed in 1977 (see Chapter 7).

In Britain, however, worker attempts in the 1950s and 1960s to improve upon the minimum substantive terms of employment in more favourable labour market conditions, together with the lack of legally-binding disputes procedures, stimulated the expansion of (fragmented) workplace bargaining over pay and a high proportion of shopfloor strikes. All of this transcended the frontiers of control and undermined the employers' ability to manage. The result was that in order to regain control over industrial relations a restructuring and formalisation of 'domestic' bargaining, especially wage-payment systems, was needed. But this reform could only feasibly be carried out within companies and plants by single employers, rather than by multi-employer associations.[7] Hence, the move towards single-employer bargaining in Britain became more firmly established, especially in large firms which had the necessary managerial expertise to undertake such reforms. There has been an increasing professionalism of industrial relations management in Britain and, as noted by Goodman:

> As company size and the internalisation of industrial relations activity have increased many companies have acquired or strengthened their own specialist personnel management function . . . thus facilitating the pursuit of more distinctive, company-specific employment policies. (Goodman, 1981, p. 606)

An accompanying development was that, from the 1960s, employers' associations in some important industries changed the emphasis of their role. From being a central coordinator determining a common line to be followed by all member firms, they became more a centre to which their members might turn for advice and industrial relations services, particularly those relating to the expanding field of labour law and other consequences of government action such as incomes policy requirements. Although there has been no mass exodus of member firms from employer bodies, nevertheless 'employers have used their associations more as advisers than negotiators and have increasingly looked after negotiations for themselves' (Brown, 1981, p. 24).

Not only has a trend towards the internalisation of negotiating activity been apparent in Britain but also in those countries such as the United States and Japan where enterprise-level bargaining has predominated labour relations issues have long been handled by the managements of individual undertakings themselves. Because employers can increase their profits when they have greater control over the labour process it has been suggested that in the USA internal 'job ladders' of promotion and wage benefits were developed by managements within some large firms as a deliberate control strategy to counter unionism and increase the dependence of workers on their companies. Similarly, the emphasis in large-scale Japanese companies has been on the creation of organisation-oriented, bureaucratic policies (emphasising job security, seniority-based promotion, incremental pay scales, etc.). In that country one of the most salient characteristics of post-World War II industrial relations has been the development of control by professional managements in the larger enterprises. Also, in Germany firms such as Siemens originally joined employers' associations yet never fully relied on them as a collective means of defending managerial prerogatives and curtailing union activities in the workplace. The association was not a substitute for, but rather a supplement to, internal company means of labour control (e.g. via a company union) (Homburg, 1983). Some discussion is needed, therefore, from the limited comparative literature which is yet available, of internal labour control mechanisms at the level of individual establishments and the strategies of managements towards employment relations.

It has been pointed out by Gospel that 'managers' themselves cannot be defined simply as being either employers or employees, since for the majority of them their role is (simultaneously) of a dual nature:

> On the one hand they are 'employers of labour' and managers because of the functions they perform, the authority they possess and the rewards they enjoy. On the other hand, they are employees in that they do not own the organisation for which they work, they are salaried agents, and they are subject to superior authority. (Gospel, 1978, p. 363)

In fact, for a number of reasons including changes in the market situation of managers (in terms of narrowing pay differentials and perceived increases in job insecurity) together with the more ready conceding of union recognition for those employed in the public sector of the economy, managerial unionism increased markedly in Western Europe during the 1970s. 'Middle managers in Britain, *cadres* in France, *Dirigenti* in Italy and *Leitende Angestellte* [senior executive staff] in West Germany joined trade unions in large numbers' (Poole *et al.*, 1983, p. 426).

In this chapter, however, our concern is with managements' authority functions and their strategies in relation to their workforce. The term 'strategy', as a way of conceptualising management actions, refers to long-term policies pursued by management and it implies, according to one common approach, that management has a choice between alternative possibilities with respect to the best ways of attaining its labour relations objectives – within the constraints set by the external environment. Thus boundaries to strategic choices will be set *inter alia* by political and economic forces. Moreover, as Poole has observed,

> the implementation of strategies will in themselves depend greatly upon a series of further conditioning variables such as managerial organisation, patterns of authority within the management hierarchy and, above all, upon the power of oppositional groups (especially trade unions). (Poole, 1980, p. 40)

Management Strategies in Industrial Relations

A number of typologies of employer strategies towards industrial relations have been suggested with the objectives of securing managerial control over the work process, obtaining the allegiance of the workforce, and negating trade union influence within the enterprise. On the basis of US experience, Edwards (1979) identified a progression of employer strategies from 'simple' (direct) control in small firms, whereby arbitrary power to issue instructions and discipline employees is accorded to foremen and supervisors,[8] through 'technical' control in which machines set the pace of work, especially in mass-production industries, to a 'bureaucratic' stage where work becomes highly stratified and employers develop a system of impersonal rules to control workers. Also, a range of managerial devices designed to enhance worker satisfaction and exclude or counter trade union influence in the undertaking may be introduced including company unions, welfare policies and paternalism. Much of the literature in this area has been of US origin, and the more general applicability of such managerial strategies to other countries needs, therefore, to be considered in the light of evidence from cross-national studies.

Gallie's (1978) comparative study of oil refineries in France and Britain highlights important differences in managerial strategies. In broad terms it was found that British managements had adopted a control system which relied little upon direct managerial intervention and allowed the workforce a greater say in decision-making, essentially as a recognition of the *de facto* power of trade unions and shopfloor organisation within the industry. Management could be faced 'with severe economic losses if it failed to take into account their views, or to win their consent on issues which were felt to be of major importance by the workforce' (p. 314). In contrast, trade unions in France had too little organisational strength in the workplace to be able to inflict major economic losses on the firm and they were considered to be too ideologically radical to be permitted a higher degree of participation. French managements were able to exercise a much tighter system of control involving a higher ratio of supervisors to workers together with the imposition of more disciplinary sanctions. At the same time there was an emphasis upon paternalism to enhance workers' motivation and promote effective work performance which might otherwise have been impaired by this control strategy.

Gallie concludes that the relatively greater emphasis upon authoritarian and paternalistic practices within the French context[9] is not solely a reflection of managerial attitudes engendered by the structural characteristics of industry, as typified by a long predominance of small, family firms in which the employer regarded himself as having a right to exclusive control. In fact, similar managerial characteristics have continued to prevail in larger, technologically-advanced firms. Thus in both the French and British refineries industrial relations are 'firmly locked into the wider institutional patterns of their societies' (p. 182), reflecting the historical development of their social structures and the differing cultural orientations of the actors. Even within highly automated, and almost identical, sectors of the refining industry no process towards similarity or 'convergence' in managerial strategies in the two countries appears to have occurred.

In addition to direct, or personal, control it has also become usual to distinguish a form of control which is incorporated within (impersonal) technological structures. Such technical control was first developed in the mechanised, mass-production industries in the United States during the 1890s and early years of the present century, as epitomised in the steel mills. Because expensive capital equipment and the attainment of a rapid through-put of production were central to this development, 'the craft skill and judgement of the workers had to be as much as possible superseded, as did the control of workers over the pace of work' (Lazonick, 1983, p. 112). Profitable mass production necessitated not only employer control over the planning and organisation of work, but also reliable, attentive and loyal workers to perform it. One management response in the USA was therefore to introduce a range of welfare policies, and employee representation plans, generally known as 'company unions'. Similarly, in some of the large industrial enterprises in Germany during the inter-war period with the introduction of standardised mass-production techniques a parallel emphasis was placed upon welfare measures (company housing, provision of leisure activities, etc.) as a means of motivation, promoting integration and worker commitment to the company.

However, in contrast to the situation in the United States and Germany, recent comparative research has shown that both technical control and corporate paternalism failed to become important long-term strategies in much of British industry in the early part of the present century because of a predominant small-firm structure together with the opposition of well-entrenched unions. In the engineering industry, for example, employers were unable completely to transform work relations towards deskilling and standardised mass production, mainly because they were not prepared to undertake the major capital investment which would have been required (Zeitlin, 1983). In the car industry, control of the labour process through machine-pacing was also not generally regarded as a viable strategy by British management in the context of the existence of powerful labour organisations at the point of production and a desire to reduce the perceived increasing antagonism of labour to capital. Instead, productivity improvements and more cooperative attitudes were to be attained by other devices such as wage incentive schemes (Lewchuk, 1983).

A third strategy used to manage and motivate employees as the size of industrial enterprises increased has been the development of bureaucratic personnel policies. These are characterised by internal company training and promotion systems, complex wage hierarchies, as well as greater job security, since most jobs are insulated from the direct effects of competitive forces in the external labour market. In the United States during the 1920s, job security and internal 'job ladders' (i.e. promotion from within the firm) began to be introduced, it has been claimed, partly in order to differentiate (the semi-skilled) labour force and break up the sense of solidarity that united a firm's workers in collective opposition to their employer – and they were to prove particularly effective in forestalling unionism (Edwards, 1979). In the case of the steel industry Stone (1974) contends that the restructuring of job hierarchies, the creation of internal job ladders and accompanying wage payments did not, in fact, reflect the attainment of technical skills derived from on-the-job training. Instead, employee loyalty and dependability could be the major factors in securing promotion through the hierarchies. (With this line of argument, however, it is possible to exaggerate the extent to which the hierarchical division of labour – fostering sectionalism among workers – was primarily a result of deliberate and purposive employer labour strategy, rather than being more an unintended consequence of technological advance.)

A similar strategy of bureaucratisation would appear to have emerged during the inter-war period among Japanese employers, which was to some extent directly influenced by developments in the United States (Taira, 1973). In order to absorb growing labour militancy, maintain and prevent turnover among their (mobile) key workers, and strengthen their right to manage, employers' labour strategy in the larger enterprises turned to establishing their own training schools and internal promotion ladders. Where necessary they were also prepared to set up enterprise works committees with employees' representatives, whilst at the same time strongly opposing external industrial or national unions.

> By differentiating in a complex fashion its own workforce management from the practices of all other firms, each firm hoped to balkanise the labour market and to tie the well-being of employees to the success of the firm. (Taira, 1973, p. 174)

In the heavy engineering industry, as well as internal labour markets, Japanese employers also chose paternalistic practices and employee welfare provisions, rather than accept the threat to their power posed by trade unions and collective bargaining (Okayama, 1983). Nevertheless, the different rewards and promotion systems appropriate to Japanese industry, founded in part upon an acceptance by management of the need to enhance the welfare of all permanent employees, reflect quite different values to those of US management: 'The example of Japan, therefore, indicates the importance of general social and cultural factors in influencing the thrust and direction of strategic managerial thinking' (Thurley and Wood, 1983, p. 213).

Conclusions

In this chapter we have examined comparative aspects of the nature and development of collective employers' associations together with the management strategies of individual firms. In many countries employers' organisations originated, often in periods of cyclical upswings in economic activity, with the intention of providing protection against onslaughts upon the position of employers and the undermining of their prerogatives, especially from trade unions. Although mainly reactive bodies at the outset, they were not slow to initiate new patterns of industrial relations in countries like Britain and Sweden. In more recent years provision by the associations of advisory services in labour matters, dispute settlement procedures and legislative issues – as well as pressure-group activities – have all become general, reflecting the increasing complexity of industrial relations and the enlarged role of government.

However, although it is possible to identify a number of common facilitating factors in the development of employers' associations in various countries there are also some important differences both between and within countries, particularly in the extent to which these bodies engage in direct negotiating activities on behalf of their members. To some extent this has been influenced by the economic structure and market factors in the particular country or industry concerned. But it also appears to depend upon the extent to which employer control over the workplace is enhanced by multi-employer bargaining rather than by independent, single-firm action. From the evidence of a 10-country study, Gladstone (1984) notes that the activities, structure and functions of employers' associations do show a good deal of inter-country variation, often a reflection of distinctive historical experiences and a particular course of industrialisation with resultant differences in the environment in which a country's industrial relations system has to operate.

Similar observations can be made in relation to the development of management strategies in industrial relations at the level of the individual enterprise. We have noted similarities in company labour strategies in the USA, Germany and Japan during the inter-war period by way of the introduction of enterprise career structures and bureaucratic internal promotion systems. Britain was something of an exception, however, not only because of the slow development of the large corporation and mass-production techniques, but also because of the effects of a long-established, powerful and horizontally-structured trade union movement which opposed such firm-specific practices and internal labour market systems.

In sum, employers are highly significant as actors in their own right and their activities are a critically important variable affecting the direction and development of industrial relations. Not least, as we have shown, an analysis of the role of employers and their organisations leads to important insights into the structure and dimensions of collective bargaining. It is this topic which will be considered in the next chapter.

Notes

1. As Windmüller (1984, p. 8) expresses it, 'Employers' associations, by contrast with trade associations, specialise in representing the interests of their members mainly or exclusively in the labour area. In European terminology their chief concerns are the so-called "social" issues.'

2. In order to prevent those employers who did not recognise and negotiate with a union enjoying a labour cost advantage over their competitors who did. Thus in certain industries in the USA multi-employer bargaining was initiated by employers faced with excess capacity and inelastic product demand.

3. A good illustration is the Engineering Employers' Federation in Britain: 'Historically, the principal function of the Federation has been to provide a defensive alliance of employers to meet actions of unions regarded as inimical to their interests, principally through the use of a nationally based "provision for avoiding disputes" ' (Marsh *et al.*, 1981, p. 9).

4. Edwards (1981) attributes this in part to the absence in the USA of a feudal tradition which required loyalty among employees. American employers had therefore to establish their own legitimacy and secure their employees' undivided loyalty. They could tolerate no threat to the achievement of that objective.

5. In Germany, Italy and Japan the associations became absorbed into the political structures of Fascist or military regimes.

6. By 1914 some 20 per cent of German manual workers were covered by collective agreements.

7. Gospel (1983a) argues, however, that the impetus to plant-level bargaining about wages and conditions occurred because of competitive, product market factors. As the scope of markets became more international they were less amenable to (multi-employer) collusive arrangements.

8. Sometimes replacing the (sub-) contracting system of labour force management, as in the nineteenth-century British and US iron industries.

9. In Italy also – until relatively recently – small, medium and large employers tended to follow paternalistic–autocratic personnel policies (Brandini, 1975).

Further Reading

The most comprehensive international survey of the functions and activities of employers' associations is Windmüller and Gladstone (1984). A more analytical investigation of a small number of Western European countries and the role of employers' organisations in collective bargaining is Sisson (1984). Systematic comparative analysis of management strategies in industrial relations has only recently begun, the major work so far being Gospel and Littler (1983) which relates to the inter-war period.

4 COLLECTIVE BARGAINING

In many industrialised market economies collective bargaining has become so firmly established that it is sometimes regarded as being virtually synonymous with the prevailing system of industrial relations. Collective bargaining determines wages and working conditions, and also regulates the relationship between the bargaining parties themselves. It has been defined as

> an institutionalised procedure . . . of joint determination of the rules to govern the terms and conditions of employment of the workers concerned and the labour-management relationship itself. (ILO, 1980, p. 25)

In this sense collective bargaining is not only confined to formalised, written agreements between trade unions and employers' bodies, it can also include informal, collective dealings and negotiations at local level, both on wage and non-wage issues, between managements and works councils or similar bodies in countries like Austria and West Germany, even though in the latter country collective bargaining and the co-determination mechanisms are supposed to be kept separate.[1]

Diverse Nature and Functions

Although it is perhaps the single most prevalent aspect of post-war industrial relations systems in advanced capitalist societies (Crouch, 1982a) collective bargaining is in fact a multifaceted institution which, on an international basis, has diverse meanings and functions. In addition to rule-making, thereby reducing the degree of uncertainty confronting workers and management, it can also be a vehicle for resolving disputes, a power relationship[2] and, where it takes place at enterprise or plant level, it may be regarded as a form of participation for workers or their representatives (see Chapter 7). Thus in Norway, employers see it as a mechanism providing for industrial peace, whereas according to the CGT in France it is a form of class struggle (Schregle, 1981). In the USA collective bargaining is viewed almost as 'the alpha and omega of trade unionism' (Reynaud, 1975). A different conception of collective bargaining in terms both of its character and role is applicable in socialist countries with centrally-planned economies. There, despite the identical name of 'collective agreements', it is regarded not as an adversary process but rather as a means of ensuring the full co-operation of management and workers in carrying out the economic and social plans and improving the management of undertakings (ILO, 1980). Also, in West Germany, Scandinavia, Switzerland and the USA the collective bargaining agreement is a legal contract, whereas in Britain, traditionally,

> collective bargaining is not typically concluded by a contract, specifying in detail the future rights and duties of either side but by an understanding [which] must depend on personal relationships and customary usages. (Burrage, 1972, p. 150)

In the case of Japan collective agreements tend to be notably more general and abstract than their western counterparts, a characteristic – so it is claimed – of the nature of Japanese personal relations in which there is reluctance to have one's rights and obligations closely defined (Hanami, 1979).

In countries where there is a large degree of regulation of the terms of employment by the state, the role of collective bargaining may be correspondingly reduced. For instance, in many Latin American countries collective bargaining is only a secondary source of rights and obligations in labour relations after legislation (Bronstein, 1978). Among European countries, in the historical development of French industrial relations the frequent intervention of public authorities gave union struggles a decidedly political flavour. Instead of bilateral employer–union agreements there developed belatedly a protective labour law which, by the very functions it fulfilled, was a hindrance to the emergence of collective bargaining (Maurice and Sellier, 1979). Nevertheless, over the past 30 years statutory regulation has diminished somewhat in importance in France and collective bargaining has developed considerably, doing much more than filling the gaps left by legislation. Collective bargaining is a flexible instrument and can build upon the minimum standards which the law lays down. Sometimes it has played a pioneering role in bringing about new developments, such as the Renault agreement on the duration of holidays which then became generalised by legislation (Despax and Rojot, 1979).

Similarly, in West Germany collective agreements have on occasion introduced new labour norms which subsequently became generalised minimum statutory standards. An example is the 'social plan' package of protective and compensating measures for workers made redundant, originally negotiated in the coal and steel industries (Günter and Leminsky, 1978). In that country legislation also maintains an important position in the setting of norms for industrial relations and working conditions, covering many fringe benefits that could be collective bargaining issues elsewhere. Moreover, some topics are placed by law within the (co-determination) jurisdiction of the works council, a formally union-independent system of interest representation in which all eligible employees may vote and stand for election regardless of union membership. The distinction between co-determination and collective bargaining is important in that works councils, as agents of co-determination, are legally forbidden to call a strike whereas unions, as collective bargaining agents, are not (Streeck,1981). Nevertheless, *de facto*, the works council forms the organisational backbone of the union within the plant and, furthermore,

> owing to its early introduction in 1920 and also because of the substantial extension of its rights in 1952 and 1972 it was able to evolve into the virtual bargaining monopolist on the employees' side at the plant level, to the extent of being considered by unions as the proper bargaining agent at that level, much more so than in other countries. (Sorge, 1976, p. 288)

Works councils have been particularly important in securing improvements in working conditions and other non-wage elements since many of these are so specific to individual workplaces that they cannot be regulated by means of a general, industry-wide agreement.

In Belgium it has been argued that there is so much social and labour legislation that there is less room for collective bargaining. Although it is true that the legal provisions are mostly protective minimum standards which can be improved upon via collective bargaining, the fact remains that collective bargaining itself does not have the same range as might be the case if legal provisions were fewer (Blanpain, 1982a). It may also appear that the scope for collective bargaining would be more severely curtailed in Australia, where the state-operated system of conciliation and compulsory arbitration has shaped labour-management relations since the turn of the century (see Chapter 5). Nevertheless, such third-party regulation often incorporates and consolidates employment terms which have already been agreed via prior negotiations between unions and employers. In this sense the Australian compulsory arbitration system, although a form of statutory regulation, may also be regarded as part of a collective bargaining system (Clegg, 1976). The compulsory arbitration system in fact emphasises conciliation, with arbitration by tribunals in the event of failed negotiations.

Bargaining Structure

The regularised patterns of union-management interaction, or the network of institutionalised bargained relationships, is referred to as the 'bargaining structure'. Although it may be contended that it is the *process* of collective bargaining as an ongoing activity which is at the heart of industrial relations, the negotiating process itself has received little attention in international studies (an exception is Smith and Turkington, 1981). Greater interest has been generated by bargaining structures which, as will be shown, establish the framework for the exercise of power within the labour market. A number of different dimensions of bargaining structure have been identified. These include the one or more levels at which negotiations take place, the extent (or coverage) of the resultant collective agreement across different sectors of employment (often termed the 'bargaining units'), and the scope of bargaining in relation to the range of subjects included therein. It may be asked, how do these structural arrangements vary across countries? and what are the determinants of the variations and what are their consequences for industrial relations systems? These questions will be considered in turn.

Bargaining structures within the international context, although extremely heterogeneous rather than conforming to any simple and tidy pattern, may be broadly classified in terms of the level at which negotiations are mainly conducted. Three modal types can be distinguished: *industry-wide*, multi-employer bargaining which is external to the firm, as practised in much of Western Europe on wage-related issues; *single enterprise* or firm bargaining, as typically found in the USA and Japan; and *economy-wide* systems between trade union and employer central confederations which have been characteristic of several countries, including Norway, Sweden, Denmark and, at times, the Netherlands. In many countries the terms and conditions of employment are the result of agreements made at two or more different levels. In France industry-wide negotiation has been the preferred level for wage bargaining, being principally confined to the fixing of minimum conditions. Yet since the late 1950s extensive progress on the negotiation of general clauses on working conditions has taken place between the central employers' organisations and large trade union confederations, along with government participation, on an economy-wide basis. But unlike the economy-wide agreements in Scandinavia, these exclude wages and deal instead with single, specific issues such as employment security or the progressive reduction of the working week (i.e. 'they deal with problems often dealt with solely by the government and amount to the development of law by collective bargaining' (Meyers, 1981)). As far as Italy is concerned, the relatively low level of institutionalisation of collective bargaining relations has meant that any matter can now be bargained at any level and any time – for instance, at shopfloor level matters already dealt with in the industry agreement can be negotiated (Treu, 1981).

How, then, may such differences in bargaining structures between national industrial relations systems be explained? Why do some countries have a structure which is characterised predominantly by either highly centralised or industry-wide agreements, whereas others have far more decentralised arrangements? There is a large measure of agreement within the literature that the structure of bargaining which becomes associated with a particular country's industrial relations system is not simply the result of chance occurrence or historical accident, but develops instead because of identifiable forces. In this respect it would appear that the preferences and relative power of the parties are especially important in shaping structure – that either unions or employers, or in some cases the government, want (and if necessary can make) it that way. Therefore, we now need to examine the explanatory factors which help determine on an inter-country basis each of the three major types of bargaining structure which have been identified. It needs to be remembered, however, that in categorising collective bargaining arrangements there are marked differences not only as between countries but within each national context as well. As Goodman has expressed it, in attempting generalisations for European industrial relations which cut across national boundaries

> collective bargaining arrangements form a multi-coloured patchwork of different styles, tones and texture which makes all-inclusive comment difficult. The search for appropriate generalisation and meaningful comparison is hazardous. (Goodman, 1978, p. 30)

Thus in Belgium, although most industrial sectors are covered by national (industry-wide) agreements providing minimum conditions which can be improved upon, in sectors such as the chemical industry these provisions are almost meaningless since the bulk of collective bargaining is carried out at the level of the plant or establishment (Blanpain, 1982a).

Industry Bargaining

Industry-wide wage bargaining between national trade unions and employers' associations, whether conducted across an entire industry or, as in West Germany, more partially for the regional sub-divisions of an industry, has been the prevailing practice in most Western European countries. This broadly-based or, as Windmüller (1977) terms it, 'macro-oriented' European bargaining structure eschewed formal negotiations at the level of the individual enterprise, in marked contrast to the enterprise-centred bargaining structures in the USA and Japan. Industry-level bargaining would seem to have corresponded most closely to the preferences of employers and their capacity to organise themselves with a view to protecting market shares and strengthening their own bargaining power. Contemporary bargaining structures are to some degree a reflection of bargaining patterns established at a fairly early stage of industrial development. In most European countries collective bargaining, whether conducted at the regional or district level, involved a group of enterprises rather than individual firms or plants.

This early development can often be related to the competitive dimensions (ease of entry and relatively low degree of concentration) within the product market, together with labour market considerations. Certainly, in Britain much of the impetus for joint action came from employers who were close competitors with each other in the sale of their products. They were anxious to help regulate competition throughout the product market by establishing uniform rates of pay and standard conditions. This interest in wage regulation, standardising and setting a floor to wage costs – thereby limiting competitive wage- and price-cutting – was especially prevalent in labour-intensive industries where labour costs formed a relatively high proportion of total costs.[3]

As well as the extent of product market concentration a further influence concerned the spatial or geographical concentration found in a number of important industries in Britain. This also favoured multi-employer bargaining arrangements because, since the workforces of geographically-concentrated industries are likely to be subject to less variation in local labour market pressures, it was possible to establish and more easily maintain a meaningful wage structure for district, or higher level, employer groupings (Beaumont *et al.*, 1980). Moreover, by the time of World War I a widening in the geographical scope of product markets themselves, and a desire to eliminate competition from low wage districts – together with government-setting of many wage awards during war-time – all these influences tended to extend the area of collective bargaining still further to the industry level.

Similar considerations were also applicable in some continental European countries. In France before World War I, collective bargaining existed only in mining and printing — both being geographically highly concentrated industries in which employers had an obvious interest in organising, in this case in order to avoid 'whipsawing'[4] by the union. In fact, Sellier (1978) attributes the generally late establishment of collective agreements in France (only since the mid-1950s for the bulk of the private sector) partly to the association by employers of workers and unions with revolutionary ideologies, but also to the marked weakness and slow development of employer organisations – the state long remaining the main partner of the unions.

Moreover, if employers had to bargain with trade unions their preference was for multi-employer bargaining at regional or industry level instead of engaging in direct enterprise dealings. In Holland and several other continental countries the unions' rightful place was very much regarded as being 'not inside the plant but beyond the gates' (Windmüller, 1967). In France 'unions were kept at a distance by the system of industry-wide bargaining which dealt with limited subjects and did not endanger the day-to-day power of management to make operating decisions' (Meyers, 1981, p. 191), although a union presence in the plant was later forced upon management by legislation as one of the consequences of the 1968 strikes. Industry bargaining was also preferable to employers in Italy since it allowed their associations to maintain a tight control on bargaining activities whilst at the same time freeing the individual employer from direct impact with the union – yet giving him ample leeway to influence his employees from outside union channels (Treu, 1981). Even in Britain Phelps Brown (1959) has shown that employers did not want to work in 'double harness' with their own men, that is to say, they would strongly resent their own workmen claiming to argue as unionists with them in their own works.

A preference by employers that bargaining relationships should follow the contours of an entire industry, or relate to some other multiple of firms, was often matched by similar union attitudes towards bargaining structure. They, too, wished to expand the size of the bargaining unit to reduce the possibilities of substitution within product and labour markets. For those unions organised on a comprehensive, industrial basis it is easy to see that they would be likely to seek bargaining arrangements founded upon the extent of the product market. According to Chamberlain,

> Here the interests of the workers cross occupational lines . . . [and] if their product must enter into competition with a substitute product made under cheaper working conditions, they will find it difficult to maintain or improve their own circumstances. If a common agreement blankets all competitors, however, none can secure an unfair advantage by undercutting the labour standards. (Chamberlain, 1961, pp. 4-5)

By ensuring the general application of minimum wage standards industry-wide bargaining could also prevent workers from competing with one another by offering to work for less. For Italian unions, in this respect, industry bargaining corresponded originally to a need to unite their scarce resources in order to guarantee uniform minimum conditions of work 'to an impoverished, fragmented and still mostly agricultural working class, privileging the weak sectors thereof with respect to the élite' (Treu, 1981, p. 135).

For the more numerous, horizontally-structured unions in Britain of the craft-type which crossed industry lines their interest during the nineteenth century lay in obtaining uniformity of conditions for the particular occupation throughout the labour market. Although, on the face of it, this might not appear to have been conducive to the development of industry-wide bargaining paradoxically such 'division by occupation promoted bargaining by industry' (Phelps Brown, 1959, p. 362). Because the various occupations in any one employment would monitor and compare their respective rates of pay, and given that the ability to pay of the employer was the same for all of them, they tended to negotiate a common bargain. It was more practicable to do this for a district or industry, since firm-by-firm bargaining was precluded for want of suitable union organisation to bring together all employees at the workplace. In this way the structure of British unions themselves contributed to the growth of industry-type bargaining. It is true that these original objectives and policies of particular types of union concerning the labour and product markets of the relevant occupation and industry have subsequently been modified as the unions amalgamated or became more diversified in terms of their recruitment. Yet they did have an important influence on the evolution of bargaining structure and the characteristic form which it assumed.

In addition to such economic influences, it has been observed that there was also an ideological basis for continental European trade unions' preference for broadly-based industrial bargaining. As we noted in Chapter 2 many unions regarded themselves as being part of a socialist-oriented labour movement directed towards a fundamental reconstruction of society. From this viewpoint any highly segmented representation of worker interests in relation to employers, such as via individual enterprise bargaining, had little appeal. Instead, the unions looked towards wider structures which would advance the interests of all workers in an entire industry, or a territorial subdivision of it, and promote as large a degree of solidarity as possible (ILO, 1974). Consequently,

> the employer tendency to favour the industry-type of bargaining was reinforced by the broad socialist, class consciousness of major European unions which probably led them to favour this approach, since it would engage 'employers through mass class action', and also extend protection to a larger part of the workforce. (Kassalow, 1982, p. 216)

On the basis of the predominance of these industry-wide agreements some observers have suggested that an actual 'European model' of collective bargaining may be delineated (Litvak and Maule, 1972; Clarke, 1980a). This is, however, a somewhat doubtful proposition since not only is it not entirely applicable to the Nordic countries without qualification (nor nowadays within manufacturing industry in Britain), but significant differences also exist even within continental countries, especially as between France and Germany. We have noted the importance in Germany of the works council as a bargaining mechanism and there are numerous characteristics which have also distinguished collective bargaining in France. Agreements there have generally been concluded for an indefinite term and (linked with this) no 'peace obligation' has arisen by the application of the agreement, in contrast to Germany. The CGT, for instance, has regarded collective bargaining as no more than a temporary measure of the balance of power between management and unions, enabling the union to obtain the best negotiating results for wage-earners at a given point in time (Goetschy, 1983). As a consequence it would appear that 'strikes are often the most practical means of renouncing an agreement' (Sellier, 1978, p. 222), although recently there have been attempts in France to institute more regularised collective relationships.

In contrast to this first basic pattern of bargaining which has been delineated, industry-wide and multi-employer agreements, we now turn to an analysis of the rationale of single-employer bargaining at the level of the enterprise or plant (not necessarily conterminous) which is typically found in the United States, Canada and Japan. In the USA it is estimated that about 80 per cent of collective agreements are confined to employees of a single company and about two-thirds are limited to a single plant (Cohen, 1975).

Enterprise Bargaining in the USA

In the United States multi-employer or association bargaining at district or regional level was by no means unknown, primarily in industries exemplified once again by highly competitive product markets. There, the large number of small employers might combine together as a defence against an otherwise predominantly unilateral union imposition of terms. For the union too multi-employer bargaining was probably the only administratively feasible form in many local product markets consisting of numerous small-scale undertakings. Multi-employer bargaining makes for simplification of effort in that separate contracts do not have to be negotiated with each individual employer. Similarly, in industries with casual employment such as building in which employees lacked permanent attachment to a given employer, the union's focus of organisation was the product or labour market rather than the individual firm. This tendency became even more pronounced as the market widened with improved means of transportation. For all these reasons multi-employer bargaining came to predominate in non-manufacturing industries and, more exceptionally, elsewhere in the concentrated industries of basic steel and the railways where government intervention seems to have been a decisive factor in shaping the bargaining process (Livernash, 1963).

On the whole, however, the trend in the USA was decidedly against broad industry bargaining arrangements, particularly in the dominant manufacturing sector, typified by large-scale firms, where single-employer bargaining units became the norm (see Chapter 3). Once more employer influences in favour of a restricted bargaining base were reinforced by congruent considerations on the union side. Livernash (1963) would even claim that the structure of bargaining in the United States has been primarily determined by union preferences and, unlike the situation in some European countries, employers appear to have exerted only a minimum positive influence. Unions might favour single-employer bargaining as a deliberate strategy since it would enhance their relative bargaining power in terms of a potential ability to whip-saw individual employers. In other instances this form of bargaining structure might prevail only as a second-best option because of the union's inability to organise the total product market – a necessary condition for the enforcement of industry-wide bargaining. Also, in terms of their aims and philosophy most US unions concentrated their attention on practical 'business unionism' improvements in the terms and conditions of employment which

> were best achieved by organisations that held secure positions inside the enterprise, and unlike their European counterparts the unions in North America insisted on establishing their presence in the plant itself and not merely outside it. (ILO, 1974, p. 95)

As well as the interests and objectives of the bargaining parties themselves, an additional influence favouring single-employer bargaining structures in the USA relates to the role of state policy. Certain kinds of employers' combinations seem to have been hindered by anti-trust legislation and this may help to explain the generally low level of organisation among employers. A more important factor, however, has been the provision of government support for collective bargaining. In the United States the 1935 Wagner Act was the watershed for trade union recognition and protection of employee collective bargaining rights, particularly in the mass-production industries of automobiles, steel and rubber. One feature of the Act was the principle of majority rule for electing the employees' bargaining representative which would then be granted exclusive jurisdiction as the negotiating agent for all the employees in the bargaining unit. The important point in this respect is that the legislative rules introduced into industrial relations emphasised the establishment of bargaining relationships plant-by-plant and enterprise-by-enterprise rather than on any wider basis. In the case of Canada, the 1944 legislation[5] was patterned on the Wagner Act and introduced certification processes compelling employers to engage in collective bargaining. Furthermore, Labour Relations Boards would usually confine certification orders to single-plant, or single-location bargaining units (Herman, 1966).

Enterprise Bargaining in Japan

Having examined the main reasons which explain the predominance of localised, single-employer bargaining on the North American continent we now consider the case of Japan, the other major country in which collective bargaining is normally conducted on an enterprise basis rather than in the form of industry-wide agreements. Despite such decentralisation, however, the structure of bargaining in Japan differs from that in the USA since unionisation and collective bargaining are heavily concentrated in large firms rather than being more widely diffused throughout the industrial structure (Levine, 1980).[6]

Japanese industrial relations display a number of singular characteristics of which the essential elements are the three so-called 'pillars' of the system, appertaining particularly to larger firms: single-enterprise trade unions, lifetime (or, more strictly, career) employment and seniority-related wages. The enterprise-based bargaining structure is closely intertwined with the structure of workers' trade unions. In Japan each union caters for workers employed within a particular enterprise and it concludes agreements with the management of that same enterprise. The emergence of the enterprise union form of organisation after World War II, and the importance attaching to its role in the industrial relations system, has its economic basis in the practice of lifetime employment for key employees.

One sort of explanation sees such practices as permanent employment and seniority wage systems as being related to Japan's unique cultural traditions and the carry-over to modern industry of patterns of social relationships and obligations which characterised feudal Japan.[7] Other, perhaps more convincing, approaches (as these practices are not characteristic of smaller-sized firms) see them as an employer response to the exigencies of the labour market and as a control device to elicit and reward loyal workforce behaviour (Jacoby, 1979), since lifetime employment is not a practice of very long standing in Japan. In fact, the system developed during the transition to industrialisation in the early part of the present century. In order to alleviate bottlenecks in the supply of skilled labour at that time, each enterprise or factory assumed the responsibility for training recruits for the emerging mass-production industries. Therefore, training became internalised within the structured organisation of the firm itself and, to reduce turnover, an internal labour market system of workforce allocation and promotion, along with a wage structure, was developed (see Chapter 3). Moreover, because employees were typically trained as single-skill operatives for a particular type of (often) enterprise-specific technology their acquired skills were largely non-transferable. Employees therefore had a vested interest in remaining with their firm since job mobility was restricted. Employers also wished to retain skilled labour to recoup their investment in training costs.

In explaining the shape of the bargaining structure in Japan, as with the industry-wide structures in Europe and the decentralised arrangements in the United States, the wishes and expressed policies of the bargaining parties themselves would appear to have been a predominant factor. Unionised workers sought employment security and income advancement primarily *within* their respective enterprises. Similarly, Japanese employers have tended to favour enterprise bargaining. They did not want outside intervention in the collective bargaining process from representatives of more broadly-based trade unions since such interference could be inimical to the preservation of paternalistic employee relations within the undertaking (Okochi *et al.*, 1973). Also, in parallel with the United States, the influence of public policy seems to have been an additional factor of some importance since it has been observed that the policy of the occupying powers after 1947 probably strengthened the tendency to form enterprise-based unions rather than alternative structures for bargaining purposes (Levine, 1981). (Collective bargaining in the public sector in Japan, however, remains more underdeveloped and problematic.)

Economy-wide Bargaining

We now turn to an examination of the third identifiable category of bargaining structure, economy-wide agreements in certain European countries. Their outstanding feature is the conduct of negotiations, not initially through the individual trade unions and employers' associations themselves but rather via the central confederations to which they are affiliated. The major agreements are drawn up between a small number of tightly-controlled organisations and the outcome of their central negotiations sets guidelines and limits to the industry-wide negotiations which then subsequently take place.

This sort of system was operative in the Netherlands from the end of World War II until the early 1960s. It resulted from government initiatives which centralised the process of wage-fixing to keep down labour costs and promote savings in an attempt to accelerate the modernisation of industry and foster economic growth. Henceforth, key negotiations on changes in the basic terms of employment took place between the union and employer confederations in close consultation with the government agencies concerned. Until its eventual collapse under the weight of accumulated economic pressures, the system operated successfully for almost 20 years. It was administratively feasible because Dutch industrial relations had always been characterised by a relatively high degree of centralised control over the bargaining process, together with a weak position of the trade unions at shop floor level.[8] Also, in that particular period, the country had been ruled by governments which by virtue of their composition and policies were able to secure trade union cooperation (Albeda, 1971).

Within the Scandinavian countries the predominant role of central organisations of employers and workers in negotiating collective agreements is best known in Sweden. The evolution of Swedish collective bargaining into a system of economy-wide agreements was greatly dependent upon the presence on both the employer and employee sides of a small number of organisations 'each large enough to bring crucial influence to bear on the development of bargaining issues across the whole labour market' (ILO, 1974, p. 340). Certainly, on the union side, the central trade union body (the LO) attained much greater power and authority than either the TUC in Britain or the AFL-CIO in the United States and the Swedish Employers' Confederation (SAF) had tightly controlled powers over its affiliates since its inception.

Before World War II and in the immediate post-war period industry-wide collective agreements continued to be negotiated beween individual employers' associations and trade unions with little intervention from their respective central organisations. During the 1950s, however, employers began to press successfully for coordinated, central wage bargaining, which has continued subsequently. Centralised negotiations between the union and employer confederations led to 'frame agreements' which then provided guidelines for industry-wide negotiations between the national unions and employers' organisations. As a final step the agreements were adjusted to local conditions via negotiations between managements and the workplace union organisations. Swedish employers believed that the greater coordination of negotiations by means of central bargaining could reduce the incidence of industrial conflict. A further consideration was that it would increase their own bargaining power since wage settlements made under the previously more decentralised system were proving increasingly expensive for employers. The unions would use the early settlements made in annual negotiations as a precedent to obtain leverage in their own bargaining and would attempt to improve upon them still further. The leap-frogging process which resulted meant that as a wage round progressed, later settlements tended to be more favourable to the unions and also more costly to the employers. In addition, unions would often delay settling in the hope of securing improvement, thus protracting wage bargaining. It was further claimed that the wage determination mechanism conducted on this basis gave a strong impetus to inflation.

For the unions one of the main inducements in favour of centralised negotiations was that they offered a better prospect for promoting the labour movement's specific policy of wage solidarity. This had originally been introduced in the 1930s with the aim of reducing what were regarded as unwarranted differentials in wages, and in particular as a means of improving the position of the lowest paid workers. Since the main differences in wage levels were to be found between, rather than within, unions an expanded role for the LO in wage negotiations had also been deemed necessary. With a central, unified system of negotiations there would be greater opportunity to reduce the wage 'spread' between industries, not least because then no bargaining group would be relatively disadvantaged for having settled in advance of the others.

The development of economy-wide agreements for both Scandinavia and the Netherlands reflects, however, not only those influences which are specific to the various countries themselves but also more general factors. Country size, for instance, appears to be related to the propensity to centralise collective bargaining authority within national confederations. As Weber (1963) points out, Sweden, Holland and Denmark are small nations with limited sized labour forces and only a few industries of major importance. Consequently, economy-wide bargaining units were more organisationally practicable and easier to establish. In addition, the economies of Holland and the Scandinavian countries are especially sensitive to international trade influences, which may also have encouraged a broad approach to wage determination. In this latter respect, government policy (or the threat of intervention) would seem to be the most significant factor tending to remove authority over collective bargaining to the national confederations.[9] Attempts to align the outcome of wage negotiations with macroeconomic policy objectives have been one factor which has tended to raise the level of bargaining and it has played a significant role at certain periods in countries such as Holland, Norway and Austria.

In summary, it is apparent from the preceding discussion of industry-wide, enterprise and centralised (or confederal) collective bargaining arrangements that in focusing upon determinants of the main forms of bargaining structure a number of diverse factors are important in explaining the marked differentiation found between countries. Their early bargaining patterns and nature of product markets at the time bargaining developed, the willingness or otherwise of employers to form bargaining coalitions in dealing with unions, the form of divisions between unions themselves, together with the role of state policy, have been the major, identifiable forces (ILO, 1974). In attempting to weight the relative importance of these individual variables some observers, despite the countervailing evidence, would maintain that on a world-wide basis economic forces have had only a limited influence in shaping bargaining structures (Beaumont *et al.*, 1980). However, it is generally recognised that economic considerations are undoubtedly important in shaping the *changes* which have occurred within existing structures over the course of time since collective bargaining itself is an evolving social institution. These changes also require discussion.

Changes in Bargaining Structures

It is true that, once established, the main elements of bargaining structures tend to persist and remain relatively stable. They do not usually break out suddenly from their traditional framework and veer off in a new direction. Yet the structures are by no means completely static. Shifts in market and technological factors, government policy and worker aspirations have been incorporated and bargaining structures gradually modified, sometimes substantially so.

In some Western European countries, where industry-wide agreements have been general, there has been a tendency in recent years towards greater decentralisation in the bargaining structure together with an extension in the scope and subject matter of agreements. (Even with the economy-wide agreements in Sweden in the 1983 negotiations no settlement could be arrived at with the union side which insisted upon separate industry level negotiations being conducted.) In Britain – outside the centralised and bureaucratic collective bargaining machinery which typifies the public sector – the trend has been towards more plant-level bargaining, more company-level agreements and generally more participation in collective bargaining by union workplace and management representatives at local level. Within private manufacturing industry as Brown (1981) has shown, multi-employer negotiations are no longer the major means of pay determination since two-thirds of manual workers now have their pay settled by single-employer bargaining – although, for the economy as a whole, 46 per cent of firms in the private sector reported multi-employer bargaining as being the most important for pay increases, as against 75 per cent for the public sector (Daniel and Millward, 1983). The recession of more recent years does not appear to have induced a reversion back towards multi-employer bargaining.

In Italy, also, although industry agreements are still important, there has been a marked growth since the 1960s of decentralised bargaining at plant and company level, in contrast to the previously highly centralised system. In companies such as Fiat and Olivetti the unions secured regulation of investment and development policy via decentralised negotiations (von Beyme, 1980). Even in Franco's Spain during the 1960s and early 1970s bargaining power also became divested from the (state-controlled) unions to the level of the workplace (Fina and Hawkesworth, 1984).

The reasons for this decentralising movement towards the growth of workplace bargaining activity in Western European countries have been in part economic, as a result of generally high employment and continuous economic growth in the post-war years to the mid-1970s along with a varying capacity to pay of separate employers. Strong competition for supplies of scarce labour encouraged managements in British industries such as engineering to negotiate additional supplementary agreements at enterprise or plant level. Similarly in Germany, industry-wide agreements (especially in boom periods) were unable to exhaust the capacity to pay of prosperous firms. As a result, enhanced earnings were negotiated informally (since technically it was illegal) by the works councils (Streek, 1981). Furthermore, in many countries the bargaining power of shopfloor workers was enhanced because of the greater capital intensity and tighter integration of industrial processes and had to be accommodated.

Other influences include a demand by workers for more participation in enterprise decision-making. When formal participation schemes have been introduced this has quickened the extension of bargaining to the enterprise level and promoted the integration of works councils into that structure (Windmüller, 1977). Underlying changes in industrial organisation, via the increasing concentration of ownership and expanded size of enterprises (Hannah, 1976), have also been important in stimulating decentralised negotiations at the expense of association bargaining. In Italy the technological renovation of industry altered the basic conditions of employment in different ways across various firms and sectors, resulting in the general clauses of national agreements becoming obsolete and moving the centre of industrial conflict towards the enterprise itself (Treu, 1981).

Another significant factor working in the same direction towards decentralised negotiations in many European countries may also have been the increased importance of foreign-owned firms, particularly US multinationals (see Chapter 8). Furthermore, in the case of the Netherlands, von Beyme (1980) sees the tendency towards decentralisation in the early 1970s as a reaction to the failure of attempts to promote a central incomes policy – which had been pursued more strongly than in other countries. Finally, the effects of the economic recession have also helped to make bargaining more decentralised in Belgium by emphasising differences between the varying sectors, regions and enterprises. (In the metalworking industry no national wage agreement for manual workers has been possible since 1974.)

It is also notable that in Australia, despite the predominance of the arbitration system, there were similar signs that during the 1970s collective bargaining had penetrated at plant and workshop level even though there was little formal institutionalised machinery for this. The arbitration system was principally concerned with settling disputes over wages and working conditions, narrowly defined, rather than with matters internal or specific to the enterprise. Also, since union officials concentrated their attention upon winning arbitration cases it was left to shop stewards to take up problems such as plant-level dismissals, work assignments and transfers (Levine, 1980).

Notwithstanding these developments, however, even in some European countries the tendency towards decentralisation in collective negotiations has been offset to some extent by cross-currents. In France, for instance, we have noted the negotiation of general, economy-wide agreements on some non-wage matters and in Belgium a more centripetal force has been the 'extension' of certain, appropriate items in collective agreements to the rest of the economy.

In countries which already have predominantly enterprise-level bargaining reverse and countervailing pressures have operated only to a more limited extent – in this case towards greater consolidation in bargaining structures. In Canada some provincial governments have encouraged moves towards broader-based, province-wide bargaining as a means of reducing the potential for damaging shutdowns (Cordova, 1978). Also in the USA one long-term influence has been an upward movement in the locus of decision-making in some business organisations, again through the creation of larger units by mergers or natural growth. The effect at corporate, if not industry, level has been the 'creation [of] enhanced bargaining power which unions will sooner or later try to match by corresponding adjustments, including an extension of the bargaining structure' (ILO, 1974, p. 129). One corporate-centred bargaining strategy in the form of 'coalition' bargaining has been adopted by a number of US unions since the 1960s. The aim is to attempt to neutralise the employers' advantage in multi-plant companies where the workers of each plant are represented by different (and otherwise uncoordinated) trade unions. With coalition bargaining, the bargaining units remain separate, but nevertheless the unions agree to act together in the pursuit of a common bargaining strategy in relation to demands and settlements. Similarly, so-called 'pattern' bargaining has occurred in certain industries. By this means a single employer is selected for the initial claim and the resultant settlement is then extended to the rest of the industry – an arrangement which, in some respects, may be regarded as a *de facto* form of industry-wide bargaining.

In the case of Japan, however, enterprise bargaining seems as yet to have been rather less affected by centralising forces (although, since 1973, there has been some *de facto* industry-wide bargaining in the major metal industries). Most enterprise-based unions remain fairly self-contained and although many do affiliate to the appropriate national, regional or industrial federations they accord them little authority for conducting collective bargaining or sanctioning agreements. An approach towards more coordinated wage negotiations has been made via the annual 'Spring Wage Offensive' which takes place on a nation-wide basis, and in which many unions participate. However, guidance only on the (varying) amounts and formulation of wage demands by the individual unions, together with a schedule of warning strikes, is centrally arranged. The actual negotiations are still carried out by the various enterprise unions themselves and the role of the national union federations remains very limited.

We may therefore conclude in relation to bargaining structures (whether centralised or decentralised) that although there are clearly forces making for change in all countries their extent should, perhaps, not be over-estimated – especially not those changes which may appear to produce convergent systems.

Consequences of Bargaining Structures

Having explored at some length the categorisation and determinants of inter-country bargaining structures it is also necessary to look at some of the implications of these structures for the conduct of industrial relations. In fact, cross-national differences in bargaining structures have been shown to produce a very significant impact upon a country's entire industrial relations system. As we discuss below, these include the degree of centralisation of union and employer bodies, the level of trade union density, strike patterns and certain economic consequences which also appertain to bargaining structures.

There is a relationship between the level at which bargaining takes place and two other variables. Bargaining levels are related to the structure of the parties themselves in collective bargaining, particularly the extent to which their own respective organisations are strongly centralised (federated) at national level, and to the extent or density of unionisation of a country's labour force (Clegg, 1976). As a means of illustrating these relationships on a multi-country basis, the OECD (1979a) has produced two scattergraphs. It is admitted that the gradings assigned to the respective countries have been done on a subjective basis and that different observers might well have come up with somewhat different rankings. There are also doubts about the validity of the linearisation of the ordinal scale which is implied in the diagrams. Nevertheless, despite such limitations, the rough relationships which are depicted are not without interest.

In Figure 4.1 the relationship between degree of centralisation and level of bargaining is shown for a number of countries. Each country is ranked into three basic grades of high, medium or low degrees of effective centralisation[10] in its union and employer federated organisations. The characteristic level of bargaining is similarly ranked according to a scale representing national, industry or regional, and enterprise or workplace levels, with intermediate values depicting cases of 'mixed' bargaining. It is clear that there is a broad correspondence between the two variables. Highly-centralised employer and union structures are related to the prevalence of national or economy-wide bargaining, and vice versa. This is shown by comparing at the extremes Sweden, Norway and Austria in the top left-hand segment, with Canada and the United States in the bottom right-hand corner. In the latter two countries there are markedly decentralised union–management structures and a large proportion of collective agreements are made at the enterprise or workplace levels. It has been argued by Clegg (1976) that

Figure 4.1: Relation of Centralisation of Structure to Level of Bargaining

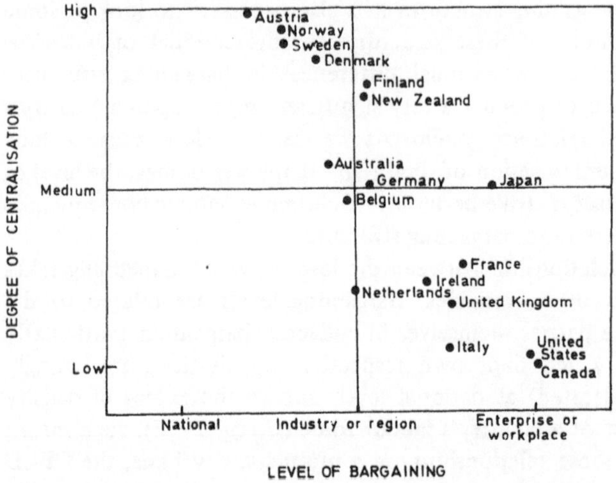

Figure 4.2: Relation of Unionisation to Level of Bargaining

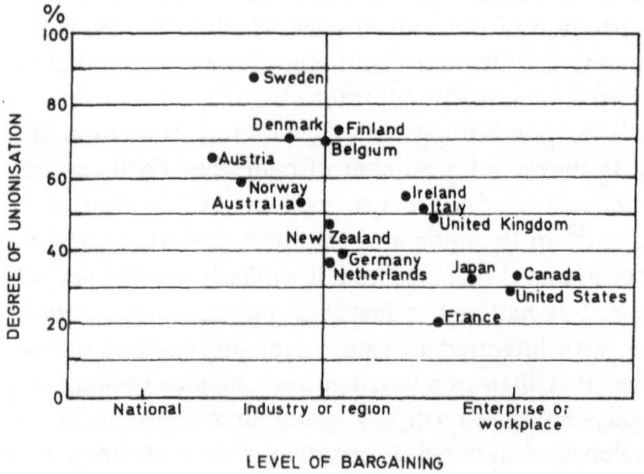

Note: + Measured by the proportion of total employees who belong to unions.
Source: C.A. Blyth, 'The interaction between collective bargaining and government policies in selected member countries', *Collective Bargaining and Government Policies* (OECD, Paris, 1979), pp. 92–3.

in terms of the causal direction of the relationship it is the level of bargaining which determines the degree of centralisation, with the result that power is decentralised within organisations when bargaining takes place at a decentralised level, and vice versa. A relationship between the bargaining level and the extent of union and employer organisational centralisation may be expected since appropriately-structured organisations are likely to be established so as to meet the requirements of a particular level of decision-making in the bargaining process.

The somewhat weaker relationship shown in Figure 4.2, however, is perhaps less intuitively apparent. Here the level of bargaining (again shown horizontally) is plotted against the level of unionisation (vertically). There is found to be a consistent tendency for higher levels of bargaining to be associated with a greater degree of union organisation. In Sweden, for instance, economy-wide bargaining arrangements are accompanied by a union density figure approaching 90 per cent, whereas the company or plant-level bargaining in the United States has a corresponding union membership density of less than 30 per cent. The explanation put forward for this relationship is that where the coverage of collective agreements is extensive, as in centralised-bargaining structures, trade union membership is thereby encouraged since the benefits of agreements are seen to accrue to union members on a wide scale. The stimulus to membership will be even greater if, in addition, local union representatives are actively involved in the administration of agreements and encourage union organisation and if employers are prepared to countenance, or even actively support, trade unionism for their employees (Clegg, 1976).

In contrast, decentralised bargaining systems have a restricting influence upon the degree of union membership attained. Thus, in the United States unionisation must precede collective bargaining rather than following it since extensions of negotiating rights take place at plant or company level, on an individual and piecemeal basis, and often have to be secured against adamant employer resistance. As regards France and West Germany, two countries with below-average union densities, the two leading trade union confederations in France (particularly the CGT) have strong reservations about collective bargaining, although its development in recent years has improved the status and authority of the unions because of the tangible results obtained. In Germany union membership was perhaps less important to employees because of the benefits obtainable from an extensive legalistic employment code together with co-determination. As a result, the scope of autonomous collective bargaining was restricted. In both these countries, therefore, collective bargaining lacks depth, in terms of the involvement of local union officials and workplace representatives in the administration of agreements, which is believed to have adversely affected union density.

In his study of collective bargaining in an international context, Clegg (1976) regards differences in the level at which agreements are concluded as an important determinant not only of membership density but also of a number of other aspects of union behaviour, at least in those countries where collective bargaining is the main method of trade union action. As we have seen, he argues that trade union government will be relatively centralised where agreements are drawn up for an industry or an entire country, and will be relatively decentralised where they are regionally- or plant-based. Accordingly, the level of bargaining influences the distribution of internal union power. In turn, this affects the extent to which union workplace organisations have independent authority to negotiate over a wide range of issues.

Furthermore, Clegg maintains that the pattern of strikes is closely associated with the structure of collective bargaining (see Chapter 6). He expresses the view that strikes will be fewer in number where collective bargaining is conducted at higher levels and more numerous where there is plant bargaining, largely because, in the latter case, since all workers within an industry or region need not be brought out, strikes can be called at much less cost to the membership as a whole. Thus the relative cost and consequences of a strike to the parties concerned will vary with the type of bargaining structure. An empirical investigation of the relationship between bargaining structure and strike activity has been carried out by Hibbs (1976) for 15 advanced industrial economies over the period 1950–69. He shows that mean man-days lost per 1000 workers were highest in decentralised systems characterised by firm-level bargaining and lowest in highly centralised systems typified by economy-wide bargaining arrangements (i.e. an apparently negative relationship between degree of centralisation and strike activity). However, when the analysis was extended from consideration of only a single variable relationship to a multiple regression model which controlled for other possible influences on strikes, such as unemployment, profits and real wages, it was then found that bargaining structures did not have a statistically significant influence.[11]

Clegg's explanatory approach, relating differences in trade union behaviour to variations in the dimensions of collective bargaining, is penetrating and wide-ranging in its integrating of contemporary international evidence and historical determinants, but it has also been subjected to criticism. In the case of particular countries such as Sweden his interpretation has been challenged. Korpi and Shalev (1979) insist that the development and pattern of collective bargaining in this country must be seen largely as a *consequence* rather than as the cause of changes in trade union density. Increasing union strength and a changing (political) power balance forced Swedish employers to deal with workers as a collectivity rather than, as Clegg suggests, the support given by employers being decisive for union recruitment. In Italy, Cella and Treu (1982) maintain that the structure and initiatives of employers' associations have tended to be a response to, rather than a determinant of, those of trade unions. More generally, it may be asked to what extent it is appropriate to regard collective bargaining – the explanatory variable in Clegg's theory – as an independent and primary determinant in its own right, rather than as a transmission mechanism for other forces. Although Clegg identifies the structure and attitudes of employers' associations and managements as the main, direct influences on the dimensions of bargaining themselves, in fact, the determinants of collective bargaining receive little detailed attention in his work. It may be that bargaining structures and processes can be more usefully approached within a broader framework as secondary, or intervening, variables which are themselves dependent upon more basic socio-economic forces within modern industrial societies (Shalev, 1980).

As well as the effects on trade union activity, a further implication of cross-national bargaining structures which has received a good deal of attention concerns their economic consequences. In this respect interest is often directed towards identifying which form of bargaining structure is the most 'efficient', where efficiency is usually defined in terms which attach primarily to managerial interests (Ogden, 1982b). Pratten (1976), for instance, concluded from a detailed comparison of Swedish and British companies that negotiating procedures in Britain, as well as more fragmented union representation, contributed to the lower labour productivity of some UK companies.

It has been claimed that company-level bargaining has advantages over, and is presumptively more efficient than, industry-wide bargaining in that wages can be related directly to the firm's performance, profitability and capacity to pay (Ulman, 1974a).[12] With industry agreements there is a wider separation of the centres of decision-making as well as more overlap in the determination of pay since it has traditionally been understood that nationally negotiated terms in some industries were minima which could be improved upon at enterprise level. In Britain it is well known that the 1968 Donovan Report identified bargaining structures as a major strategic variable in determining the effectiveness of industrial relations. Rationalisation and reform were felt to be needed, and it was assumed that the resulting improvements would benefit all the interested parties.[13] Particular attention was directed to the lack of accordance between bargaining outcomes and national, economic policy objectives. The multi-level and fragmented bargaining which occurred in the private sector was seen as fuelling inflation and making the implementation of incomes policy more difficult. Indeed, a radical reform of collective bargaining in the interests of acquiring greater control of the wage-determination process is still regarded as a prerequisite for any long-term, effective incomes policy. This would seem to point to the need for more centralised bargaining since a government can most effectively pursue its policy of encouraging responsive bargaining if it can deal with the leaders of unions and employers who represent highly centralised structures, themselves have adequate authority and can expect appropriate support and consent from their memberships (OECD, 1979a).

Industry-level and Workplace Studies

So far in this chapter we have been concerned with the determinants and consequences of collective bargaining structures as they appertain on an inter-country basis at national level. However, bargaining structures may also be compared at the disaggregated industry or workplace levels which vary greatly within countries as well as between them. We therefore conclude with a brief examination of a number of studies which either explicitly compare bargaining structures of different countries at a sub-national level, or which seek to identify systematically by means of quantitative methods inter-industry determinants within a single, national industrial relations system – the results of which may then be compared as between countries.

In an interesting comparative study of the US and British steel industries (Elbaum and Wilkinson, 1979), explanations are sought in the historical development of the two industries for their pronounced industrial relations differences – a long period of violent conflict in the United States in contrast with more orderly procedures and fewer strikes in Britain. From the common starting point of an industrial structure typified by similarities in basic technology, fragmented and competitive product markets, with sub-contracting to organise production and the labour process, marked divergencies occurred in subsequent developments. In both countries collective bargaining had emerged in a form strongly influenced by product market considerations. Demand was unstable and in the highly competitive market prices fluctuated widely, thus requiring firms to be able to reduce costs quickly in a recession in order to avoid losses. Sliding-scale arrangements provided the solution since,

> by joining with the skilled workers in agreements linking wages and prices, employers could hope to regulate competitive wage cutting amongst themselves in recession and end costly stoppages as the workers recouped these losses in booms. Such arrangements suited the mutual interests firms shared both with each other and with skilled workers. (Elbaum and Wilkinson, 1979, p. 286)

A transformation took place, however, in the US industry in the late nineteenth century from a small scale, competitive structure towards a large-scale and increasingly concentrated one, controlled ultimately by a handful of firms. The main influences were innovations in steel-making technology whose production indivisibilities meant that the minimum efficient scale of operations was greatly increased. Also, an expansion in the level of demand occurred particularly for steel rails within a market well protected by tariffs from the effects of foreign competition. In Britain, on the other hand, technical change was slower, plants remained relatively small-scale and demand conditions were far less favourable in competition with foreign steel industries. As a result, the early system of collective bargaining continued intact. In contrast, in the USA the development of large-scale steel production both weakened the craft basis of unionism and correspondingly enhanced the power of individual firms in relation both to the unions and product market.

> The large firm could, by securing more effective control of its labour costs, use its massive productive resources to capture larger and larger shares of the market and consequently the benefits of collusion with rival producers and trade unions rapidly declined. (ibid., p. 301)

Therefore in the USA the methods of collective bargaining associated with the heyday of competitive capitalism were outmoded and eventually destroyed along with the breaking by employers of union control of the labour process.

In an investigation of industrial relations arrangements at *workplace* level Marsh *et al*. (1981) compared a number of plants in the engineering industry in Britain and West Germany. Although there are important variations within each country, on a cross-national comparison two principal structural differences are noted. First, in Britain the primary basis of relationships is centred on the workplace itself where unions and managements function largely autonomously with no substantive, external, regulative framework. This is attributed mainly to historical reasons whereby the function of external agreements in the UK has been largely procedural, rather than substantive. In contrast, in Germany workplace relations are essentially dependent upon external regulation in the form of regional agreements. Although informal plant bargaining does take place, the additions and amendments are not regarded as being competitive with external agreements. A second difference concerns the single union-management channel for handling regulative issues in Britain as opposed to the dual, but clearly differentiated, system in Germany between the works council structure and that provided by the union and employer.

As a consequence of these differing structures of job regulation, notable differences in the behaviour of workplace representatives are apparent. Shop stewards in the UK enjoy greater freedom in pursuing their own domestic negotiating relationships with their managements, especially since there is no alternative workplace structure to provide a competing focus of authority or regulation. In Germany, workplace representatives in this industry see themselves as part of the administrative framework for the smooth conduct of industrial relations and work within given administrative and legal constraints. By way of contrast, the British shop steward reacts to, and is more prepared to challenge, management decisions, regarding himself 'less as an agent of regulation than as a tactician in pursuit of tangible, if elusive improvements for the rank and file' (ibid., p. 185).

A further analysis of workplace bargaining in the metalworking industry, but in this case as between Britain and Sweden, has been carried out by Korpi (1978b). He emphasises the actual similarities in the pattern of bargaining despite the differences which exist in the formal structures. Although the scope of workplace negotiations has been more restricted (by law) in Sweden than in Britain, in both countries the bargaining which occurs relies largely upon informal agreements and tacit understandings. Similarly, although the works clubs which are in charge of workplace negotiations in Sweden are sub-organisations of the branches of the national unions and less loosely linked to union organisation than the equivalent shop steward system in Britain (at least before the expansion of single-employer bargaining), nevertheless they act independently of the branch and national union headquarters. In both countries the high levels of unionisation and low unemployment rates for much of the post-war period gave workers significant leverage in workplace negotiations. Korpi concludes that workplace bargaining is not more under the control of the central union organs in Swedish manufacturing industry than has been the case with its British counterpart.

In addition to such single-industry, cross-country studies the recent availability of quantitative survey data in Britain and the United States has now made it possible to test some explanatory hypotheses of bargaining structures more systematically across a much broader cross-section of industries. In the absence of a fully-developed theoretical model, Deaton and Beaumont (1980) use a number of *ad hoc* explanatory variables derived from the case-study literature of bargaining structure in an examination of almost 1000 establishments in the manufacturing sector in Britain. The objective is to identify the determinants of multi-employer or single-employer structures. Utilising the statistical technique of discriminant analysis they find that 'high regional concentration, high union density,[14] and multi-unionism are associated with multi-employer bargaining whereas larger establishments, multi-plant firms, foreign-owned firms, high [product market] concentration industries and firms with industrial relations management tend to have single-employer bargaining' (p. 210). Within each industry group high labour costs were associated with multi-employer bargaining, although as between industries no such relationship between labour costs and bargaining level was apparent. Broadly similar findings emerged from an empirical study of US manufacturing industries (Hendricks and Kahn, 1982). Their results indicate that bargaining structure is systematically related to product and labour market considerations and that high concentration and large plant size are found to be strongly associated with single-firm, as opposed to multi-firm, agreements. The authors conclude that their findings support the hypothesis that 'unions and management consider choices of bargaining structure in a systematic way that reflects the basic environment in which negotiations take place' (p. 182).

Summary

Throughout this chapter the emphasis has been directed towards the determinants and consequences of bargaining structure since this is a concept which has been accorded a considerable role in explaining a number of important collective bargaining phenomena both within and between national industrial relations systems. It has been shown that the structural dimensions of collective bargaining vary greatly between industrialised countries, since they reflect the distinctive economic and social contexts in which they are embedded. Moreover, as the ILO (1974) points out, although many aspects of collective bargaining are usually discussed within the confines of specific national contexts, comparative analysis can provide important insights into the operation of collective bargaining and the ways in which different systems respond and adapt both in convergent and divergent ways to the environmental changes generated within modern societies. In particular, as collective bargaining becomes more wide-ranging in its functions and content so the levels at which bargaining is conducted tend to increase (Cordova, 1978). We have also noted in passing the important and increasing role which public authorities have come to play in many countries in the bargaining process. In the next chapter the role of the state itself in industrial relations is considered more systematically within the international context.

Notes

1. In most European countries there has existed a formal distinction (greatly blurred in practice) between matters on which employer and union interests clearly differed and those on which it was assumed that they were broadly shared. Basically, conflictual matters – such as wage determination – were to be dealt with by collective bargaining carried on outside the enterprise so that unions had no direct role within the enterprise itself. 'Common' interests, however, would be discussed internally via such bodies as works councils or joint consultation committees.

2. Because, for example, the negotiation of topics such as labour utilisation necessarily entails an erosion of management authority (Barbash, 1977).

3. 'A given percentage increase in wages translates itself into a higher percentage increase in unit labour costs in firms with lower proportions of capital to labour than in firms with higher proportions of capital to labour' (Ulman, 1974a, p. 105).

4. The practice of 'whipsawing' by a union refers to the playing-off of one employer against another. The strategy is designed to obtain benefits from a number of employers by applying pressure initially on one and then using the settlement as a base from which to obtain the same, or better, benefits elsewhere.

5. *Order in Council PC 1003.*

6. In 1974 within the private sector 64 per cent of all Japanese workers in establishments with 500+ employees were union members, as against 9 per cent in establishments with less than 100 employees.

7. Thus 'the stirring and spicing and baking process of industrialisation may have been the same [as elsewhere], but if you start off with a different cultural dough you end up with a different social cake' (Dore, 1973, p. 375).

8. The weak position of trade unions at the workplace level has been attributed to the relatively late industrialisation of the country and slow development of the trade union movement, together with its division into separate federations, thereby making representation within firms difficult.

9. It is possible, however, that government intervention in some cases might weaken any tendency towards centralisation by reducing the authority of the central union and employer bodies themselves.

10. 'By centralisation of structure is meant the extent to which trade unions and employer organisations are federated or joined into strong central bodies at the national level with substantial executive (and negotiating) powers capable for instance of negotiating with one another and dealing with government on behalf of their members' (OECD, 1979a, p. 75).

11. This finding at the cross-national level does not necessarily eliminate the possibility that bargaining structure might still be a significant determinant within the context of a single country's industrial relations system.

12. Ulman points out that in connecting company-wide settlements via pattern bargaining, as in the USA, the union members' demand for *uniformity* of pay throughout an industrial jurisdiction can also be satisfied.

13. For a critical assessment of this position, see Goldthorpe (1974).

14. This is used as a proxy for the extent of union power.

Further Reading

A succinct discussion of comparative aspects of collective bargaining is Cordova (1978). An earlier, and still very useful, book-length exposition is the volume published by the International Labour Office (1974), whilst for the EEC countries there is the survey of the Commission of the European Communities (1979). The relationship between collective bargaining and trade union behaviour is analysed in the well-known study by Clegg (1976).

5 THE ROLE OF THE STATE

In this chapter we consider the role of the state in industrial relations, primarily from the standpoint of the approach and involvement of government. Although the state also includes parliament and the judiciary, as well as the police and military, it is government which is now the most significant element in determining the legal environment within which industrial relations operates. The government can be regarded as an actor within industrial relations performing a number of distinct roles. A primary purpose has been to act as a third-party regulator promoting a legal framework which establishes general ground-rules for union–management interaction, particularly in the procedures for collective bargaining: 'All modern states try to fix the rules of the game by, at a minimum, specifying tactics which are not permitted and by facilitating the coming-together of the parties for negotiation' (Shorter and Tilly, 1974, p. 24). Secondly, and additionally, as a means of supporting and underpinning collective bargaining – or as a supplement to it – governments make statutory provisions relating to minimum conditions of employment, including health and safety and, in some countries, wages and working hours. In relation to these substantive conditions of employment Clegg notes that

> the law can be used to establish minimum standards while collective bargaining exploits particular advantages to secure higher standards wherever it can . . . The law can also be used to generalise concessions gained through collective bargaining and to enforce them on recalcitrant employers. (Clegg, 1976, p. 101)

A third well-established function in many countries is the provision of state services for conciliation, mediation and arbitration[1] with a view to facilitating the settlement of industrial disputes. In Britain and the United States there is a wide variety of public peace-making machinery, whereas in France and West Germany institutional provision of government assistance in dispute resolution has been minimal.

More latterly, a fourth aspect of the role of the state has become increasingly important – that of a direct and primary participant as a major employer within the public sector. In this respect the greater the importance of government as an employer the more pervasive is its influence likely to be on bargaining developments and the content of agreements since it may then influence the pattern of industrial relations by its own behaviour and example. In fact, the enlarged role of government as employer, together with the greater responsibility which it has come to accept for overall economic management, has led to increased concern for the substantive outcomes of collective bargaining as well as for the smooth functioning of the bargaining machinery. In this respect we may also identify a fifth role of government, as a regulator of incomes. In many countries incomes policies have been used in an attempt to modify or neutralise the results of collective agreements and public sector workers, whose wage increases are highly visible, required to conform to the government's pay guidelines in order to influence private sector wage settlements. As a result, direct and active government involvement in industrial relations has become much more pronounced in recent years (Flanagan *et al*., 1983).

Industrial countries differ, however, in the extent to which they rely on government legislation to determine the procedures of collective bargaining, to fix the substantive terms of employment and to settle disputes. In the United States the law has been markedly influential in shaping the industrial relations system particularly in regulating the contours and tactics of bargaining, although less reliance has been placed on legislation to fix substantive employment conditions. In West Germany, also, the law has assumed a central importance and extensive influence in the relations between capital and labour – partly as a result of pressure from the collective bargaining parties. In France the Collective Agreements Act 1950 similarly provided a comprehensive legal framework for collective bargaining. By contrast, in Britain until the 1970s industrial relations was less regulated by law than in other western countries since there was an enduring tradition of voluntarism and self-determination by the parties which had become a part of the British cultural heritage. In the case of Australia an industrial relations mechanism in the form of a government arbitration tribunal system was set up at an early stage in the country's industrial development. The main intention was to institutionalise industrial conflict and thereby protect society from the effect of large-scale industrial struggles. As a consequence of such heavy dependence upon state intervention for more than three-quarters of a century it might be claimed, arguably, that 'by international standards Australia . . . is the most legal and legalistic system in the western developed world' (Niland, 1978, p. 79).

Given such marked diversities in the nature and scope of government involvement we need to analyse more fully some of the major cross-national differences within the various areas of government activity in industrial relations which have been identified. We begin with the development of public policy towards collective bargaining.

Development of Collective Bargaining Regulation

In attempting to explain the extent of legal intervention in the bargaining process on a cross-national basis the degree to which collective bargaining was accepted and well established at an early stage, or else underdeveloped, is an important factor. This is because, in historical terms, the intention of government intervention – once unions had been conceded lawful status – was typically to promote collective bargaining. Since any appearance of formal symmetry in the individual employment contract conceals a real inequality of bargaining power between the parties[2] collective worker action came to be seen as necessary to countervail superior employer power and thereby establish a rough equilibrium of forces. It was only later legislation aimed at reforming and conditioning, rather than being enabling and supportive, which has taken the view that collective bargaining and union activities require to be curbed rather than encouraged (Clegg, 1976).

Rimlinger (1977), in a comparative analysis of Britain, the United States and France, has shown that government relations with the labour movement have undergone a similar historical evolution from an initial phase of suppression of workers' organisations and collective action at the onset of industrialisation, moving to one of toleration and encouragement, to be followed by a later period of greater detailed regulation by the state. Nevertheless, because of differences in prevailing social and economic conditions as well as the extent and pace of industrialisation this common evolution has taken a markedly distinctive form within each of these three countries, which requires closer examination.

Britain

In comparison with other countries industrial relations in Britain, the first nation to experience an industrial revolution, developed on the basis of arrangements that relied little upon the intervention of the law as a regulatory device. The special and peculiar situation of Britain in respect of a very extensive period of government abstention from detailed involvement in collective bargaining has been attributed to the influence of the prevailing economic and social philosophy during the formative years of trade unionism in the early nineteenth century. The establishment of unions coincided with a period in which *laissez-faire* liberalism was predominant in economic life. Initially, the application of this doctrine meant that the law was used in various degrees to persecute unions. Collective organisations of work-people for economic purposes were against the interests of property-owners since they restricted competition and freedom of individual contract within the labour market. Because at this period the role of the state was that of enforcing a legal structure necessary for the functioning of the market, specific pieces of statutory legislation such as the Combination Acts were used to repress unionism, and the common law – made and interpreted by judges – was usually implacably opposed to union activity.

However, the application of legal penalties by no means prevented the continuation of trade unions and after the 1820s the state no longer contemplated serious attempts at further suppression. Not only was it ultimately conceded that trade unions would no longer be unlawful bodies but equally importantly a growing number of employers were prepared to deal with them. Unlike the situation in, say, the Scandinavian countries[3] where the later development of industrialisation had precluded the predominance of autonomous craft unionism, in Britain trade unions acquired and maintained substantial bargaining power at an early date in important sectors of the economy. However, they never mounted a sustained campaign in favour of legal, procedural intervention as a means of promoting collective bargaining. The main reason appears to be that in large parts of industry, particularly the skilled trades and coal mining, the union movement had developed substantial industrial strength and already achieved bargaining status prior to the extension of the franchise in the second half of the nineteenth century and the subsequent growth of union political influence. Once the more repressive restrictions on workers' organisations and collective labour actions had been removed the unions then had the basis and capability to promote and further extend collective bargaining by their own efforts. During the last quarter of the nineteenth century collective bargaining spread even to the unskilled in the service and transport industries.

There can also be little doubt that their long history of struggle for legal recognition – in contrast to Swedish unions, for instance, where the resources of the state were not used to impede their development[4] and which did not have to endure long periods in which the courts treated them as conspiracies (Johnston, 1962) – had made

British trade unions deeply suspicious of any attempts to interfere with collective bargaining. The same was true of Germany where unions had also relied on autonomous action and voluntary organisation, opposing the introduction of a positive collective bargaining law because of the belief that an inescapable corollary of such legislation would be legal regulation of their activities (Kahn-Freund, 1981). Unlike British unions, however, they had failed in the pre-1914 period to achieve recognition in heavy industry because of determined employer resistance. Consequently, many of them were then prepared to relinquish reliance on their own organisational autonomy when the state promised, at the beginning of the Weimar period, to deliver recognition through legal guarantees.

It was Kahn-Freund who pointed out that the organic relationship between law and industrial relations in the 'formative period' in Britain (i.e. 1850–1906) was unique because of a combination of three circumstances found in no other comparable labour movements in the formative period of their labour laws:

> First the labour movement was relatively strong. Trade unions achieved bargaining status without legal assistance at a relatively early stage. Secondly, this was achieved without the aid of a working-class political party. Pressure was applied on the bourgeois parties in Parliament. The Labour Party was born only in 1906. Thirdly, the basic trade union laws were established before universal male franchise. (Wedderburn, 1983, p. 37)

One important consequence was that the legal form of collective trade union rights consisted largely of negative statutory protection, or 'immunities' from the sanctions that would otherwise attach in law, rather than positive legal rights to associate, to bargain and to strike as in many comparable countries. As a result of all these factors, Hyman (1975) has suggested that in Britain the *laissez-faire* doctrine itself came to be reinterpreted – certainly by the 1890s – to imply that unions and employers should carry on their relations with a minimum of state interference. It was not so much that the government was averse to regulation in principle. Rather, the problem was the practical one of finding appropriate measures which could be enforced and which would not do more harm than good (Phelps Brown, 1959). Until the 1970s, therefore, when more stringent and detailed government intervention was introduced, the industrial relations system in Britain continued to be conducted predominantly on the basis of voluntary collective bargaining without legal compulsion on either side and implemented through unenforceable agreements.

USA

In the United States collective bargaining had experienced an early development somewhat parallel to that in Britain. Both countries had entered into modern economic development at least several decades ahead of Western Europe and in the USA unionism not only remained confined largely to skilled workers for an even more extensive period of time than was the case in Britain but it also continued as a purely industrial force without any serious ties to political parties. The narrow craft foundation of American unionism and its failure to penetrate the basic manufacturing industries was a major reason why, apart from a brief spurt in World War I, membership never rose much above 10 per cent of non-agricultural employment until the late 1930s (Reynolds, 1978). Although unions favoured voluntary collective bargaining, their weakness in major sections of the economy made any extension a slow process since employers were far more reluctant to engage in it than their European counterparts for reasons which have already been examined (see Chapter 3). Indeed, employer resistance was the major force in accounting for the long years of union failure in the mass-production sector and the fact that by the early 1930s American organised labour could be described as an 'arrested' movement in that it

> had not breached the industries characterised by the giant firm, by multi-plant operations for a national market; by an advanced technology involving mechanization and division of labour; and by a workforce composed primarily of unskilled and semi-skilled men. (Brody, 1980, p. 82)

Employers had again been assisted in the suppression of unionism by a sympathetic judiciary and in the United States, in contrast to much of Europe, it was predominantly the common law rather than the legislature which defined the rights of workers. In Britain Parliament would intervene at crucial times (under political pressure) to restate the rights of workers after conservative court rulings had undermined them, whereas in the USA statutory laws bearing upon industrial relations were more sparse. Before the 1930s, when Congress took charge of public policy in this area, labour's rights had been decided mainly by court decisions which were much less liberal than those in Britain

(Rimlinger, 1977). Before 1931 the courts had issued some 10,000 anti-labour injunctions to prevent unions from committing specific acts of interference with employers' business and property rights. So-called 'yellow-dog' contracts, whereby an employee undertook not to join a union as a condition of employment, were enforceable in the federal courts as well.

The depression of the 1930s was to have a major impact in altering the climate of public opinion and in promoting state intervention in support of union organisation and collective bargaining to redress a serious and continuing imbalance of power. An important underlying assumption of the New Deal was that unequal bargaining power between employers and unorganised workers (or weak unions) had not only encouraged labour unrest but actually aggravated the depression by reducing and destabilising wage rates and thereby restricting purchasing power. As a consequence of these changing public policy orientations the first major and comprehensive piece of federal legislation to be applied to collective bargaining, the Norris–La Guardia Act 1932, gave protection to unions against court injunctions and yellow-dog contracts and a further 'balancing' law, the National Labour Relations (Wagner) Act 1935 became the most important landmark in this field of US regulatory legislation. The law was henceforth to be used as a positive force in shaping bargaining relations between labour and employers, such that the latter were required to bargain over specific subject areas. The extensive legal framework introduced by the Act established and protected employees' rights to organise and bargain collectively (excluding the public sector to which it did not apply) by means of the banning of certain forms of management conduct as 'unfair labour practices'. It also laid down the principle of exclusive representation,[5] whereby one union would serve as the sole representative for all employees in the designated bargaining unit, as well as majority rule for selecting the representative.

The need to take administrative decisions on the selection of exclusive bargaining agents is partly a reflection of the fact that in the USA competition and jurisdictional rivalries within the union movement have been heightened by the uneasy coexistence of craft and (later) industrial unions. By contrast, in those European countries where the main emphasis centres on industrial unions the potential for inter-union conflict has been less. Even in Britain, where craft and general unions have coexisted, the willingness of unions to be jointly represented in collective bargaining has obviated the need for such decisions to select exclusive bargaining agents (ILO, 1974). In fact, the more general emphasis on detailed procedural regulation and administration of collective bargaining in the USA[6] than exists elsewhere may also be explained in terms of structural factors in the form of a predominance of bargaining at the enterprise level. Regulation was required because the specific items of negotiation characteristic of this arrangement – determining effective employment conditions and involving a union presence within the enterprise – are more likely to produce disputes than European industry-wide bargaining on more general issues and minimum standards.

The fact that enterprise bargaining also takes place in Japan, yet largely without such external procedural regulation, does not invalidate this observation of an apparent relationship between decentralised bargaining and a high degree of state intervention. Japanese collective bargaining displays unusual characteristics as regards its late development in comparison with its western counterparts. Other notable features (as we saw in the last chapter) relate to the internalisation of skill acquisition within large firms and lack of entrenched and sharp occupational differentiation, together with the enterprise form of union organisation whereby most union officers are regular employees of the enterprise, or 'insiders', who are assigned to union business. Since most collective agreements are negotiated between an enterprise union and its responding enterprise there was little cause to necessitate the involvement of government agencies (Shirai and Shimada, 1978). Furthermore, because in this kind of decentralised structure – unlike that of the USA – issues were negotiated relating to enterprise workforces as single entities, such as general wage increases rather than wage structures as between sectional job groupings, there was less need for administering detailed collective agreements via external control (Levine, 1980).

Finally, in relation to the USA, and unlike some European countries, the absence of statutory authority to extend collective bargaining agreements to non-signatory parties is also rooted in US industrial relations structures. It is relatively easy to extend an agreement containing a limited number of minimum terms and conditions to encompass employers and workers at the economic and geographical limits of the industry, especially where such an agreement has been negotiated by an employers' association broadly representative of a large number of firms:

> In the United States, however, where rival unions may coexist in a single industry, where contract terms set actual rather than

> minimum requirements, and where provisions are highly complex and often vary from one firm to another, it would be very difficult to find a single set of terms that would be suitable for all firms in the industry. (Dunlop, 1976, p. 238)

France

In contrast to both Britain and (more latterly) the United States, collective bargaining in continental Europe before World War II was less developed and in France, certainly before 1914, it played a negligible role in the determination of wages and working conditions. In that country state action towards labour was especially repressive during the nineteenth century. Legislation forbidding worker combination, such as the Chapelier Act, was similar in substance to British and US doctrines of common law conspiracy but even when French labour laws were relaxed after the 1860s recognition was accorded only to the right of association and not the right (with an implicit obligation upon the employer) to bargain. Concurrently, however, state intervention was introduced at times of serious industrial conflict so that state agents in local areas (*préfets*) would not only seek to promote arbitration but also induce employers to negotiate. Moreover, in the major social crises, 'the [national] government intervened in order to settle conflicts whose intensity and violence could have had serious political consequences' (Sellier, 1978, p. 218). Notably in 1936, after the election of a Popular Front government and widespread strikes for the right to organise and bargain collectively the Matignon Agreement resulted in the promotion and extensive state regulation of collective bargaining and union rights in the enterprise. In effect, the government became the major party to collective bargaining since it could convoke unions, and more particularly employers, to the bargaining table, and it prescribed much of the subject-matter of collective agreements.

Although the new legislation gave the 'most representative' unions at plant level the right to bargain (thereby tending to prevent the organisation of non-independent, company unions) it was actually the government rather than the workers via a ballot, as in the USA, that determined which organisations *were* the most representative. Again, unlike US practice, the legislation on union recognition did not adopt the rule of the majority since the most representative union might have only a minority of the organised workforce. Nor did it adopt the principle of exclusive union representation, largely because of ideological differences within the labour movement. Yet for the first time the coverage of agreements could be extended to include companies not represented at the bargaining table. It would thereby compensate for the organisational weakness of employers' associations in sectors such as agriculture, commerce and textiles where – in a country whose economic development had been marked by slowness of industrial concentration – there were many small, non-affiliated establishments over which employers' organisations could exercise little authority. By means of this device the terms of negotiated agreements could be elevated by government sanction from private contract to public regulation (Meyers, 1981).

It has been contended by Sewell (1977) that the origins of the distinctive French interventionist and regulatory attitude by the state towards industrial relations may be partially ascribed to the 1789 revolution and its attack on any form of private privilege. Since that time the state had retained an abhorrence for publicly-recognised, voluntary associations which were unregulated because, within the French context, this necessarily smacked of privilege:

> In short, the French interventionist approach to labour relations reflects peculiarly French definitions of the limits of private and public spheres, definitions that automatically made the state a potential party to any agreements negotiated between employers and unions. (ibid., p. 229)

It is apparent from the above discussion that the distinctive methods developed for regulating industrial relations in Britain, the United States and France reflect basic social and economic differences and the respective power positions of the parties, together with a particular historical conjuncture of events. Similar influences may also be delineated in the very different regulatory approach which has evolved in Australia. The industrial relations system in that country (along with a similar, and even earlier, pioneering innovation in New Zealand) is unique within developed market economies in that it has utilised conciliation and compulsory arbitration over an extensive time period as the major form of conflict resolution with a government body as a direct participant in industrial relations rule-making processes. This applies not only to dispute settlements but also to the fixing of wages and working conditions by means of legally-enforceable awards. We now turn to an analysis of the determinants of this particular form of state regulation.

Compulsory Arbitration in Australasia

The Australian arbitration system employs third-party decision-making in the adjudication of substantive issues – unlike US labour law which, although it sets out detailed procedural rules for the conduct of bargaining and establishes the right to union recognition, does not usually prescribe what the results of those bargains should be. However, compulsory arbitration in Australia does not exclude, nor is it incompatible with, collective bargaining. On the contrary, its founders hoped that it would help to achieve the recognition of collective bargaining. As Walker (1970, p. 15) has expressed it, compulsory arbitration 'in effect granted the unions' demand for collective bargaining, but at the same time placed a check upon their power by restricting strikes.' In practical terms, where the parties arrived at an agreement prior to a dispute being referred to arbitration 'consent' awards could then be applied for in order to give effect to that agreement.[7] As a result, agreements directly negotiated by unions may coexist with, or take the place of, arbitration awards in a hybrid form of quasi-collective bargaining (Lansbury, 1978a).

The historical determinants of this system relate particularly to the great strikes which occurred during the 1890s concerning the right of unions to bargain collectively in the face of a concerted attempt by employers to replace newly-developing collective agreements in certain sectors of the economy, such as the pastoral (sheep-raising) industry as well as shipping and docks, with individually negotiated (non-union) contracts. Although compulsory arbitration had been under discussion for some years, prior to these particular events the savagery of the ensuing conflicts and utter defeat of the unions provided a backdrop for the introduction of a legalistic framework for handling industrial relations. As a direct heritage of its formative years this was to reflect 'an inordinate preoccupation with strike prevention and settlement' (Niland, 1978, p. 27). One of the main objectives in establishing compulsory arbitration in Australia was to make strikes unnecessary, with the expressed intention of protecting the public by avoiding a repetition of the dislocations of the economy occasioned by lengthy industrial stoppages. At the same time, with the unions' power to force employers to bargain collectively virtually eliminated as a result of events which from their viewpoint 'epitomised desperation, defeat and disillusionment' (Cupper and Hearn, 1981, p. 15), they recognised that political action in the form of government intervention would be needed to secure the benefits which industrial weakness had denied them.

The vital significance of these early conflictual events in giving a particular and distinctive direction to the Australian system[8] has been stressed by Isaac (1973). He speculates that had the strikes not occurred and collective bargaining been allowed to continue to establish itself, then the course of Australian industrial relations might well have developed more closely upon the lines of the British pattern. On the other hand, Phelps Brown (1959) has suggested that although it had been decided by the late 1890s not to adopt compulsory arbitration in Britain, mainly because of the practical difficulty of enforcement where the unions were strong and might not accept its awards, nevertheless 'if disputes had been more costly in the 1890s, or the international outlook more threatening, or the unions passing through a phase of weakness, Britain might have come to it then' (p. 189).

As regards Australia and New Zealand, however, it is worth noting the importance of environmental conditioning factors, as well as particular events, in facilitating the introduction of governmental arbitration. Both countries had small populations together with large agricultural and pastoral sectors which were at the heart of the economy. In New Zealand the predominance of small-scale industries and scattered and isolated communities was hardly conducive to the development of strong, well-organised unions. It was not surprising that the unions 'dissolved like snowflakes' in the face of a serious employer offensive so that the labour movement then turned to political action (Roth, 1974). Similarly in Australia, a pragmatic labour movement concerned with securing practical results was quite sympathetic to social reform via state action.

Arbitration as a method of centralised wage-fixing was also to utilise social and equity criteria in terms of setting a structure of basic wages providing for minimum needs together with a superstructure of largely historically-determined differential margins for skills. It was the favourable economic circumstances of these countries which helped to ensure the viability of such a system. New Zealand had no industries manufacturing for export (except those processing agricultural produce) and therefore in competition with other manufacturers in foreign markets, and its home industries also had tariff protection against competition from imports (Hare, 1946). Similarly, in Australia manufacturing employers were sheltered by tariffs from foreign competition and sometimes would be given full tariff protection only if the Commonwealth Arbitration Commission certified that their industries paid 'fair and reasonable' wages (Walker, 1970). As a result, wage levels could be set broadly by the government with less regard to the profitability or external competitive position of the individual industries concerned.

It is clear from this consideration of the early development of public policy in a number of countries that some common features may be discerned in relation to its objectives, notably a desire to maintain industrial peace and the support of collective bargaining directed towards that end – with the timing of the measures frequently being determined by the occurrence of national crises. In this respect it has been suggested (Strinati, 1982) that, fundamentally, state intervention in industrial relations derives from the logic of capitalist development in terms of the need to provide for the maintenance and continuity of production and capital accumulation, which in turn necessitates state intervention in the management of industrial conflict. Yet, as has been shown, considerable national variations are to be found in the ways in which the attainment of these objectives has been sought, according to the particular circumstances of individual countries. Moreover, although the historical origins of government intervention were important in helping to determine the subsequent shape of cross-national industrial relations, including the structure of collective bargaining itself (Clegg, 1976), the course of public policy in this area has been characterised by significant shifts of direction and, in some cases, a certain volatility over the course of time. It has been particularly influenced by changing economic conditions which affect the balance of power in collective labour market relations as well as by the political complexion of governments. To some extent it has also been a reaction to the (sometimes unforeseen) consequences of earlier government intervention. Some of these policy changes which were introduced will now be examined.

Consequences and Evolution of Public Policy Measures

In both the USA and Australia – two countries with extensive regulation where it had been decided that collective bargaining was underdeveloped – the objective of bringing the parties together via legislative measures and thereby forcing employer–union interaction and dealings was attained. Also, the expectation of a consequential marked increase in trade union growth proved to be well founded. In the United States the legal protection accorded to trade unions under the Wagner Act was undoubtedly a crucial factor in hastening trade union growth, with total membership increasing almost threefold between 1934 and 1939.

The legislation was successful in encouraging collective bargaining and it underwrote the decentralised structure of agreements made at plant level. Similarly, in Australia the regularisation of industrial relations together with the according of legitimacy to organisations of workers was greatly facilitated by the introduction of the government-operated arbitration system. Since dealing with large numbers of employees who were not well organised might have swamped the federal or state arbitration tribunals with business a first step was to require employees to be organised so that their representative body could be covered by a single award (Howard, 1980). In this way the arbitration system created an institutional need for unions to promote administrative efficiency. Since it depended upon unions for its operation it was to prove a major stimulus to union growth (see Chapter 2).

In terms of the level at which bargaining was conducted, unlike United States procedural legislation, Australian arbitration also helped to widen the bargaining unit and extend it even to an economy-wide basis in the case of federal awards on minimum wages and standard hours of work. Furthermore, as with the supportive legislation in the USA whereby what had previously been non-negotiable matters could be designated as 'bargaining issues', it also extended (although to a more limited extent) the scope and subject areas of collective bargaining since the tribunals determined which claims were appropriate and therefore acceptable. In the USA favourable experience of legal support measures in terms of the results obtained had helped convert US unions, including most of the older craft organisations, from a belief in the virtues of unbridled voluntarism (Flanders, 1974). In Australia, however, the unions' attitude to the arbitration system remained more ambivalent. With around 300 employees' organisations covering a workforce of some 6 million, Australian unions were highly fragmented and the weaker ones (originally in the pastoral and manufacturing sectors) supported arbitration since they had much to gain. Unwilling employers could be taken to a tribunal whose award could be legally enforced. Yet some unions with strong bargaining power, due either to their strategic position or to more favourable economic circumstances consequent on a rising market, came to support a greater emphasis upon directly-negotiated agreements. The object was to secure better wages and conditions from particular employers than could be obtained from tribunal awards. In fact, from the 1960s until the mid-1970s the relative importance of such direct agreements increased substantially, and more generally the tribunals themselves adopted a pragmatic approach in making awards which would prove acceptable by reflecting the unions' enhanced bargaining power under full employment (Isaac, 1973). Subsequently the prominence and authority of the arbitration system has been reasserted against a changed background of large-scale unemployment and inflation in which privately negotiated 'over-awards' have become more difficult to obtain from employers. In a country dependent upon foreign trade and investment, the economic crisis also prompted a changed government after 1975 to institute a shift from encouraging collective bargaining to more stringent legislation penalising failures to abide by compulsory arbitration awards. (In New Zealand there was also an initial departure, in 1973, from a central role for conciliation and arbitration, followed by a subsequent return to it four years later.)

As we have noted, one of the main intentions of legal intervention in both the USA and Australia had been to reduce the incidence of strikes. In the United States, with the exception of recognition disputes, this objective remained unattained and in the immediate post-war period a further strike wave was an important contributory factor in the introduction of restrictive, and what were felt to be required 'balancing', measures in the form of the Taft–Hartley Act 1947. A basic premiss of this legislation was that conflict may result not only from employer activities but also from those of unions. The concept of 'unfair labour practices' was therefore extended to embrace aspects of the collective bargaining conduct of unions (secondary boycotts, jurisdictional disputes, etc.), and agreements themselves were made legally binding. Additionally, greater government control was imposed over the internal affairs of unions – reflecting a long-standing attitude on the part of policy-makers that unions could not be left to their own devices.[9]

In Australia, a legal framework of arbitration awards also failed to reduce strike incidence, but rather reduced the level of moral obligation towards upholding the settlements which purely voluntary agreements could have been expected to engender (Niland, 1978). As a result the parties did not consider themselves to be bound by the awards. This may help to explain the typical pattern of frequent short strikes which has predominated in Australia (and New Zealand) as a response to unacceptable awards, and as a tactical weapon for securing over-awards from employers. However, short strikes are also a response to unattended shopfloor grievances and highlight one of the shortcomings of the arbitration system in that plant-level grievance procedures are not well developed. In contrast, to the USA, where plant-level procedures are well established and adhered to, a much larger proportion of strikes in Australia have concerned the local-level issues of working conditions and managerial policy.

Interestingly, in Canada – another country with a long history of statutory dispute regulation in the form of a compulsory delay for purposes of conciliation before strikes and lock-outs can take place – there has been an *increased* duration of stoppages over interest disputes (Huxley, 1979). The contrast between Australia and Canada in this respect might, in some measure, be a result of differences in the stage of industrialisation of the two countries when the legislation was first introduced. In Australia it occurred when unions were weak and a pattern of continuing protest was therefore established, whereas its later introduction in Canada coincided with the growth of stronger, transnational organisations having access to the resources of their US parent unions. Also, it could be that such legislation merely exacerbates the existing pattern of stoppages rather than altering the shape of strikes (Waters, 1982).

Significant shifts over time in public policy towards collective bargaining have taken place, however, not only in the United States and (to a lesser extent) in Australia – two countries with extensive state regulation – but also at the other end of the continuum, including Sweden after the unofficial strike wave in the 1960s. Most notably in Britain a view shared by all the actors that industrial relations are conducted most effectively and peacefully when unions and employers make their own voluntary arrangements was not inviolate for all time. Although it set a pattern of continuity which was enduring for many decades, it became modified in the early 1970s, largely under the exigencies of a relatively deteriorating national economic performance, towards a much more interventionist government strategy. In more recent years even the long-standing public policy of support for collective bargaining itself and the use of the law to bolster it appear to have ended (Wedderburn, 1982).

A belief in Britain that the balance of power in industrial relations had moved excessively in favour of trade unions and groups of shopfloor employees with resultant adverse economic consequences, together with concern for certain alleged infringements of the rights and freedoms of individual union members, prompted a Conservative government to attempt to generate counter-pressures, particularly to reduce shopfloor bargaining power. The intention of the Industrial Relations Act (1971-74) was 'the replacement of collectivist *laissez-faire* in labour law with a comprehensive and strongly interventionist legal framework which featured legal concepts drawn from North

American legislation' (Lewis, 1976, p. 12).[10] The Act, nevertheless, failed to achieve its major objectives since not only did the trade unions actively resist its operation and many employers fail to utilise its provisions but, more especially, where the Act ran up against established customs and traditions then it was singularly unsuccessful. As Clegg (1976) has observed, 'it is easier for the law to mould collective bargaining where it is immature and unformed than where it has grown up and taken shape' (p. 112).

One major exception, however, to the capacity of state intervention to make effective a previously weak and underdeveloped system of private sector collective bargaining is the case of France. Collective bargaining was installed in that country with great difficulty because of employer resistance, partly in response to the radicalism of the trade unions (Sellier, 1978), and although legislative intervention was forthcoming, the growth of collective bargaining remained stunted. Clegg (1976) suggests that a requirement along US lines for employers to bargain in good faith with unions which could demonstrate their support in a ballot might have proved more effective. Yet that sort of provision would have promoted the membership and power of the CGT and therefore probably have been unacceptable. Also, although the 1950 law on collective agreements recognised 'representative' unions for bargaining purposes, agreements were usually confined on the union side to those organisations recognised as being representative at the national level. It is now generally considered that the law was, in fact, far too restrictive in this respect thereby discouraging bargaining and the growth of union membership. Since only a minority of employers actually negotiate at the level of the undertaking recent (1982) reforms of collective bargaining law (the first for 30 years) represent a further legislative attempt to stimulate local-level bargaining and ensure that more workers benefit from collective agreements. Where unions already have workplace representatives there is a new requirement on the employer to negotiate annually on pay levels within the undertaking. By giving the unions an opportunity to obtain negotiated agreements and thereby enlarge their recruitment platform, the government hopes for a greater commitment by them to contractual collective bargaining.

Having examined the role of the state in establishing ground-rules for the collective bargaining process we now consider a second major function, in the form of legislative provisions concerning the terms and conditions of employment.

Regulation of Employment Terms

As well as legislation relating to procedural aspects of collective bargaining negotiations there are also cross-national differences in the extent to which countries provide statutory regulation of the substantive terms of the employment relationship. In all countries the state sets certain minimum standards in relation to areas such as occupational safety and health, but regulative legislation dealing with wages, hours and other major conditions is more uneven. In Britain (and more especially in the USA) a greater reliance has traditionally been placed on collective bargaining than on legal enactment. In the USA substantive norms (such as length of the working week, paid holidays, fringe benefits and health insurance), which elsewhere are often handled by legislation, are regularly dealt with through collective bargaining. Originally in both countries well-entrenched and self-centred craft unions relied upon autonomous employment regulation and opposed state intervention, fearing that it would weaken their strength and solidarity (Clegg, 1976). Such attitudes have, however, long since been eroded, and Lewis (1976) notes that in the case of Britain the unions had campaigned unsuccessfully up to the early years of the present century for the introduction of a legal minimum wage and maximum daily hours of work.[11] Yet statutory protection was not extended more widely than safety, health and welfare measures largely because the unions themselves ceased to press for it. Instead, they came to rely increasingly upon the domain of collective bargaining as the single most important method for regulating their members' terms of employment, since

> over a period of time employers were prepared to concede what Parliament denied, and consequently through experience unions became deeply attached to the efficacy of industrial negotiations over the method of legal enactment [although the two] were never regarded as mutually exclusive. (Lewis, 1976, p. 8)

In the United States the preference for collective bargaining over legislative enactment was also enhanced by its high pay-off, in part a result of a long-run scarcity of labour which strengthened workers' market power together with rising productivity and real wages. At the same time a split between federal and state levels under the US political system, as well as the willingness of the courts to declare unconstitutional legislation which was felt to hinder inter-state commerce, made it more difficult to obtain effective protective legislation (Edwards,

1978). In contrast, in recent years a good deal of regulatory legislation in the areas of equal pay, employment discrimination and pensions has been actively sought by unions and enacted. It would appear that as a means of obtaining their objectives the focus of US unions may be shifting away from an overwhelming reliance upon collective bargaining, with its restricted and diminishing coverage, towards increasing support for the method of legal enactment. In this respect the introduction of government wage controls in 1971 seems to have been a significant event since the unions 'learned the importance of a political counterpart to bargaining effectiveness' (Rosen, 1975).

In continental European countries state regulation has played a greater part in determining wages, working conditions and fringe benefits than in either Britain or the USA and therefore the political process has assumed a critical role. This greater statutory emphasis derives in part from the close linkage of continental European labour movements with political parties whereby legislation was seen as being able to provide universal benefits common to the working class as a whole. There was also an old tradition of state intervention and regulation in economic life. In the case of Germany, for instance, although the state had opposed the development of collective labour organisations the nineteenth-century social security policies of Bismarck (on insurance for health, accidents and old age), along with their sequel in the Weimar Republic, created a system of protective legislation and welfare provisions for individual workers then unknown in other countries. At the present time statutory norms provide a floor of minimum standards for German workers including wages, hours, vacations, job security and safety provisions which the unions have come to regard as a body of irreversible social rights (Günter and Leminsky, 1978).

Kahn-Freund (1972) has made the broad generalisation that regulatory legislation concerning the terms of employment has tended to prevail over collective bargaining where the political power pressure of workers exceeds their industrial power pressure (i.e. on issues which the unions have felt unable to resolve on their own account). Thus in the relatively favourable market conditions of pre-1914 Germany the economic power of the unions was greater than their political power, whereas in the new political democracy established after 1918 the reverse was the case, so that they then relied to a greater degree upon legislative measures. Similarly, for France Lange (1982) notes the duality of focus of French unions which having achieved only modest success in relation to their labour market objectives because of industrial weakness looked to the political process through pressure on the state. Questions which might elsewhere become matters for collective bargaining have therefore been the object of politics, legislation and state regulation. Nevertheless, this contrast should not be overdrawn since the more recent growth of French collective bargaining implied that less was expected from government legislation and more from direct negotiations (Reynaud, 1975). Also, the view that employment legislation and collective bargaining are necessarily alternative and competing routes to the achievement of labour's objectives often seems nowadays to be misplaced. They can be more usefully regarded as supplementary and mutually reinforcing since, as in both Germany and France, collective bargaining achievements may be incorporated into law, extended and passed on to labour as a whole.

As well as provisions concerning the substantive conditions of employment a further well-developed function of the state has been the establishment of procedures to assist in the resolution of industrial disputes, to which we now turn.

Disputes Settlement Mechanisms

Negotiations of employment conditions presuppose the possibility of disagreements occurring. Even where an agreement has been concluded and relations between management and workers regularised at the level of the undertaking, grievances are inevitable. It therefore became recognised that third-party, peace-keeping procedures would be both useful and necessary to help resolve disputes with a view to the avoidance of industrial action. These could take place by means of judicial settlement via courts of law in the case of those agreements with legally-binding rules or by government-sponsored conciliation, mediation and voluntary arbitration for these and other categories of labour dispute.

In a number of European countries (e.g. Austria, Germany, Luxembourg, Switzerland and Scandinavia) the right to strike is circumscribed by the legally-binding obligation to keep the peace during the life of a collective agreement whose terms are legally binding. In these countries an important distinction is drawn between disputes of 'right' and disputes of 'interest'. These are considered to be of a different order in the belief that the problems arising in the negotiation and the application of a collective agreement – although closely related – are distinct processes requiring different procedures of settlement. Rights disputes relate to the interpretation of the existing collective agreement and the parties may not resort to pressure tactics such as strikes and lock-outs for resolving the issues. Instead, they must do so through negotiations or, in the last resort, by the binding decision of a specialist Labour Court which exists in most European countries (Aaron, 1971). In contrast, interest disputes concern matters as yet ungoverned by law or contract such as the negotiation of a new agreement or the renewal of an existing one. In these cases the parties may resort to industrial action once the old agreement has expired.[12] The issues involved here are regarded as being inappropriate for judicial settlement, whereas the making available of third-party conciliation or mediation devices is a principal means to help ensure their peaceful settlement. Thus the 'peace obligation' during the term of the contract is central to this distinction between disputes of right and disputes of interest (Elvander, 1974).

In the USA and Canada, although a similar distinction is observed with conciliation and mediation procedures being used for helping to settle economic or interest disputes, the institution of the Labour Court does not exist. Instead, as a means of resolving rights disputes under the collective agreement, there has evolved a unique system of private grievance arbitration – informal, yet binding, industrial jurisprudence – in which the arbitrators are jointly selected and paid for by both parties. This was a logical development since, unlike industry-wide bargaining arrangements in European countries, in the USA the parties were immediately and closely involved in the administration and application of the collective agreement at local level. By way of contrast, in Britain no such rights/interest distinction is made. Indeed, it would scarcely be possible since the parties do not usually intend their agreements to be legally-binding contracts and informal (unwritten) 'custom and practice' has often governed their more detailed terms. A further impediment relates to the unspecified and indefinite duration of many agreements which makes collective bargaining something of a continuous process in which differences relating to the interpretation of an agreement merge imperceptibly into differences concerning claims to change its effects (Donovan, 1968).

A comparative study of dispute settlement mechanisms within the Nordic group of countries (Elvander, 1974) maintains that the particular pattern of the state's conflict-resolving function is largely determined by a combination of historical factors of a political and economic nature (concerning the date and character of the industrialisation process), together with the resultant structure and power position of labour market organisations. In Finland, the 1918 civil war helped to weaken and politically split the labour movement which, because of its reduced ability to participate constructively in conflict resolution, in turn facilitated state intervention. In contrast, Sweden differs from its Scandinavian neighbours in that the Basic (Saltsjöbaden) Agreement of 1938 between the central union and employer federations, whereby the negotiation of disputes became obligatory and the responsibility for preserving industrial peace rested with the parties themselves, had the effect (as was the intention) of obviating the need for extensive interventionist state legislation for conflict resolution. The defeat of the Swedish unions in the 1909 general strike was an event which had made them particularly hostile to all forms of state intervention on labour disputes, in contrast to the labour movements in Norway and Denmark which never experienced a setback of such proportions. However, the reliance upon their own system of regulation was only possible because of the strongly centralising tendencies of the union and employer federations facilitated by the earlier development of large-scale, concentrated industry in that country.

Later industrialisation in Norway, which thereafter developed at a faster pace, led not only to industrial unrest but was also a factor in the labour movement's assumption of a more radical character and greater factional tendencies than occurred in Sweden and Denmark. This helps to explain the more active role of subsequent state intervention in disputes in that country (often in the form of compulsory arbitration) as compared with other Nordic countries. In the case of Denmark a consequence of early and slowly-developing industrialisation, with small-scale production units, was that the organisational structure of the labour movement assumed an aspect of a guild tradition expressed in the form of only a limited concentration of centralised power within the LO. In contrast with the other Nordic countries there was a predominance of horizontal craft unions whose locus of internal power also resided less at the centre. Once again, the resultant splintered organisational structure impeded the achievement of self-regulation and helped promote the conferring of substantial powers upon the state's mediation system.

Although this particular comparative study is highly perceptive in its analysis of the effects of industrialisation and political factors, it neglects somewhat consideration of possible market factor determinants, such as differing degrees of export dependence among the various Scandinavian countries. These may also have been important variables in their own right in helping to shape industrial infrastructure and therefore the extent to which this facilitated the development of more (or less) powerful employers' organisations capable of assuming regulatory functions.

As well as the traditional background role performed by the state in making provisions to assist dispute resolution in the bargaining process we have also noted that governments themselves have become increasingly involved in the outcomes of (particularly wage) bargaining. We therefore need to consider some of the industrial relations consequences of the more active role assumed by the state in managing the economy.

Government Intervention in the Economy

Miliband (1969) has argued that in those instances where governments have felt it incumbent to intervene directly in disputes between employers and wage-earners, the result has tended to be to the disadvantage of the latter, even though it may well have been done ostensibly in the name of the 'national interest'. This view strongly challenges pluralist interpretations of the role of the state which is seen as being by-and-large neutral in relation to the various (and competing) groups in society, merely 'holding the ring' around them. In particular, the approach maintains that there is no third, separate element at the bargaining table representing the 'national' interest – according to which the interests of society as a whole are claimed to transcend narrow sectional interests – since behind its everyday usage lurk distinctive material interests and, more precisely, class interests (Hyman, 1982a).[13] The thrust of this standpoint is that the growth rates of western capitalist economies have deteriorated in more recent years, thereby reducing the margin for a positive-sum resolution of industrial conflicts by means of the granting of economic concessions. Greater state intervention in industrial relations (especially in wage bargaining) has therefore appeared more attractive to governments increasingly and actively involved in the management of economic affairs.

A major problem for governments in the post-World War II period was that the increased industrial strength of workers' organisations consequent upon a long period of full employment had given them more power to raise money wages. If these were passed on in price increases the country's foreign competitiveness would be impaired, and if they were not then profits (the source of capital accumulation) would tend to be squeezed. It was this problem which provided the spur to state action directed towards inducing (or compelling) trade unions to cooperate in a voluntary (or statutory) incomes policy so as to restrain money-wage demands in collective bargaining (Panitch, 1977).

One response of the state in dealing with the economic behaviour of trade unions has been to develop a corporatist strategy which 'integrates organised socio-economic producer groups through a system of representation and cooperative mutual interaction at the leadership level and mobilisation and social control at the mass level' (Panitch, 1980, p. 173). This involves the non-conflictual integration of central trade union and business organisations into tripartite economic planning bodies directed particularly towards agreement on incomes policy programmes in which the unions become involved in the support and administration of wage restraint on their members. Corporatist structures can most clearly be identified in early post-war Holland (and to a lesser extent in Belgium) where the unions became integrated into incomes policy institutions for the formulation of national economic policy, and later in West Germany where there was a long tradition of a corporatist legal framework aimed at checking conflicts of interests. In the latter country a programme of 'concerted action' was instituted in the mid 1960s, concerned in principle with achieving congruence between the macro-economic goals of state policy and those of the major collective organisations. In practice the emphasis was upon moderating wage settlements to pay guidelines and with cooperation rather than conflict in industrial relations.

Although a critical factor accounting for the development of corporatist structures in the first two decades after World War II was undoubtedly the high level of employment, one effect of full employment in Britain was to shift power down to the shopfloor. As a result, an attempted corporatist mode of state intervention was less appropriate since it had become more difficult for union leaders to be able to 'deliver' on incomes policy requirements. Similarly in the United States, with highly decentralised bargaining, a corporatist structure has been comparatively the least developed – unions being largely excluded from participation in state policy-making. In the case of France and Italy the weakness and isolation of the unions meant that it was neither possible nor necessary for the state to use them as instruments of national cohesion (Crouch, 1978). The potential for corporatism was also limited in these two countries by the unwillingness of the large communist movement to become involved in planning bodies. On the other hand, ideological considerations could sometimes be an important facilitating factor since corporatist structures became much more developed in those countries where the labour movement had been dominated by collaborative, confessional and social democratic unions with highly-centralised confederations such as the Netherlands, and Austria, Scandinavia (and to a lesser extent Britain) where the unions also became drawn into the state's economic apparatus.

Corporatist arrangements were, however, characterised by instability in these countries since although union leaderships (because of their isolation from the workplace) tended to be insulated from the rank and file, membership pressures at plant level caused them on occasion to withdraw their cooperation, as in the Netherlands and West Germany. Panitch (1981) contends that as a means of resuscitating the structures, one response of the state has been to attempt to institutionalise bargaining and shop steward committees at the local level. This might be done via legislation to strengthen union organisation together with control of its membership and – although there were other motivations (see Chapter 7) – to provide for formalised and non-conflictual workers' participation at plant and company level, as occurred in Sweden and was intended in Britain in the mid-1970s. Also, where unions at national level have become too strong for consensual policies with the state to be achieved, then a form of 'bargained corporatism' (Crouch, 1979) may be introduced. Here union support for wage restraint requires that the government makes bargained concessions by way of improvements in items such as hours of work together with non-work issues relating to pensions and other social benefits. The best illustrations of this approach are the social contracts negotiated in Britain and in the Netherlands during the 1970s, although there were also parallels in the Scandinavian countries, as well as in Austria, Ireland and Finland. The *quid pro quo* for restraint in nominal wage increases usually focused on tax reductions, price controls and subsidies together with social policy measures and employment schemes (OECD, 1979).

Where, however, governments are not prepared to bargain with the trade union movement a policy alternative for the ordering of government–union relations is what has been termed 'neo-*laissez-faire*'. With this alternative, as characterised by the 1980s Conservative government in Britain, trade union strength is pushed back and the outcomes of collective bargaining controlled not by compromises and agreements but rather by indirect means such as strict money supply control and the level of unemployment, buttressed by selective pieces of legislation (to restrict picketing, the closed shop, etc.).

Summary

In this chapter we have examined the role of the state in providing a more (or less) comprehensive legal framework for industrial relations, dependent in part upon a country's own history and its national traditions, and in many cases making limited provisions relating to minimum wages, hours and working conditions. It has been shown that in recent years the state has become increasingly and actively involved in regulating the conduct of industrial relations particularly with a view to influencing the outcome of negotiations. A large number of countries (although not all) also have long-established state services for conciliation, mediation and arbitration to facilitate dispute settlement and further collective bargaining. Additionally, it has been usual to provide special measures for regulating strikes and lock-outs in essential community services in order to protect the safety and health of the public. A diversity of methods has in fact been used for handling such disputes, including a requirement for advanced notice of industrial action (Japan and India), statutory conciliation (Denmark and Japan) and cooling-off periods (USA), as well as insistence on at least a partial operation of the service concerned (Belgium and Portugal). Yet in this respect it has become more difficult in an increasing number of countries to separate the problem of 'essential' services, as traditionally understood, from that of the industrial relations role of the public authorities in 'emergency' disputes relating to potential disruption of the national economy (Pankert, 1980).

It has been suggested that in general terms the role of the state in industrial relations may be viewed within the context of the need to permit the process of capital accumulation to continue, without disruption from industrial conflict, in order to promote the successful operation of the economy. However, the extent of state intervention as directed towards this end has varied considerably among countries reflecting diversities in their own economic and political developments. In relation to the procedural aspects of collective bargaining 'the degree of state regulation . . . tends to increase as the prevailing level of negotiations moves closer to the workplace' (ILO, 1974, p. 140). This has been particularly apparent in the USA and Canada, but there has also been relatively detailed procedural regulation of relations between works councils and managements in West Germany and Holland.

In Britain, the growth in militancy of powerful groups of shopfloor workers who were 'estranged from the control, influence and policies of the leadership of their official union hierarchies' (Strinati, 1982,

p. 203) was much more marked than in most other European countries and it took place against the background of a weakening and under-capitalised economy. Thus state regulation increased in an effort to promote a more orderly system of industrial relations in which industrial conflict could more readily be contained.

The incidence and determinants of industrial conflict itself, as expressed mainly in strike activity, are examined from a comparative perspective in the next chapter.

Notes

1. Conciliation is a procedure whereby a third party brings union and employer representatives together when negotiations have reached an impasse or have broken down, to find their own solution. With mediation his role is more active and he may submit settlement proposals to them. In the case of arbitration the third party takes a decision which disposes of the dispute.

2. 'One Law for the Lion and Ox is Oppression' (Clark, 1971, p. 425).

3. In Sweden, for instance, the first modern unions were not founded until the late 1870s.

4. Schmidt (1972) maintains that, historically, in Sweden business interests have never been able to exert as much political and economic influence as they have in many other parts of Europe and in the USA. In the Swedish Parliament it was farmers and small entrepreneurs who played the leading part until the Social Democrats came to power in 1932. Also, the multi-party constellation of power in the Swedish Parliament produced by a proportional representative voting system meant that although repressive legislation was proposed it could not attract the necessary parliamentary support (Jackson and Sisson, 1976).

5. This principle had been adopted by the American Federation of Labor since the 1880s to prevent disputes among its affiliated unions.

6. Including delineation of the appropriate bargaining unit, election of bargaining agents and the requirement upon employers to furnish necessary bargaining information and bargain 'in good faith'.

7. Between 1965 and 1975 about 20 per cent of all new awards were 'consent' awards.

8. Walker (1976) notes that because of the distinctive feature of compulsory arbitration the Australian industrial relations system was for long regarded by most other countries as 'an antipodean curiosity as exotic as the kangaroo or the boomerang' (p. 1).

9. This control was further strengthened by the Landrum–Griffin Act 1959.

10. This feature prompted a distinguished labour lawyer to comment that 'the importation of foreign labour law without due regard to lessons learned in its mother country is a remarkable event' (Wedderburn, 1972, p. 275).

11. However, the establishment of statutory Trade Boards (subsequently Wages Councils) in low-paid industries fulfilled some of the same functions.

12. In Belgium, however, although the rights/interest distinction is made, it is of little practical consequence as either type of dispute may be settled by strike action.

13. He emphasises that the direct involvement of government in contemporary industrial relations requires *legitimation* so as to avoid the charge of systematic

bias in favour of capital – a function which is performed by the ideological identification of the interests of capital with the 'national' interest.

Further Reading

There are useful general chapters on the state's role in the ILO's (1974) study of collective bargaining in industrialised market economies, and by Crouch (1978) concerning the changing role of the state in industrial relations in Western Europe. A recent, full-length study within the British context is Strinati (1982), whilst corporatist policies are well elucidated in Panitch (1977, 1981). Conciliation and arbitration provisions under governmental auspices are considered in ILO (1980).

6 INDUSTRIAL CONFLICT AND STRIKES

Some observers would contend that conflict – latent or manifest – is the essence of industrial relations (Barbash, 1979) or at least most would agree that it is a deeply-rooted, enduring and essential feature of the employment relationship. Within the shifting complex of economic and technical forces in market economies job security, the price of labour and control of its uses (power relations as exemplified in command and subordination) the conditions of production as well as its results, all these are sources of tension and latent conflict. In given circumstances they become manifest in one or more forms of overt conflict. In fact, the conflict universe encompasses both collective and individual responses, including not only strikes (i.e. concerted, temporary cessations of work) but sabotage, work slow-downs and boycotts as well as individual actions such as absenteeism and quitting. In Japan, the diverse, demonstrative forms of conflict incorporate 'sick-outs, leave taking . . . rallies, billboards, flyers, armbands, headbands [displaying union demands and other slogans]' (Levine and Taira, 1980, p. 68). Also, within the Soviet-type communist system, dissatisfied workers respond not only on occasion by spontaneous strikes and sometimes rebellion, but more frequently with actions located on the fringes of, or beyond, institutional networks including late arrival at work, indifferent performance, absenteeism and high labour turnover (Porket, 1978). In consequence, although strikes are usually the most visible and conspicuous expressions of industrial conflict, and in a country like the United States have dominated other forms of protest, they are not the only medium through which conflict of interests and values can be expressed.

Cross-National Strike Differences

Despite their partial nature, strikes are frequently used in comparative studies as an index of conflict for which statistical data are readily available. In addition, the quantitative analysis of strike activity which proceeds via model-building and testing techniques is sometimes regarded as being a particularly fruitful area for the development of theory since it lends itself most readily to the use of formalised data (von Beyme, 1980). An immediate problem, however, in the cross-national comparative analysis of strikes is not only that it may be of limited value if industrial conflict takes diverse and uncorrelated forms between countries, but also the fact that the strike itself is not a homogeneous phenomenon. It can have different meanings and significance in different parts of the world, as well as fulfilling varying functions over the course of time. As Dunlop (1978) has observed, it may be used 'as an organising device, a means of general protest, as a political demonstration, or it may be regarded as an integral part of the collective bargaining process used to induce agreement' (p. 7).

In the United States, for instance, the strike, as the most typical form of labour dispute, is a pivotal aspect of the union-management relationship, and a major component of the collective bargaining process when an impasse has been reached. (Although, this is not true in the public sector where strikes have generally been prohibited in favour of third-party procedures to resolve a negotiating impasse.) Because in an unorganised plant a union has to win an election contest in order to gain recognition rights from the often unwilling employer an adversary position is encouraged from the outset, so that 'in a real sense a conflict situation is the midwife of almost all new American unions' (Kassalow, 1977, p. 120). In West Germany, unlike the position in Belgium where in principle the strike is subject to no legal regulation, only strikes called by unions within the collective bargaining context upon the expiry of a collective agreement are legalised. 'Political', as well as solidarity and sympathetic strikes are illegal. Thus Maurice and Sellier (1979) have characterised the strike in Germany as being a 'legal bureaucratic phenomenon' called upon the authoritative decision of the union to set it in motion and support it financially. In the case of Japan, however, the strike performs a somewhat different role and is not the final weapon in collective bargaining, or the most usual form of labour dispute. Frequently it will be called at the onset rather than the breakdown of negotiations (before any bargaining has taken place) to warn employers and demonstrate the union's seriousness about its demands, as well as the extent of union membership support and solidarity. Typically it will be carried out with the employees remaining at the work site, and thus resembles the sit-down strikes found in some western countries (Hanami, 1979).

In contrast to such purely collective bargaining orientations of the strike, the situation in countries such as France and Italy may be differentiated, with the strike fulfilling other additional functions. It has been contended that in France strikes are a 'charismatic' phenomenon

(Maurice and Sellier, 1979) and that more generally within the Latin countries, as manifestations of worker protest they often possess a 'mystical quality' (von Beyme, 1980). The right to strike has been enshrined in the constitution both in France and Italy, being a human right belonging to a political tradition and comparable to the freedom of speech and association. Moreover, in France the

> strike has been regarded as an action by individual employees joined by other employees. Sometimes it is initiated by a union, but just as often it is spontaneous in its initial stages and later on is made a matter of concern to one or more unions but often without financial commitment. It has been looked upon as a revolt by the individuals against the power of the employer. (Schmidt, 1972)

Certainly, in the pre-World War II period when French employers would not generally acccept unions for bargaining purposes one prime objective of strikes appears to have been to compel public intervention in order to make recalcitrant employers more pliable (Shorter and Tilly, 1974). In the post-war period strikes in that country could also assume an enlarged role as a symbolic protest, as 'displays of power and organisational ability' (Crouch, 1978) to impress the strikers' case upon decision-makers in the legislature. Similarly, in Italy strikes were often regarded less as a means of winning specific economic demands than as an exercise in mass mobilisation and propaganda (Kendall, 1975).

Instead of treating strikes as an incident in the bargaining process the orientation of this kind of approach views them within a wider context as having an important role in broader societal struggles for power, whereby industrial conflict itself assumes a larger, socio-political significance. Nevertheless, as we shall show, this interpretation within the French context is more applicable to certain kinds of strike undertaken at particular periods of time, rather than to all strike activity. It would, perhaps, be more accurate to say that in France a 'strike' covers a whole range of different phenomena. It can be a symbolic expression of protest, as with political strikes directed against unfavourable government decisions for instance, whereupon union members have frequently marched and demonstrated in the streets of Paris. But equally, in more recent years, it has also been concerned with enterprise-related issues such as wages and conditions, including newer forms of worker action such as *grèves bouchons* (selective strikes by various groups of employees occupying strategic positions in the production process, engaging in many short stops and starts) (Delamotte, 1982).

In some of the Third World countries Hyman has noted certain features which tend to differentiate strikes there from the typical Anglo-Saxon collective bargaining strike:

> Commonly they are a form of pressure or protest directed against the government rather than individual private employers; accordingly they are likely to possess an overt political dimension . . . strikes which are an explicit challenge to established authority are commonly intimately linked with other forms of popular protest; thus upsurges of strike action normally occur in periods of more general social and political turbulence. (Hyman, 1979, p. 323)

As well as such differences in the function and significance of strikes viewed from a comparative perspective there are also marked variations in their form, level and trends over both the short and longer terms. von Beyme (1980) has distinguished three broad typologies of conflict behaviour within capitalist countries, since generalisations are possible only if types are established. (Some disaggregation within the categories may be necessary, however, because particular countries can display divergent traits.) The West European type is distinguished by a large number of relatively short strikes, although in this latter respect Britain is something of an exception. It is also argued that within this category political motivation often plays an important part in addition to questions relating to income distribution since strikes may be symbolic or undertaken to exert pressure upon political bodies. Secondly, a North European type has been delineated. There the number of strikes tends to be low and, although widespread, they are of short duration (with the exception of Sweden). Also, Social Democratic parties are influential and there is a long tradition of negotiation by the labour movement with political bodies, as in the Scandinavian countries and to some extent in West Germany. Finally, with the North American type strikes are relatively frequent and long-lasting, but are used predominantly for economic purposes (with political influence being exerted mainly via organised lobbying).

Not only are there cross-national differences in the level and patterns of work stoppages but also divergences in the trend of strikes over the longer term. From 1900–72, for instance, strike activity in Canada, France, Italy and the United States either increased or fluctuated around a constant mean level, yet it decreased to negligible amounts in Denmark, the Netherlands, Norway and Sweden (Hibbs, 1978).

In the light of these preliminary considerations we may ask, what accounts for such differential levels and cross-national patterns of strike activity in western countries? A number of general explanations have been put forward which, although they include several variants, may conveniently be grouped into three major categories. These comprise institutional approaches, which relate particularly to collective bargaining arrangements, and also 'organisational–political' theories emphasising the capacity of labour to mount strike action, together with an insistence that collective bargaining must be seen within the context of wider and longer-term societal changes. Both these approaches focus upon the medium and longer timespan characteristics of strike levels and patterns. Thirdly, however, there are explanations embedded in prevailing economic conditions and primarily applicable to short-run variations in the incidence of strikes. The salient features of each of these perspectives need to be considered in turn.

We begin with the approach which maintains that strike activity is not independent of institutional arrangements in that, although conflict may be inevitable, 'the particular structure and process of bargaining play a major role in determining the extent to which this conflict can be settled short of strike action' (Kaufman, 1982, p. 482).

Institutional Explanations

A general link has been postulated between the nature of the industrialisation process and patterns of worker protest and reaction as manifested in strike action. Strikes are expected to peak during the early stages of industrialisation as a result of protests against the difficult adjustments required of the labour force in moving from traditional society to the discipline and pace of industrial production (Kerr *et al.*, 1962). Thereafter, as industrialisation evolves, the amount of worker protest tends to decline. Emerging worker organisations control spontaneous protest expressions and they themselves become accommodated within the system. Institutional mechanisms of negotiation such as collective bargaining and grievance procedures are set up to resolve industrial relations differences so that, although conflict continues to exist within the employment relationship, its magnitude is reduced and its assumes a less open form.

There are, however, severe doubts about some aspects of this particular line of argument. It cannot explain why heightened strike activity is marked by discontinuous phases and strikes may not peak in the early stages of industrialism if workers are insufficiently mobilised for collective action. Moreover, at the empirical level it has been shown that in the United States and a number of other countries there has been no tendency for strike activity to decline. Instead, the outstanding feature of US strike levels has been their 'long-term constancy with measures of worker involvement and duration showing no general upward or downward trend' (Edwards, 1981, p. 51). Nevertheless, the 'institutionalisation' thesis itself has remained an important strand in the comparative literature on strike activity. It was originally used by Ross and Hartman (1960) to help explain what they saw as a tendency towards a long-term decline in strike activity throughout much of the industrialised world. Their extrapolative prediction that, with some exceptions, the strike would continue to 'wither away' was based on mistaking a subsidence in their measures of strike activity during a particular period of relative quiescence, especially in the early post-war years, for an established trend. It is well known that they therefore missed predicting the subsequent, general break-out and acceleration which occurred at the end of the 1960s. Thus far from having withered away the strike 'is alive and flourishing in a high proportion of countries' (Clarke, 1980b, p. 23).

From a specific comparative standpoint, however, Ross and Hartman sought the determinant influences on relative strike activity within particular countries in aspects of their industrial relations systems. They emphasised the reduction in organisational, and to some extent economic, influences on conflict as a consequence of the acceptance of trade unions by employers, mutual accommodation and the resultant institutionalisation of collective bargaining. Centralised bargaining systems, in particular, would contain or reduce the level of industrial conflict since worker and employer organisations are enabled to impose real behavioural constraints upon their respective memberships. In essence, it was postulated that countries with stable and unified union movements, accepted by employers and locked into centralised and well-developed collective bargaining machinery were those which would enjoy the greatest peace in industry. High strike activity in Italy and France (West European type), therefore, could be explained largely in terms of low levels of unionisation, union movements riven by disunity and internal factions and mainly unrecognised by employers – resulting in weak and unstable labour-management relations. By way of contrast, the much lower strike propensities in Scandinavian countries (Northern European type) were attributed to the facts that their labour movements had firm and stable memberships and that collective bargaining, which became institutionalised early in the present century, had become well consolidated and centralised.

Some more recent studies of cross-national patterns of industrial conflict continue to reflect this institutional orientation. The wave of strikes from 1968 to 1970 in Western European countries and their form, in terms both of spontaneity of action and long duration, have been related to the imperfections and shortcomings of industrial relations institutions at the lower level, that of the enterprise to which power had tended to gravitate (Dubois, 1978). In Italy, for example, the series of strikes in 1968-69 originated mainly as a spontaneous, rank-and-file development at workplace level, and the rash of strikes in Belgium in 1970 has also been attributed to a similar expression of worker frustration at developments during the 1960s. In Sweden there was an outbreak of mainly unofficial stoppages towards the end of the 1960s, and similarly in West Germany an unprecedented wave of spontaneous wildcat strikes.

More generally, the greater incidence of industrial conflict in the United States (North American type) in broad comparison to that in many European countries has been explained as a function of the level and scope of collective bargaining (Kassalow, 1977). The wide coverage of collective agreements in Europe is seen as encouraging more consensual tendencies. Bargaining along a broad industry front lowers the negotiating stakes in line with the ability to pay of marginal producers, thus reducing the potential resistance of many firms. In addition, less of a direct challenge to job control and managerial prerogatives at plant level is involved. The very extensiveness of industry- (or regionally-) wide negotiations may inhibit bargainers from allowing bargaining to break down because of the more widespread effects of any ensuing strike – particularly where negotiations are economy-wide, as in the case of Sweden. In the United States, on the other hand, conflict becomes exacerbated by decentralised bargaining since strikes involve crucial and fundamental battles over the control of the workplace (Edwards, 1981). In consequence, employers have been more hostile to unions which have frequently been unable to establish a permanent and stable position (i.e. the thrust of this position is that industrial relations in the USA have been less than fully institutionalised).

Furthermore, Kassalow argues that generally in Western Europe because of a considerable dependence upon international trade the parties have always appreciated the importance of exports for their economies' well-being, a fact which is also used as one explanation for the lower strike propensity of many Western European countries in comparison with the United States. Yet the importance of this particular factor can be overstated since severe export dependence has not prevented rising levels of industrial conflict in countries like New Zealand, which are actually concentrated in the export-related sectors of the economy (Korpi and Shalev, 1979).

Clegg (1976) has also put forward an institutional theory to account for the varying status and dimensions of strikes based upon evidence from six major industrial countries. He contends that strike patterns are closely associated with the structure of collective bargaining in each country in terms of the bargaining level and disputes procedure, together with the indirect effect of the level of bargaining through factional competition within trade unions. Thus the relatively high proportion of union-sanctioned, official strikes in the United States is explained by the predominance of plant-level bargaining. With this form of bargaining structure a strike can be called at relatively little cost to the membership as a whole in terms of the payment of strike benefit because only a limited number of workers need be called out, that is, strikes can be called in particular plants without bringing out all the workers from an entire industry (as in Holland), or region (as in Germany). Clegg also regards the extent and development of disputes mechanisms and procedural norms within a country as important dampening influences, especially in reducing the number of unofficial strikes, since these devices function as an alternative to striking during the currency of the agreement. Comprehensive procedural arrangements in Sweden are seen as helping to explain the relative infrequency of strikes in that country[1] whereas their absence in France is associated with a high strike incidence. As Despax and Rojot have expressed it, in France

> the absence of a peace obligation, the freedom for unions or groups of employees to engage in industrial action at any time, and the failure of legal procedures for the resolution of conflicts combine to produce a rather high level of industrial conflicts. (Despax and Rojot, 1979, p. 217)

In the case of Germany the substitution of the works council (with a statutory peace obligation) for union in-plant bargaining may also have helped reduce the level of stoppages – although possibly at the price of reducing the employees' degree of job control at the point of production (Kendall, 1975). Finally, high strike activity can, according to Clegg, be partially related to factional competition both within and between trade unions being particularly marked in the USA but not in Sweden or West Germany. For internal political reasons a successful strike is a means of impressing sections of the unions' membership, or potential membership, and securing their allegiance. In Clegg's theory, therefore, differences in strike levels and patterns across countries are related mainly to the institutional structure and characteristics of collective bargaining.

Infrastructural Variations

A somewhat different institutionalist approach is that adopted by Ingham (1974) in his comparative study of industrial conflict in Britain and Scandinavia, of which Sweden is taken as the main example. His analysis goes beyond identifying and relating salient differences in bargaining structures between countries to their respective levels of conflict since he attempts to explain the origins of the institutional arrangements themselves. His thesis is that institutional variations in industrial relations systems depend primarily upon differences in the industrial infrastructure (i.e. economic structure and mode of production of the countries concerned). The dominant features of contemporary industrial relations are seen as being crucially influenced by the early stages of the course of industrialisation in the countries investigated. Three particular dimensions of infrastructure are selected as being the most relevant to the development of industrial relations systems: the extent of industrial concentration, the degree of product differentiation and specialisation, and the complexity of technical and organisational structure.

The first determinant – a high degree of industrial concentration in which output in the major sectors of the economy comes to be dominated by a small number of large concerns – is particularly apparent in the case of Sweden. In that country the small size of its own domestic market meant that in the late nineteenth century expansion had necessarily to be geared to foreign demand in export markets. The highly competitive nature of the export sector tended to force out smaller, inefficient firms, leaving a markedly concentrated industrial structure. This particular aspect of infrastructure, in turn, affected industrial relations. Since the various industrial sectors had become dominated by a small number of large firms operating within oligopolistic market structures (characterised by low levels of price competition within and between the sectors), Ingham argues that collective organisation among employers was facilitated. Strong, centralised employers' organisations could be established leading to the growth of formal institutions for the regulation of conflict since, if necessary, the employers' body was sufficiently powerful to be able to impose such regulation. In this exposition, therefore, a crucial role in the development of institutional regulation in industrial relations is attributed to employers. By way of contrast with Sweden, in nineteenth-century Britain there existed a large, diversified and highly competitive home, as well as overseas, market which was supplied by a preponderance of smaller- and medium-sized firms. The result was less commonality of interest among (more fragmented) employers so that combination to form strong centralised institutions was far less possible than in Scandinavia.

As well as the effects of industrial concentration a second, and related, source of infrastructural variation concerns the degree of product specialisation within an economy. In this respect Ingham suggests that

> those societies which were among the first to industrialise and which possess large domestic markets have tended to produce a wider range of goods than smaller countries which successfully industrialised later to a large extent through the export of highly specialised products (Ingham, 1974, p. 42)

This particular dimension also helps determine the capacity of a society for developing centralised institutions for the regulation of conflict. In Sweden the crucial significance of exports dictated the production of a small range of products (ball-bearings and other specialist engineering products) for highly specialised markets, and therefore a relatively undifferentiated industrial structure. In the case of Britain product diversity and differentiation, by producing a vast range of goods for both domestic and foreign markets, were added to the industrial infrastructure during the nineteenth century, thereby inhibiting the development of formal and centralised regulatory organisations.

A third important feature of industrial infrastructure is the complexity of the production system itself, which affects the structure of the trade union movement. A country such as Britain, which was the first to industrialise, tends to have a complex production system. It has passed through and incorporated a number of different technological and organisational phases, beginning with a craft and workshop technology, moving through mass production and ultimately on to automated systems. The effect of this structural development upon the labour force is to produce a vast range of occupational skills and specialisms and, correspondingly, a large number of highly differentiated trade unions organised along occupational lines in order to cater for them. Such a structure precipitates sectionalism and conflicts of interest within the labour movement reducing cohesiveness, solidarity and the growth of powerful, central union bodies.

As a contrasting development, industrialisation took place in Sweden at a later date and could therefore take immediate advantage of factory production technology. Because craft-based workshop technology never became predominant in its manufacturing industry, the Swedish labour movement developed a more homogeneous structure. Workers became organised principally on an industrial basis since the emergence of powerful and autonomous craft unions was precluded. These factors made it easier for the central union organisation (the LO) ultimately to assume a strong degree of control over its affiliated unions. The authority of the LO was also reinforced since its permission has been required before major strikes can be called (in order to secure access to the central strike fund) and it has the right to be present at industry-level negotiations.

In Ingham's exposition these structural tendencies within the labour movement complement the centralisation achieved on the employers' side and further reinforce the institutionalisation of conflict. It would appear, however, that the main credit for the greater adherence to agreements in Sweden belongs to the employers' side (Clegg, 1976). Employers have been less prepared than their British counterparts to make concessions at local level which overrode agreements because of the stronger discipline within Swedish employers' bodies. As a result, open conflict is more inhibited in Sweden because it becomes channelled through the highly-developed and formalised institutional framework.

A more recent study by Waters (1982) along similar lines contends that the mode of production and accompanying structure of industrial society are the main generators of different patterns (or 'shapes') of strikes in capitalist societies. His model, which focuses on the identification of a number of historical phases (accompanied by particular patterns of conflict) in the process of industrialisation, is developed against the background of Australian experience, although its general outlines are also applied to Sweden, the USA, Britain and France. He distinguishes craft, mechanised factory, assembly line and service and automated production phases, each of which is characterised by a specific mode of production organisation.

Theories which purport to account for variations in particular dimensions of strike activity as between countries by means of differences in the social organisation of production have, however, been subjected to some criticism. In particular, Ingham's explanation of the institutional contrasts between Britain and Sweden, in terms of differences between their economic sub-structures, although original, is also somewhat problematic in relating these divergences to trends in industrial conflict. It can be misleading to draw too sharp a contrast between the flourishing of the strike in Britain and its decline in Sweden since in the latter country the frequency of unofficial strikes has increased significantly since the late 1960s (Korpi and Shalev, 1979). It may be the case that strike reduction in Scandinavia has been of a cyclical, rather than a secular nature. That Ingham exaggerates the amount of control over wage negotiations exercised by the central institutions in Sweden is also evidenced by the amount of 'wage drift' occurring at plant level outside the control of the central organisations (Fulcher, 1975). Furthermore, the analysis is essentially in terms of an assumed mechanistic relationship with no account of the processes which may mediate the effect of infrastructural considerations upon actual behaviour (Jackson and Sisson, 1976). It has also been pointed out by von Beyme (1980) that this approach – if extended beyond Britain and Scandinavia – does not explain why Canada, with a similar level of concentration to Swedish industry, has a high strike incidence[2] whereas Germany, towards the lower end of the concentration scale, has been relatively strike-free.

As regards Sweden, the main difficulty, however, for the thesis relating changes in the long-term number of disputes to the growth of institutions for the regulation of conflict concerns the *timing* of the respective changes. Korpi (1980) has shown that as early as the first decade of the present century Sweden had some well-developed institutions for containing and regulating conflict, yet the level of disputes was not reduced at that period. Rather, along with Norway, man-days lost continued to be the highest in the western world. The dramatic change to very low, relative dispute levels came suddenly in the mid-1930s. Korpi contends that although institutions are significant they must not be taken as being the primary cause of any substantial decrease in manifest conflict. In the case of Sweden the decisive changes in the level of conflict manifestations appear to lie elsewhere, outside the orbit of the industrial relations institutions themselves. He claims that the explanation is to be found in political changes in the coming to power of the Social Democrats in 1932 and their remaining in office for many years subsequently. This gave the unions access to political and legislative power with the result that there was then less need to fight costly battles in the industrial sphere. Political means had become available for securing a more favourable distribution of economic rewards since 'to the extent that labour is successful in acquiring control over political institutions it can exercise its power through these means and will not be limited to the industrial arena' (Korpi and Shalev, 1979, p. 170). At the same time, the political power resources of Swedish employers became correspondingly depleted in that they could no longer rely on having a friendly government to intervene on their behalf, as and when necessary. Thus, as with the labour movement, a change also took place in the employers' conflict strategy. It was decided to seek an accommodation with the LO with a view to promoting economic growth. By renegotiating their interrelations in this way conflict of interest might be converted from a zero-sum to a positive-sum type, to enable both parties to improve their positions – even if their relative shares did not change very much.

In summary, critics of the institutionalisation of conflict thesis would maintain that although it can be a valid explanation of the form and type of conflict as expressed through strikes, it overstates the role and importance of industrial relations institutions themselves in accounting for inter-country diversities in the levels of industrial conflict. On this view institutional arrangements for conflict resolution should be seen more as *intervening*, than as independent, variables affecting the level of conflict. It is too facile to identify the institutional framework as the major cause of any decrease in overt conflict levels. Rather, the institutional arrangements themselves reflect, and are dependent upon, the power structure of society, as well as on changes therein. Therefore, for Korpi the development of such institutions, together with any accompanying decline in conflict levels, are jointly attributable to a third variable – the underlying differences in power resources between the contending parties. That is to say,

> the extent of dissatisfaction with inequalities in work-related rewards will depend on the aspiration level of the workers, which in turn can be expected to reflect their power position in relation to the employers. If the power position of the workers continues to improve, this can be expected to affect their social consciousness and to generate a desire for improvements. (Korpi, 1978a, p. 47)

In this respect it is widely recognised that an emphasis solely upon structural determinants of industrial conflict is insufficient since it is also necessary to consider attitudes and consciousness. Workers respond not simply to the objective features of a situation but to their own perceptions and interpretations of it. In addition, the labour force needs to be mobilised to undertake collective action. It is therefore claimed that the political process approach to industrial conflict is particularly valuable since the workers' power position can also affect their social consciousness and their will to mobilise.

We shall now examine on a cross-national basis the broad category of organisational-political theories, in which strikes are seen as being determined by wider social and political forces, as a contrasting approach to those which stress the primacy of conflict-regulating institutions.

Organisational and Political Theories

The work of Shorter and Tilly (1974) for France is particularly notable for its emphasis on the organisational and political positions of labour as factors influencing the level of strike activity. Trade unions are viewed as a mediating influence between workers' dissatisfactions and the translation of those grievances into overt protest since prior organisation is regarded as a precondition of strike activity. For Shorter and Tilly, each of the periodic waves of strike activity in France reflected an increase in the organisational capacities of the labour movement, with the timing of the waves being determined to take advantage of crises at critical junctures of French political history. They portray the strike as an instrument of political action, a means of putting pressure on the political centre when the industrial working class, as a contender for power, has not yet been admitted into the polity and does not participate in the government process. In this sense the strike becomes a means of involving workers in political processes – and not only by compelling government action on behalf of the strikers in the dispute itself.[3] At particular periods of political crisis such as 1936, 1947 and 1968 it was a method of impressing upon the public the force and vigour of demands from a temporarily highly-mobilised labour movement for a greater share of national production and a louder voice for a working class 'avid for representation within the magic circle of centre stage politics' (Shorter and Tilly, 1974, p. 74).

This approach is best seen, however, as a partial rather than universal explanation of strike activity in France. In that country not only have strikes been undertaken by unorganised workers but also, by way of determining factors, it is vital to distinguish between 'waves' of strikes and 'ordinary' strikes. Strike waves within particular years represent an exceptional spread of strikes to many companies throughout all regions and all industries and their timing has coincided with political events. By contrast, economic factors are the precipitating cause of ordinary strikes directed at the employer and have a set of demands related to the subject of bargaining (on wages, employment, etc.). Especially since the late 1960s some long strikes during phases of economic recession have been undertaken in order to protect employment, thus making 'a transition from the symbolic or admonitory strike [at low average cost per striker] to the resistance strike' (Sellier, 1978, p. 226). In addition, short strikes have been geared not only to symbolic political protest but have also been used in the collective bargaining process – for example, for the reopening of agreements (of indefinite duration) where employers have been unwilling to take the initiative to renew them. In recent years conflicts have become longer in duration and smaller, reflecting an intensification at workplace level.

Shorter and Tilly's analysis of the more political character of many strikes in France leads them to ask whether it is possible to explain broader trends in international conflict patterns on a similar basis. They recognise that in examining the complex phenomenon of strike differences among nations other influences as well as political factors will need consideration. Yet they claim to be able to discern aspects of French strikes which reflect universal trends, running parallel in all western countries in the past century. They point to an essential comparability of conflict patterns among countries with similar modes of worker representation in the central polity. Before the depression of the 1930s the strike profiles of most countries in Western Europe were very similar in terms of frequency, extent of worker involvement, and duration as the working classes mobilised themselves for political action. Subsequently, in the post-war period, a divergence occurred and in countries where the working class had succeeded to political power, such as Scandinavia, the strike underwent a transformation. The strike rate became negligible since it was no longer necessary to attempt to affect political decision-making through the medium of strikes.

In contrast, where such changes did not take place as in France, it is claimed that strikes continued to be a vehicle for political protest, with wage demands being merely a mobilising device in the push towards broader objectives. Hence the finding that after 1945 French strikes (at least until 1974) became shorter in duration – since only a brief stoppage was required to make a symbolic, political point – but large in terms of the number of workers involved. In short, politicised unions were 'able to interest a wide range of workers in limited commitments of time and energy for collective enterprises' (Shorter and Tilly, 1974, p. 307). It is worth reiterating, however, that somewhat different interpretations of the frequency of short strikes as a dominant characteristic of industrial conflict in France are possible, such as relating this type of stoppage to features of the prevailing system of collective bargaining, together with an inability on the part of the unions to finance lengthy strikes.

Korpi and Shalev (1979) have extended and developed the line of approach in which strike trends are grounded in a political explanation towards further comparative perspectives. For them, the wider relevance of the political interpretation evolves out of an original analysis of the Swedish case, rather than the French. They view industrial conflict as an important symptom of societal change, with a central role being assigned to changes in the distribution of power resources between the contending parties. As we have indicated, in the case of Sweden after the coming to power of the Social Democrats in the 1930s,

> The unions had . . . access to a relatively efficient, political alternative [to strikes] which they could use to achieve important goals, primarily through changes in employment, fiscal and social policies. (Korpi, 1978a, p. 99)

Thus, via what has been termed a process of 'political exchange' (Pizzorno, 1978), the centre of gravity of distributional conflict moved from the industrial to the political sphere. Swedish labour practically renounced the strike weapon to pursue more effectively, and at less cost, its long-term class interests in the latter arena. For such an exchange to be possible, however, the power of labour within government has to be secure and likely to be enduring, not only so that the unions may be convinced of the benefits of a less militant industrial policy, but also to persuade employers to reach a lasting accommodation with them. (It may be more than coincidence that after the exclusion of the Social Democrats from government in the mid-1970s there was some resurgence of industrial conflict.) Similarly, in order to be able to 'deliver' its part of the bargain the labour movement requires a good deal of organisational unity between and within its industrial and political wings together with internal control and discipline over its constituents. In effect, the emphasis of these institutional prerequisites is upon a high degree of coordination and organisational centralisation.

In seeking to substantiate this thesis on the basis of wider, international comparisons, Korpi and Shalev look for parallels and contrasts to the Swedish case in which Social Democratic governments of other countries have achieved durable power, the labour movement is united and organisationally strong, and the level of industrial conflict has declined. A number of groups of countries are then identified, the first consisting of Austria and Norway which most closely follow the Swedish model. Since World War II both these countries have had Social Democratic rule – or at least a strong presence in government – centralised and unified labour movements, and have experienced a marked decline in the level of industrial conflict. At the opposite extreme are the USA, Canada and Ireland whose socialist parties enjoyed little electoral support and have not played a significant role in national politics. Furthermore, their labour movements are not highly coordinated nor organisationally centralised, and levels of conflict have remained high since 1945, as well as being largely retained within the employment context.

There are also a number of intermediate countries such as France (up to 1981 when the socialists came to power), Italy and Japan where, although the labour movement enjoyed significant electoral support and was relatively highly mobilised, it remained excluded from the executive branch of government and totally lacked the prerequisites for political exchange. It is argued that with these conditions the effect is actually to *increase* the level of industrial conflict. Finally, there is a group of 'exceptional' countries including West Germany, the Netherlands and Switzerland (both of the latter two countries having somewhat weak labour movements and yet also low levels of industrial conflict) whose experience does not easily seem to fit the hypothesis. West Germany, for instance, is a country in which it is readily conceded that although the Social Democrats remained outside the government until the mid-1960s, nevertheless the level of industrial disputes also remained very low – among the lowest in the industrialised world.

A further, related approach towards explaining long-run comparative trends in industrial conflict, and one which also views strike activity in terms of political factors, is Hibbs' (1978) general comparative study of 11 countries. His explanation for the differential strike-trend experience of these countries concerns the 'political economy of distribution' of the national product. In countries in which a major reduction in the volume (man-days lost) of industrial conflict has taken place, such as Norway and Sweden, this is explained largely by the effectiveness of Social Democratic and Labour governments in socialising the consumption and final distribution of national income. The crucial factor is not the coming to power of Social Democratic regimes *per se*, but the change in the locus of the distribution of national income produced by their welfare state policies. In these countries governments have created a large public sector and a high proportion of the national income has become socialised so that there is collective consumption in the form of extensive provision of public services and a high 'social wage'. Thus the political process dominates the shaping of the final allocation of the national product. In these circumstances it is argued that the distributional struggle thereby becomes removed from the private market place where allocation takes place through collective bargaining and industrial conflict and where labour's economic well-being is determined predominantly by market outcomes. Instead, the struggle is shifted to the political arena where labour and capital now compete through political negotiation and electoral mobilisation. On the other hand, those countries which have experienced little change in average strike volume during the twentieth century, or where strike activity increased – France, Italy, the USA and Canada – are those in which Centre and Right governments have predominated.

The major specific criticism, however, which has been directed at Hibbs' thesis is that by concentrating upon a single variable – the allocative role of the state – and regarding strikes as being a consequence solely of a distributional conflict over national income, it adopts too limiting a focus. It appears to deny that strikes may serve as a protest against the existing order of society itself and overlooks the fact that the conflict between workers and employers relates not only to 'price' but also to 'power' (Barbash, 1977). This power struggle will continue regardless of whether the public or private sector predominates in determining income distribution. Furthermore, an empirical study has been undertaken for 15 industrial countries over the period 1956–65 (Gifford, 1974) of the relationship between days lost by work stoppages and the nature and role of government under varying degrees of socialism. Measures such as the proportion of public ownership, the ratio of public welfare expenditure to GNP, and the number of years in which socialist parties had been in power were found, in fact, not to be significantly related to the strike rates of individual countries.

Such reservations notwithstanding, it has been claimed that the political models which have been discussed 'are probably the most ambitious, imaginative and provocative to have recently graced a field which has long been starved of theoretical innovation' (Shalev, 1978b, p. 491). They do provide a useful counterbalance to previous approaches which, by concentrating upon bargaining structures and procedures within labour market institutions, give insufficient attention to social aspirations and mobilising factors in strike movements. In contrast, political theories insist that the system of industrial relations 'is placed firmly in the context of the political economy, the class system and the power structure of society' (Korpi, 1981, p. 209). Yet political interpretations themselves are not immune to criticism. Edwards (1981), for instance, suggests that in playing down the role of collective bargaining as a means of resolving disputes in favour of broader socio-political variables they are too dogmatic, replacing one overarching explanation for another. He also questions their implication that the working class in certain European countries has achieved genuine access to political power. His position is that although the political environment needs to be taken into account, the effect of that environment on strikes is usually mediated through the bargaining system.

Although the institutional and organisational-political theories which have so far been considered may help to explain longer-term comparative strike characteristics and trends they will not explain year-by-year variations in strike activity. Instead, these strike fluctuations need to be related to variables which themselves fluctuate markedly on a short-term basis – those of an economic nature.

Economic Determinants

Few aspects of strike activity have received greater attention than the relationship between changing economic conditions and changes in the frequency of strikes. Numerous individual country studies have examined the relationship between strike frequency (number of stoppages) and some indicator of changes in economic activity, or business cycle influences. They have generally found that there is a significant, positive association between the two, with the number of strikes moving pro-cyclically. The role of economic influences is developed within a collective bargaining framework in terms of variables which will lead to a changed propensity of workers' organisations to undertake strike action and of firms being prepared to incur a strike.

It is assumed that strikes occur over wage (or similarly related) issues, thereby abstracting from the multi-dimensional nature of collective bargaining by concentrating on only a single aspect of the wide range of bargaining issues, as well as doing scant justice to the strikers' complexities of motivation.

Rees (1952) originally pointed out that economic conditions in the form of business prosperity, especially of tight labour markets, would affect the timing of strikes – assuming some given existing stock of grievances. Unions are more likely to press their demands in prosperous periods when the costs for their members will be reduced. As a later researcher has expressed it,

> The success of a strike depends on the extent to which workers can minimise costs to themselves while imposing large costs on the employer. Periods of low unemployment increase the bargaining power of workers on both counts; employees have greater alternative sources of work while the costs to the firm both in the form of profits foregone and of difficulty of attracting substitute workers are increased. (Kaufman, 1982, p. 479)

More recent studies over the past decade in countries such as Canada, the USA, Britain and Australia have used econometric, multivariate techniques in the form of single-equation strike models to examine the relationship between strike frequency and some set of explanatory variables, including real wage changes, unemployment and company profits. The prototype for these was the bargaining model developed by Ashenfelter and Johnson (1969) to explain aggregate strike frequency in the United States over the post-World War II period. An economic explanation has also been put forward to account for the timing of the strike wave which occurred throughout much of Western Europe from 1968 to 1970.[4] Although wage improvements were central to the demands in Britain, Italy and Germany, Soskice (1978) has shown that it is too oversimplified to attribute the cause of the strikes purely to the effects of the more rapid inflationary pressures of the late 1960s. Rather, there were a number of relevant influences including

> government deflationary or wage-restraint policies between 1963 and 1965 (e.g. in France and the Federal Republic of Germany), corporate policies to reduce wage costs and increase productivity in order to restore profit margins and inflationary pressure coming

from the United States (reflected in Italy and Germany by an actual boom). What his economic interpretation revealed was the combination of these factors of frustration. (Reynaud, 1980, p. 4)

Having identified a number of perspectives which seek to explain the longer-term patterns and changes in strike activity together with short-term, year-to-year fluctuations, we can also examine the translation of these approaches into testable models for empirical evaluation via quantitative techniques utilising strike statistics.

International Strike Statistics

Because strikes are a highly complex social phenomenon there are not only problems in adequately explaining their causes, but even in measuring their magnitude. These difficulties are increased in cross-national comparisons since there are significant methodological differences between countries in the collection and processing of strike data which also vary over time. Shalev (1978a) contends that strike statistics may usefully be assessed in terms of two criteria: their *validity* – how far they measure what they set out to measure; and their *reliability* – to what extent they continue to perform in an equivalent or consistent way on different occasions. As regards their validity, in no country do the official statistics constitute a complete sample of the entire universe of work stoppages. Some countries (such as France, Britain and the USA) concentrate exclusively on industrial disputes, and explicitly exclude 'political' strikes, whereas Australia, West Germany and Sweden include them (Creigh *et al*., 1980). Most countries have certain minimum threshold levels below which strikes are not recorded, although Belgium, France and Italy have no such eligibility criteria and include all stoppages regardless of their size or duration. As a generalisation we can say that, other things being equal, the smaller, shorter and more localised disputes are less likely to secure statistical inclusion in the official figures. Of the three basic strike series, number of stoppages (frequency), extent or size (number of workers involved) and scale (or volume), in terms of the number of working-days lost, the latter measure – defined on a standardised basis as the number of working-(man-) days lost per 1000 employees – is usually regarded as being particularly useful in cross-national comparative studies (Walsh, 1983). It is less likely to be distorted since it is principally affected by large-scale stoppages which are more likely to be recorded whatever the statistical system used. In contrast, the number of strikes is especially sensitive to national differences in the criteria used in order to determine which industrial disputes are too small to be classified as strikes.

There are also problems concerning the reliability of strike series over time. Territorial adjustments in boundaries of certain countries are one possible source of difficulty – such as the inclusion of Algeria in the French statistics, or Eire in those for the United Kingdom, over particular historical periods. Similarly, changes in the threshold inclusion level can be of major consequence. In Israel when the minimum duration for recorded stoppages was reduced from one day to two hours the number of stoppages increased almost threefold (Shalev, 1978a). However, if it can be assumed – as seems reasonable in most cases – that these measurement errors are either constant or have a random influence on the final statistics over time, then strike trends as between countries can (with caution) be meaningfully compared.

Empirical Studies of Cross-National Strike Determination

A number of statistical studies of the time-pattern of strikes on an international basis have recently been carried out utilising the economic, institutional and political-organisational perspectives which we have examined. Clarke (1980b) ranked six western countries (five in Europe and Canada) in ascending order of their stoppage incidence via working-days lost on average over a three-year period between 1975 and 1977, together with the corresponding behaviour of two macroeconomic variables. He noted that highly strike-prone countries also tended to be high inflation and high unemployment countries. Creigh (1982) tested these suggested relationships further by means of regression analysis for a larger sample of 20 countries, using annual averages over a six-year period in the 1970s. He confirms the apparent importance of economic variables in short-run strike fluctuations since a positive and statistically significant relationship was found between stoppage incidence and both the rate of price inflation and the unemployment level.

A more ambitious study investigating the relationship between macroeconomic variables and aggregate strike activity across a broad data base for 17 countries was undertaken by Padlam and Pederson (1982). They employed annual observations for a longer, 20-year postwar period into the 1960s, and in this case the dependent variable is specified as the number of strikes. It was found that for a majority of countries previous increases in money (and to a lesser extent real) wages were positively and significantly related to strike frequency. The unemployment variable was less successful in that only a third of the countries were found to have significant coefficients and the sign (direction of influence) on the variable also differed among countries. Interestingly, when the 17 countries themselves are broadly grouped into 'low conflict' countries, such as those in Scandinavia with strong, centralised and unified labour movements whose party is frequently in office, and 'high conflict' countries with weaker and decentralised labour movements (including the USA, Australia, France and Italy) the economic variables perform consistently poorly for the low conflict countries. The authors also suggest that although the unemployment and wage change variables are found to be 'correctly' (negatively) signed and significant for the USA, in fact the Ashenfelter and Johnson-type, bargaining model which has dominated the construction of economic strike models appears to be inapplicable to many of the other countries in their sample. This model was developed within the context of the US industrial relations system and might therefore be less directly applicable to other national industrial relations environments.

Snyder (1976) has put forward the view that the economic models of strike fluctuations which have been tested within individual countries are theoretically incomplete and empirically mis-specified since they neglect, as potentially important determinants, the organisational capacity of the labour movement to press its demands, the institutional setting, and the influence of the political environment. Although this criticism is undoubtedly overstated, it is true that the data for most longitudinal studies comprise only a relatively limited and homogeneous time-span (usually of less than two decades). Snyder therefore contends that the findings will be valid only for the particular institutional context within which a country's industrial relations are conducted and furthermore, a context which can be considered to be constant over such a restricted period. Conversely, it is hypothesised that variations in the institutional setting over the longer term will produce marked variations in the determinants of strike activity, which can be demonstrated empirically using both international and inter-temporal data. Thus, for Snyder, the institutional contexts themselves must be placed at the centre of the analysis.

Snyder's Model

In his formulation, Snyder distinguishes between two types of institutional setting. The first is where union membership is large and relatively stable, the political position of labour firmly established, and collective bargaining itself is well institutionalised. Under these conditions he maintains that the assumptions underlying the economic bargaining model will hold well in terms of calculations by the parties of short-run gains and costs. The second type of setting, however, reverses these conditions – union membership is low and unstable, labour organisations are not legitimate interest groups with regular influence over political decision-making in resource allocation, and collective bargaining is underdeveloped. Within these particular arrangements the assumptions of the 'economic' model will not hold, and Snyder believes that longer-run political objectives, such as polity membership, become more important to labour than short-run economic costs and benefits. Equally, the organisational strength of labour is problematic under these conditions in that although low unemployment, for example, may increase the propensity of workers to take strike action, their opportunity to do so may be impaired by insufficient prior organisation. Following Shorter and Tilly (1974), Snyder therefore maintains that in uninstitutionalised settings the strike is a political more than an economic weapon and that it will fluctuate with political changes and labour's organisational strength.

The hypothesis is then tested inter-temporally, using both strike frequency and size as dependent variables for three countries, France (1876-1937 and 1946-66), Italy (1901-24, and 1947-70) and the United States (1900–48 and 1949-70). The large break in the series for Italy (1925–46) is a consequence of the absence of reliable strike information for the Fascist period when strikes were illegal and were systematically suppressed by Mussolini. It does mean, however, that for Italy the sample size of the earlier period is somewhat small and it also includes the (probably distorting) effects of World War I.

The orientation of Snyder's approach is that in France and Italy it is expected that because industrial relations have remained relatively less institutionalised, political and organisational factors will be of predominant importance in explaining fluctuations in strike activity in *both* periods. In the United States, however, there have been substantial changes over the course of time in the institutional parameters affecting industrial relations structure, from an uninstitutionalised environment in the pre-World War II period to a more institutionalised setting thereafter. Consequently, in terms of this dichotomy, there should be a corresponding and observable shift in the determinants of strikes between the two periods.

The empirical results obtained for the United States appear to be consistent with the hypothesis. For the earlier period the economic variables utilised – unemployment, as an indicator of labour market tightness, and the (lagged) percentage change in real wages – are both found to be statistically insignificant and the latter variable also manifests the 'wrong' (positive) sign. Conversely, a unionisation variable is significant, as are two political variables, namely the percentage of Democrats in Congress and a 'dummy' variable to represent the years of Democratic presidents.[5] The rationale for the inclusion of the political party affiliation variables is that governments which are favourable to labour have the (unintended) effect of encouraging labour demands, possibly because of the greater likelihood of success. Also in uninstitutionalised conditions, by lacking an 'inside track' to the state legislature, labour's collective demands find expression through the strike.

The major finding of the study for the USA is that for the post-war period the regression coefficients change markedly from those of earlier years. After 1949 both economic variables are statistically significant and in the expected direction, whereas the effects of unionisation and the political indicators become insignificant and are incorrectly signed. Thus in the post-war years the effect of organisational and political influences on fluctuations in strike activity do not seem to be important. Snyder's explanation for the lack of impact of the political variables is not that Democratic officials had by then become less sympathetic to labour but that, with improved political representation of labour's interest, political demands were no longer channelled through strikes. If it is true, however, that these changes have occurred over time in the parameters affecting industrial conflict, it is difficult to see why there has not been a corresponding shift in the overall volume of strikes over the long term and in their composition in terms of size and duration.

Although Snyder's evidence for the United States appears consistent with the institutionalisation hypothesis his empirical results for France and Italy, with less well-institutionalised relations throughout both time periods, are more mixed. Because of the different political systems in Europe as well as data limitations for these countries, some of the explanatory variables are changed. National income rather than unemployment is used as a measure of economic activity since reliable unemployment statistics for France and Italy are not available for the whole of the earlier period. The political variables also represent a different dimension to those representing political 'attitudes' employed in the analysis for the USA. Following Shorter and Tilly a 'dummy' variable is included for election years throughout the period, together with a second variable relating to the number of Cabinet changes which have taken place. The basis of the argument is that political crisis or change, as proxied by these measures, will increase the vulnerability of governments to labour demands which are themselves expressed through strike action.

The results obtained for France are consistent with Snyder's explanation for the pre-1938 period. As anticipated, the economic determinants of strikes perform poorly whereas the election year (political) variable and especially the organisational, union membership variable are significant. Similarly, in Italy (given the data limitations) there is no significant influence of economic factors but there is a significant, positive relationship between strikes and union membership. For the post-war period, however, the explanatory power of the model is far less satisfactory. Although there are no substantial changes in the economic parameters – which still remain insignificant, as expected – in post-war France both the political and organisational determinants also become insignificant. In the case of Italy, union membership remains, as in the pre-war period, the only significant predictor of fluctuations in strike activity. Snyder concludes that his findings are, nevertheless, broadly consistent with the hypothesis concerning the impact of institutional setting on the determinants of strike activity and

> to the extent that national labour relations systems move toward increased size and stability of union membership, institutionalisation of collective bargaining and political integration of labour, the determination of strike fluctuations shifts from a primary political to an economic process. (ibid., p. 275)

Although the results of this study are interesting there are a number of criticisms which can be directed at the specification of the model itself and also the interpretation of the results.[6] As Edwards (1978) points out, there are obvious problems in attempting to measure satisfactorily the political components of industrial conflict. To use the frequency of Cabinet changes as an indicator of alterations in the national political position of labour has been described by one critic as 'downright silly' (Gallie, 1975), since formal government changes need not necessarily involve heightened conflict. For the USA, however, Snyder uses a somewhat different political measure in terms of the actual composition of the political centre itself. In consequence, any direct comparison between the results for the three countries must be somewhat suspect. Also, an underlying relationship between the composition of the political centre and strike activity is by no means easy to rationalise in a convincing way – 'There are obvious reasons why the level of unemployment should affect workers' willingness and ability to strike, but the influence of such things as political upheaval and the party of the President is much less clear' (Edwards, 1978, p. 325). A further possible limitation is that the level of trade union membership might also be mainly determined by the economic influences incorporated in the model, rather than having (as assumed) an independent effect.[7] Similarly, although the model presupposes that strike activity depends partly upon the extent of trade union membership there could well be simultaneous determination between strikes and unionisation – that is, greater strike activity which is successful might itself give rise to an increased density of trade union membership.[8]

To test for these sorts of possibility two further studies relating to strike determination in the United States have been carried out by Kaufman (1982) and Skeels (1982). Their results throw doubt on some of Snyder's conclusions for that country. For the 1900–48 period it is found that both economic factors (at least as measured by unemployment together with price changes) and organisational factors do seem to affect the level of strike frequency, whereas political factors appear unimportant. In the post-1948 period, however, fluctuations in union organisation ceased to be important in explaining annual movements in strike activity, and economic factors did become relatively more important – as Snyder originally showed. Skeels employs a two-equation model in order to overcome the difficulties caused by any mutual determination of strikes and union membership by economic factors. He finds that in the pre-war period strikes were not a significant determinant of union membership growth but that a good deal of union growth can be explained by the same economic factors which influence strike activity. Nevertheless, when he estimates the residual proportion of union organisation which can only be explained by non-economic factors this residual variable is found to be positively and significantly related to strike frequency. Thus it appears that the union organisation variable does more than merely pass on the influence of economic forces to strike activity without adding any additional explanation in its own right.

Conclusion

It is hardly surprising that some of the evidence from quantitative, empirical strike studies is conflicting. With this research methodology there are problems in selecting appropriate empirical counterparts for theoretical constructs as well as a considerable distance between the occurrence of strike behaviour at the micro level and testing its determinants by means of aggregative data.[9] Moreover, whilst the empirical results may be consistent with the causal hypotheses advanced, the fact remains that 'an infinite number of hypotheses may "fit" any given set of observations with equally good results' (Evans, 1976, p. 74). An even more telling criticism of the validity of this methodology, when employed on a comparative basis in the form of undifferentiated multi-country studies, is Dunlop's (1978). He believes that such studies are not likely to produce important findings because not only does the role of the strike differ as between various countries – and a strike which has a political purpose is not likely to have the same determinants as one designed to secure immediate economic improvements – but also with respect to longitudinal studies sample periods incorporating several decades often reflect industrial relations systems at various stages of development and are therefore qualitatively different. The causes and meaning of strikes can shift over the course of time, as we have noted. In short, 'the logic of industrial conflict is conditioned by nation- and time-specific institutional settings [so that] we should be wary of attempts to apply a fixed explanatory model to multi-national data sets' (Shalev, 1983, p. 428).

However, one of the major benefits of studies such as Snyder's (in which the countries to be compared are not only more carefully focused but the sample periods themselves subdivided and differentiated) and the ensuing debate which has been generated, is the reorientation of analytical work on strike activity away from one-dimensional theories towards a fuller appreciation of the total environment in which industrial relations takes place. This incorporates not only economic conditions but also the institutional framework of collective bargaining, the parties' organisational strength, power resources and attitudinal characteristcs, together with political events and the broader political climate. Nevertheless, it remains true that although the various theories which have been discussed in this chapter may explain conflict behaviour in certain countries and at particular time-periods they do not amount to general theories which are universally valid in all national settings. Possibly, however, politically-grounded theories are the most generally applicable in attempting to understand the complex changes which have occurred in the manifestations, trends and counter-trends of industrial conflict in western countries during the twentieth century and they undoubtedly afford considerable potential for further research.

Notes

1. Korpi (1981) has shown, however, that official statistics greatly underestimated the number of (unofficial) stoppages in Sweden up to the 1970s.

2. In the case of Canada the explanation may relate to its high degree of integration with the US economy (which has a lower concentration) and consequently with its labour movement in the form of bi-national unions, i.e. in this case the degree of concentration in the North American continent *as a whole* may be the decisive factor.

3. The early development in nineteenth-century France of a centralised but wide ranging state organisation seems to have been the major factor in explaining the important part played by public authority intervention in strikes (via the prefect, inspector of labour, or local Deputy of the National Assembly), and the use by workers of political weapons for economic objectives (Sellier, 1973).

4. An upheaval of this magnitude, however, would appear to require other causal explanations in addition to purely economic factors – including qualitative changes in industrial relations, possibly reflecting the influence of weakened social controls and power shifts to the shopfloor (see Reynaud, 1980).

5. This variable assumes a numerical value of 1 when the president belongs to the Democratic Party and 0 when he is a Republican.

6. Snyder's empirical results have been challenged by more recent studies which attempt to improve the specification of his equations. They suggest it may be that strike action is more, rather than less, sensitive to labour market conditions in uninstitutionalised settings since under those conditions workers' ability to pursue industrial action is most directly dependent upon their market situation (Shalev, 1983).

7. Also, the 'political' determinants of strikes may themselves be influenced by economic factors.

8. At the technical level, if simultaneous effects exist then estimating the model via the usual technique of ordinary least squares will result in biased and inconsistent coefficients.

9. The general emphasis on external influences in quantitative studies and neglect of the internal dynamics of the strike itself lead Strauss (1982) to comment, 'It appears that few recent strike researchers have ever walked a picket line or even passed through one' (p. 16).

Further Reading

A useful paper which considers the various approaches to the comparative study of industrial conflict is Shalev (1980a). Politically-grounded theories are well expounded in Shalev and Korpi (1979), and economic theories in Shalev (1980b). The question of international strike statistics is dealt with in Fisher (1973) and

Walsh (1983). A well-known critical assessment of quantitative strike analysis is that of Stern (1978), and there is a critical commentary and interchange on macro level studies of strike determination in the *industrial and Labor Relations Review*, Vol. 37, 1984.

7 WORKERS' PARTICIPATION IN DECISION-MAKING

In recent years there has been a widespread and increasing preoccupation with various schemes for employees' participation in decisions within undertakings, especially in Western Europe where it has achieved major social, economic and political significance.[1] One important change which occurred during the 1970s was the strengthening of participatory mechanisms via legislation in West Germany, Sweden and the Netherlands. It is intended in this chapter to attempt to explain the (varying) objectives and rationale of participation between countries, why its structural forms may differ and, on the basis of cross-national evidence, to elucidate some of the influences which determine the outcomes and effectiveness of participation.

There are a variety of definitions, terminological variations and differing views as to precisely what the concept of 'participation' entails.[2] According to Walker (1974) 'workers' participation in management occurs when those at the bottom of an enterprise hierarchy take part in the authority and managerial functions of the enterprise' (p. 6) that is, employees become involved in extended areas of decision-making and control which had previously been reserved exclusively as management prerogatives. Thus institutionalised workers' participation emphasises changing the balance of decision-making within the firm.

Collective Bargaining

On this definition collective bargaining at the level of the undertaking is undoubtedly a form of participation since it implies not only informing and consulting workers but also negotiating with them on matters which otherwise would be the subject of unilateral decisions (ILO, 1981b). As Schregle (1981) has emphasised, the concept of participation should not be too closely identified with the existence of specific participative machinery. The important point is whether, and to what extent, workers normally acting through their representatives have an influence on the decision-making process within the firm. This may be achieved through collective bargaining which can be said to remain the major form of workers' participation in the USA, Britain and to a significant extent in Japan, as well as in most of the countries in English-speaking Africa. The overwhelming reliance by unions in the United States on collective bargaining, *ex-post* reaction to management initiatives, and the use of countervailing power means that the line of interest-conflict between labour and management does not become blurred. This avoids possible role-conflict for the office-holder and the problems of double representation for the employee which may occur with formalised schemes for participation in management (Herding, 1972). In Australia, also, unions have preferred to rely on negotiation along with the regulation of employment conditions through the industrial (arbitration) tribunals.

Where more formalised and explicit arrangements for employees' participation have been introduced they assume a wide diversity of forms of either a legalistic or voluntary nature. These include co-determination and worker directors (employee representatives on corporate policy-making boards), works councils or similar bodies at plant level,[3] joint consultation and communications, together with workers' self-management systems and individual producer cooperatives. Yet, as the ILO (1981b) has shown, in countries such as India and Pakistan the introduction of other types of machinery has generally not slowed down the development of collective bargaining, which continues to remain the fundamental element of worker participation within undertakings.[4] Also, in the well-known case of Germany, participation in enterprise decisions has not destroyed collective bargaining. Rather, research findings suggest a certain division of responsibility for the protection of workers' interests between collective bargaining and co-determination. In this respect 'collective bargaining provides the basic pattern of working conditions on a regional and/or industry wide level; co-determination fills out this pattern on the plant and firm level' (Adams and Rummel, 1977, p. 20). A comparison is sometimes made between British shop stewards' committees and German works councils since they carry out many of the same activities, such as negotiating the application of wage payment systems, job grading, short-time working and redundancies. Such parallels should not, however, be overdrawn since there are some important differences. Not only has the works council no right to strike but also

> It is carefully regulated, protected and restrained, and lives behind a formidable high fence of elaborate and minute statutes and a gigantic wall of case law, whilst the shop stewards' committee

thrives in the open country of 'custom and practice'. (Kahn-Freund, 1979, p. 12)

Formalised Participation Schemes

Because workers' participation is a multi-dimensional concept there are a number of ways in which its various forms may be distinguished from each other and classified. Formal schemes of participation may incorporate either the direct involvement of employees at workplace level via production conferences and similar arrangements, as in Hungary and some other Eastern bloc countries, or be indirect by means of the representatives of workers on decision-making bodies within the enterprise, as in the West German co-determination scheme. At the lowest (shopfloor) level participation may take the form of semi-autonomous work groups being given a large element of responsibility for the organisation, supervision and sometimes redesign of their jobs. Poole (1979) maintains, however, that it is doubtful whether such job enrichment programmes and the like constitute genuine participatory institutions rather than a series of *ad hoc* experiments. At plant level, participatory decision-making through institutions is mainly concerned with routine, day-to-day matters whereas at the corporate level it involves broader and long-term issues. The range of decisions and subject-matter which workers may influence can therefore extend *inter alia* from wages, employment conditions and welfare activities to investment and the distribution of profits.

A further dimension relates to the 'depth' of participation regarding the extent of decision-making powers that are transferred to workers, which may be negative (vetoing management decisions) or positive and initiating. Strauss (1979) makes a basic distinction between three major participation models in terms of the degree of workers' influence or control over management (along an implicit scale), namely, consultative participation, co-management or decision-making and workers' self-management. In both industrialised and developing countries joint consultation committees or works councils are by far the most common type of body for associating workers with decisions in undertakings. With joint consultation, management makes the final decision but workers have the right to information and can offer advice and objections. In most European countries works councils originally developed along the lines of this model although they have since acquired decision-making powers on certain matters (requiring their prior agreement) such as hours of work, vocational training and safety and welfare, as well as rights to information and consultation. Secondly joint decision-making bodies may be distinguished, in the pure form of which the parties have equality of power and the consent of each side is required before action can be taken. Co-determination schemes follow this model and collective bargaining, although it is 'disjunctive' – emphasising the distinctiveness rather than the commonality of management and worker interests – may, as we have observed, also be viewed as a meaningful form of workers' participation by way of influencing the exercise of managerial power and achieving a measure of joint regulation over workplace decisions. The third and most far-reaching category is that of workers' control, as typified (in principle) by the Yugoslav self-management system within a framework of social ownership in which the assets of an enterprise are owned not by the state or private owners but by society as a whole. There is also the communal Kibbutz organisation in Israel and some producer-cooperatives in Western Europe in which workers or their representatives have final authority.[5]

Objectives

There are important and related differences in the purposes which the particular type of participation is intended to promote and from which its institutionalised forms cannot be abstracted. In Germany, although the concept itself has a long history, special considerations were applicable in that 'control over capital' was one important reason for union pressure towards co-determination in the iron and steel industries immediately after World War II 'to make certain that German industrialists would never again finance an extremist party' (Hartman, 1975, p. 55). More generally, some observers have attributed either an 'integrative' or a 'transformative' function to the objectives of workers' participation schemes. The integrative function, premised upon the basis of unitary or pluralist conceptualisations of the enterprise, attempts to foster an identification of workers with their own particular firm so as to secure 'more compliant and supportive responses from employees to managerially-defined purposes and achievement of managerially defined goals' (Ogden, 1982, p. 547). From this managerial standpoint the rationale for encouraging participation is directed towards the realisation of a number of pragmatic ends, such as the achievement of greater organisational effectiveness and a reduction in industrial conflict, or more generally as part of the managerial control system in getting decisions accepted by employees.

Alternatively, participation may be viewed as an important objective in its own right as a means of promoting individual worker satisfaction or extending the rights or benefits of political democracy to the industrial sphere. In Germany, for instance, 'the federal legal code encapsulates the concept of citizenship in all areas of social life' (Loveridge, 1980, p. 305). For the labour movement participatory schemes may be part of a transformative strategy either towards promoting a more generally participative society, as in Yugoslavia or Chile in the early 1970s, or by mobilising workers to demand a radical expansion of influence towards full control, thereby generating pressures for a transformation of the existing social order (Stephens, 1980). In the case of India, the introduction of participation in industry was seen as a prerequisite for the establishment of a socialist society (ILO, 1981b).

In Western Europe some of the strongest opponents of participatory models under capitalism have been the communist parties – certainly up to the mid-1970s, although more recently a reappraisal has been taking place. It was contended that 'worker militance must be channelled into confrontation with management not collaboration with management or acceptance of managerial responsibilities' (Garson, 1977, p. 215).[6] In Italy trade unions have also traditionally shown an attitude of strong diffidence not only towards workers' participation within private enterprise, but towards any other form of bilateral institution set up to co-determine working conditions with management – viewing collective bargaining as being the primary way to regulate labour-management relations (Treu, 1981). Nevertheless, workers' participation in that country has gained momentum in recent years not only via an extension in the subject-matter of collective agreements but even as a result of a new and more positive approach towards enterprise profitability and productive efficiency on the part of the Left (Caloia, 1979).

Interestingly, in Belgium three different representative workers' organs operate at the level of the enterprise – a triad which is the result of a compromise between the competitive attitudes of the major unions. The Christian unions favoured the idea of collaboration between workers and management through the works council. In contrast, the socialist trade unions emphasised the competition between labour and capital through the 'union delegation' (which is somewhat akin to the British shop steward committee although with less independence and scope for bargaining). The Belgian solution was to create not two but three overlapping organs within the enterprise: the union delegation, the works council and the statutory committee for safety, health and embellishment of the workplace (Blanpain, 1974). Similarly in France, there is a complex and somewhat overlapping representative system within the enterprise, again with three sets of institutions: statutory works councils (to foster cooperation between management and employee representatives), together with workers' representatives (to present individual or collective grievances), and unions also have their own designated representatives.

In developing countries government initiatives in associating workers with enterprise decision-making are often viewed as an important tool for assisting economic development, for example, by mobilising support for modernisation and attainment of the objectives of national development plans. It was for this reason that workers' self-management was assigned an important role by socialist and nationalist governments in countries such as Chile, Peru and Algeria (Strauss, 1979). In some communist countries greater enterprise democracy has been introduced, along with economic reforms, at times of labour crises. In China the 'workers' congress' system has recently been revived to give a new vitality to workers' participation in enterprise management and to emulate the Yugoslav model of self-management, although the workers' congress cannot intervene in state-prescribed pay or hiring and transfer decisions (Hong, 1984).

It would therefore appear that the causes of major international variations in institutional types of participation may in part be located 'in the wider political implications, value systems, beliefs and ideologies held by both trade unions and employers' organisations and the country at large' (Sorge, 1976).

Explanations of Cross-national Differences

We now turn to a more detailed analysis of the origins of similarity and diversity in the national institutions for workers' participation. Several comparative perspectives may be delineated in this respect. As discussed below, these include cultural and ideological influences, collective bargaining structures and power relations between the industrial relations actors themselves.

Specific cultural and ideological factors have been widely employed as important explanatory devices in national comparisons. The workers' self-management system in Yugoslavia, for instance, introduced after 1950, reflects a social and ideological background which is distinctively significant. Historically, the ethnically-differentiated peasant population of Yugoslavia had evinced a deep distrust of central authority which, together with the political instability and poor communications of the country, resulted in a good deal of local self-sufficiency and autonomy (Riddell, 1968). During World War II the pluralist and decentralised partisan movement also formed part of a pattern of resistance to distrusted central authority. Thus, although the political and economic system set up after 1945 was patterned on that of the Soviet Union, after the break with the USSR there was a switch from administrative centralism back to more traditional decentralisation. In this respect the new self-management system could be viewed as being

> not only the voluntary act of the political élite . . . but at the same time a transformation of the [war-time] liberation movement, based on political participation, into a labour movement which was henceforth based on the economic participation of those employed. (IDE, 1981a, p. 219)

The West German participation system in many ways assumes a harmony of interest between management and labour and has been described as 'basically a strategy of cooperative unionism' (Fürstenberg, 1980). It is marked by a concern for consensus and its important legal characteristics by an integrating element such that the (purely employee-constituted) works councils are required to collaborate with management, have no right to resort to strike action and, indeed, are forbidden to encourage strikes. These features have also been interpreted as a reflection of cultural and ideological influences in which not only is there a preference for statutory regulation enforced by the courts, but also 'accommodation and integration, as well as order and authority, occupy an important place in the [German] system of national values' (Schregle, 1978, p. 88). Dahrendorf (1968) views the emergence of co-determination as a consequence of the German tradition of avoiding and abolishing conflict at its roots rather than containing it by institutionalisation – a preference which may be traced back to German socio-philosophical thought in the nineteenth century.[7] This view, however, appears somewhat oversimplified since, although in the last few decades German trade unions have become well integrated into society, prior to World War I they were as radical and Marxist-oriented as those in France, Italy and Belgium (Sorge, 1976).[8]

Fox (1978) also sees the origins of German co-determination as being rooted historically in (somewhat different) features of the culture and social relations of that country. In particular, industrialisation and the factory system developed within a society which, because of its late development in the closing decades of the nineteenth century, still retained the structure of 'vertical bonding' between employer and employee. This was carried over into industry and was facilitated by the early emergence of large economic units, leaving no room for an infrastructure of medium-sized enterprises and bourgeois entrepreneurs. Whereas in contrast,

> in Britain the rising class of bourgeois entrepreneurs were creatures of a society and culture in which feudal and manorial vertical bondings, underpinned by paternalist dependence relations and ideology, had been undermined and corroded for a period of two centuries or more. (ibid., p. 22)

A further illustration of the importance which is accorded to special factors of this kind is the commercial success of the Mondragon producer-cooperatives in the Basque region of Northern Spain. This group of enterprises was established in 1956 and produces a wide range of manufactured, and some agricultural, products. A number of studies have noted the importance of Basque nationalism and its distinctive culture as a binding force encouraging mutual cooperation between capital and labour directed against a repressive Spanish central government (Thomas and Logan, 1982). A further significant feature that is often claimed to provide a foundation which is receptive to the economic requirements of self-management is a relatively high propensity to save on the part of the Basque population. However, the relevance of such ethnic considerations as a major determining factor in Mondragon's success has recently been questioned by Bradley and Gelb (1982). Their empirical work points to the greater significance of other influences – in particular, the limited labour mobility which exists partially insulates the cooperatives from competitive pressures of the external labour market. This permits more compressed wage differentials and, since workers are required to contribute to the financing of the enterprise, helps ensure economic viability by retaining savings and equity capital intact to sustain growth and accommodate to technical change.

In a broader comparative analysis of the United States and continental Western Europe Kassalow (1982) again suggests that the different forms taken by workers' participation can be partially explained by differences in the ideological background of their respective labour movements. The demands of US unions have usually been expressed in terms of the strengthening of collective bargaining, in contrast to the wider social thrust of European union policies whereby democratisation of the enterprise has often been regarded as a step towards the broader transformation of authority and power within society. Kassalow traces the origins of this difference, and the direct identification of European labour movements with the democratisation of the political process, to the fact that the rise of trade unionism in Europe in the latter part of the nineteenth century was itself an important part of the struggle for political democracy – especially the attainment of universal suffrage. By way of contrast, the union movement in the USA came into being several decades after universal male suffrage had been established.

As well as cultural and ideological influences a second comparative perspective points to differences in collective bargaining structures within the different countries as an important explanatory variable affecting the kinds of participatory mechanisms which develop. Clegg (1976) sees the level at which bargaining is conducted – either at plant level or industry-wide – as a vital factor in explaining the differences between the attitudes of US and continental European unions towards workers' participation schemes. Industry bargaining can regulate only general matters common to all the enterprises which it encompasses. Detailed topics which are specific to each undertaking require regulation at plant level. As a result, in the absence of such bargaining arrangements, alternative machinery needs to be introduced if unions are to exercise a degree of control over these matters. In West Germany, for instance, some of the topics which in other countries would be processed through collective bargaining agreements are handled by works councils. According to this line of argument, therefore,

> so long as adequate arrangements are made for collective bargaining within the plant, collective bargaining may be regarded as a satisfactory form of industrial democracy. But where regional or industry agreements fail to provide for plant bargaining, there are demands for alternative arrangements to allow workers to exercise some influence over those matters which concern them and which cannot be adequately regulated in regional or industry agreements. (Clegg, 1976, p. 97)

Windmüller (1977) adopts a similar approach by stating that institutionalised workers' participation in Europe is a reasonable fascimile of the US pattern of decentralised collective bargaining (although much more universal in its coverage), as adapted to the historically different circumstances of Western European countries. In other words, some of the main purposes of workers' participation have been achieved in the USA through an enterprise-centred system of collective bargaining with a wide range of negotiable issues which may include the location of new plants, automation and changes in work processes (Willman, 1983). Procedures for dealing with grievances in the typical US collective agreement also give workers considerable influence over the regulation of their employment conditions. That is to say, participation via collective bargaining occurs not only in the original negotiation of the agreement but in the continuing role of the union in administering the agreement during its lifetime.

In the case of Japan the opportunities for workers' participation have also been primarily conditioned by the extent, enterprise-based structure and influence of trade unions. The opportunities have been expanded by a widening in the scope of collective bargaining as well as by more formally prescribed methods such as joint consultation committees. In practice, the latter are usually set up under the terms of the collective agreement and may therefore be regarded in varying degrees as pre-negotiating bodies (Okamoto, 1979).

In continental Europe there is no doubt that workers' participation schemes may be regarded in some essential respects as an extension of collective bargaining to the individual enterprise. They tend to promote the integration of statutory works councils into the bargaining structure by allocating them explicit bargaining rights in certain subject areas, and sometimes according them responsibility for overseeing the implementation at plant level of the industry agreement. In Germany works councils – in practice the major co-determination institution – may also use their right to exercise veto powers over issues such as overtime working as a counter to get concessions on particular collective bargaining matters where they have weak powers or none at all (Crouch, 1982b). Conversely, in Britain the importance of joint consultative machinery declined in the 1950s and 1960s, mainly as a consequence of the growth of collective bargaining at workplace level. There is some evidence, however, of its more recent revival as a result of a number of factors, including a weakening of the market basis for local shop stewards[1] organisations due to the (1970s–1980s) economic recession. In any case, although consultation was supposed to be restricted to matters of common rather than of conflicting interests, such as safety and welfare, these could also become issues for negotiation, thereby making it difficult to draw a firm dividing-line between them.

The level at which collective bargaining is conducted also affects the extent to which trade union power is centralised. This is an important consideration because a prerequisite for the institutionalisation of participation appears to be the existence of a unified rather than fragmented trade union structure whose central body occupies a dominant position as in Scandinavia, where it was established prior to World War II, and in both Germany and Austria, where a single union centre emerged in the post-war period. In West Germany the relative centralisation of bargaining functions has been held to be conducive to the evolution of works councils and board-level co-determination. In Holland a further result of a high degree of centralisation was the tendency before 1960 to prefer forms of participation which operated at the national or industry, rather than enterprise, level (Albeda, 1977). By contrast, in Britain the presence of powerful and semi-independent organisations of workers at the local level tended to render works and consultative machinery ineffective unless it was formally integrated into the union channel. In the case of India government-sponsored workers' participation was weakened by the long-standing conflicts between rival organisations concerning rights to representation (Kannappan and Krishnan, 1977).

A third explanatory approach towards the development of participatory mechanisms concerns the nature of the power relations between the state, trade unions and employers. A strong and markedly repressive state (in historical terms) has been identified with the evolution of highly-regulated and legally-based participative machinery at plant level as in Germany, France, the Netherlands and Luxembourg. Conversely, the less severe the restrictions placed on unions in their early stages the more probable it was that, as in Britain, a powerful labour movement would ensure that plant-level representation would be based on a single channel of trade union organisation instead of statutory works council machinery (Sorge, 1976). The existence of powerful employers' organisations in the case of Germany succeeded for a long period in keeping the shopfloor free from union activities in favour of works council machinery (Leminsky, 1980). On the other hand, where both the state and trade union movement are powerful but the employers' bodies correspondingly weak there has been greater experimentation with a diversity of participative arrangements. In Israel, for instance, the existence of three major sectors in the economy (private, state and central – *Histadrut* – labour federation-operated) has weakened the position of the employers *vis-à-vis* the centralised trade union organisation. Participative arrangements include workers' committees, plant councils, productivity councils and in some *Histadrut*-owned cooperatives a joint management system. A further variant is that of the United States where, because

> the role of government has been notably constrained and the density of unionisation has recently declined, the bulk of initiatives have been in the form of managerially inspired programmes of an *ad hoc* character. (Poole, 1982, p. 196)

Broader political factors have also been adduced as contributory explanations. In Chile it has been claimed that the establishment of a comprehensive system of industrial democracy has been retarded not by technical considerations of economic performance but by the threat it poses to the power of dominant socio-economic groups (Espinoza and Zimbalist, 1978). In the case of Italy Caloia (1979) also believes that institutionalised schemes for participation sanctioned by law are less viable than elsewhere in Western Europe because of the large disparities in, and radically contraposed, political views of the various classes.

A related approach towards explaining the divergent evolution of either statutory or voluntary modes of participation at plant level is to look at differences in the particular historical circumstances and constraints which prevailed in various countries at the time when the decisions to create such institutions were first made. Sorge (1976) points out that innovations in participative machinery in Western Europe are clustered around the same critical points in time, namely the aftermath of two world wars at a period of deep-seated changes in social values, followed by another subsequent burst of activity after the late 1960s.[9] According to his explanation the strong repression of trade unionism by the state in the nineteenth century in much of continental Europe (notably France, Luxembourg, Austria and Germany) meant that with a weakened, yet radicalised, union movement and recalcitrant employers voluntary workplace institutions were subsequently more difficult to establish: if participatory mechanisms were to be introduced they would have to be on a statutory basis. They tended to emerge later – usually post-1945 – in conjunction with national crises when the position of employers was less strong and the state was attempting to integrate opposing forces by providing for works councils or committees. In contrast, where state repression of unionism had been relatively less severe (as in Britain, Scandinavia and Switzerland) voluntary institutions in the form of either contractually, or informally, recognised shop stewards and their committees became established at an earlier date, around World War I.

Although this particular thesis is insightful it is, nevertheless, by no means all-embracing. Belgium is something of an exception to the pattern since shop steward committees and statutory works councils became established there at roughly the same time. Germany is also a special case in that its works councils were instituted at an early date (1920) and also consisted, unusually (along with Austria), solely of employee representatives. This may be attributed to the late temporal location of Germany democracy which occurred only after World War I and the resultant greater relative influence of the labour movement on state legislation than was the case in other comparable countries.

Empirical Data

A comprehensive empirical study which systematically examines a number of possible determinants of formal participative arrangements across 11 Western European countries, together with Israel, has recently been carried out by an international research group (IDE, 1981a). In an attempt to identify the forces to which 'participative structures' (i.e. the formal framework of participation within industrial relations) are a response, they employ a combination of political, economic, social and related contextual factors which are assumed to operate jointly as determining influences. It is hypothesised first that an appropriate political background will facilitate the setting-up of participative structures. The argument is that the development of industrial democracy measures is likely to follow, after a time-lag, the achievement of political democracy. A second possible background variable relates to favourable economic conditions so that, other things being equal, the extent to which participative structures are introduced will depend upon the level of economic development (as measured by GNP). The rationale for this might be that the advanced technology which usually characterises well-developed economies may require the greater involvement of operatives to avoid costly mistakes. Or it could be that the richer the country then the more it can 'afford' participation – if this is seen as having certain accompanying costs in terms of a possible efficiency loss – so that there would be less resistance to its introduction.

A third explanatory hypothesis concerns the extent of social differentiation in the countries concerned. The notion is that the distribution of GNP as well as its level is likely to be important, thereby distinguishing Nordic from Latin European countries, for instance. In this respect we might expect countries with greater equality of incomes and less social stratification to be more favourably disposed towards participation. Fourthly, there is a related argument in terms of dominant cultural (value-system) influences. A conjecture in the study is that participation will be more highly developed within a country if its industrial culture emphasises the value of cooperative norms between labour and employers, that is, if the parties are regarded as having at least some interests in common rather than being defined as having totally divergent and irreconcilable interests.

Although it is suggested that these contextual variables will help determine the extent of prescribed employee participation what the study emphasises is that they are only contingent, or facilitating, conditions which are not in themselves capable of bringing about participative arrangements. Instead, they can only promote – or alternatively frustrate – the attempts of the parties in industrial relations to introduce participation. The actors themselves are therefore seen as the driving-force behind the development of participative structures. More specifically, it is contended that a strong, well-organised, centralised trade union movement could exert pressure upon both employers and the government for the introduction of participatory mechanisms either in the form of negotiated agreements or via legislation. Similarly, a strong, centralised employers' body, although it is better able to resist participation should it so wish, is not likely to stand out against its introduction. Such an organisation will usually have a professionalised and more forward-looking orientation towards industrial relations and will foresee the potential gains to be secured from adopting a positive strategy. (These would include a greater ability to shape participatory structures in accordance with its own wishes by becoming involved at an early stage.) As regards the role of government it is anticipated that a left-of-centre government will be another favourable condition. Not only will it have a close affinity with the trade union movement but measures promoting democratisation are also likely to be significant objectives of a socialist party in their own right.

As the IDE study points out, however, although these hypotheses are cast in the form of *a priori* arguments they were themselves formulated on the basis of the existing participation literature and preliminary individual-country surveys. The empirical evidence therefore can hardly be expected to falsify any of the hypotheses, but it can indicate to what extent they may be considered generalised propositions across a preponderance of the 12 countries investigated.

Each of the countries is given an overall relative ranking (from high to low) according to the degree of prescribed involvement of workers or their representatives in decision-making at various hierarchical levels of the enterprise. Yugoslavia is accorded first place, with Germany, Sweden and Norway also having a high standing. Holland and France occupy intermediate positions, while Belgium, Finland, Israel and Denmark are in the lower half of the ranking order. The two countries identified as having the weakest provisions for formalised worker participation are Italy and Britain. This ordering is, of course, only a very rough measure since it glosses over some quite important differences between individual systems of participation.

In order to explain the rank ordering subjective estimates are made of strength indicators (strong/average/weak) for the union and employer variables, together with more objective measures for some of the contextual variables. Gini coefficients are employed as an indicator of income inequality, *per capita* GNP is a measure of economic wealth and – more questionably – strike rates are used to indicate the degree of cooperation in the industrial relations system. The findings provide broad support for the importance of an appropriate industrial relations structure in that a combination of strong union and employer organisations along with a 'leftish' government does seem to be conducive to the attainment of a high degree of prescribed participation (*viz.* Yugoslavia, Sweden, Norway and Germany). In contrast, there is a lower degree of prescribed participation where one or more of these requirements has generally not existed, such as in Israel and Britain (weak employers' body), and Italy (right-of-centre government).

Although the hypotheses relating to an appropriate industrial relations structure, assumed to be the critical conditioning variable, are reasonably well supported by the empirical evidence, the contextual variables appear to be less systematically related to the extensiveness of participative arrangements. Only economic growth and cooperativeness of the industrial relations system are (positively) related to participative structures. (Those countries with well-developed workers' participation have generally experienced a more rapid increase in living standards and a relatively peaceful industrial climate.) In contrast, the remaining indices for wealth, economic inequality and political democracy do not correspond at all well on an inter-country basis to the relative extent of prescribed worker involvement in enterprise decision-making. These particular dimensions turn out to be, at best, much more random influences on participatory arrangements.

Outcomes of Participation

The introduction of formal schemes for workers' participation does not in itself guarantee that their objectives will, in practice, be realised since 'the process of participation is as equally important as the constitutional structure' (Loveridge, 1980, p. 309). Also, as Strauss (1979) makes clear, the important consideration is not whether participation ever works but rather, under what conditions it will best function. It is therefore necessary to look at a number of what are termed 'contingency' conditions which have been shown to influence the *results* of participation in various countries. As we discuss below, these include the strength of trade unions, enterprise size and hierarchical organisation, worker and management perceptions towards participation as well as a conducive external environment.

The effect of trade unions upon the outcomes of participation has been found to be significant in a number of individual country studies. For the more limited forms of participation, as embodied for instance in joint consultation schemes, findings from both the USA and Britain indicate that consultation is likely to be perceived by employers as being most effective in establishments where unions either do not exist or else are weakly organised (Clarke, Fatchett and Roberts, 1972). It would appear that, as a further Australian study points out, 'management usually regard such committees as a means of fostering employee motivation without infringing managerial prerogatives' (Lansbury, 1978b, p. 77). In the case of statutory works councils, however, numerous studies indicate that participation is most effective in representing the interests of workers in those enterprises which are highly unionised. For one thing union members are often more interested in participative bodies and want more influence in company decision-making than workers who are not unionised (IDE, 1981b).

In Germany a high degree of correlation has been found between unionisation and participation in works council elections and works meetings. Also, a union presence was found to be necessary since without the protection of a union workers in small firms might be victimised if they took the initiative to form a works council (Adams and Rummel, 1977). In this respect although the establishment of a council is required in enterprises where there are more than five employees, in fact there is no legal penalty for failure to do so. Furthermore, although the works councils are not trade union bodies, since they are elected by all workers within an enterprise regardless of union membership, the distinction is often more apparent than real. Both in

Germany and Austria more than 80 per cent of the works council members are active trade unionists. A close relationship is to be expected since the union is the works councillors' principal source of legal and technical expertise; it provides them with training courses, and election to the works council may constitute the first step towards a union career. By way of contrast to a strong union presence for ensuring effective participation in Germany it was found that in the Netherlands the fragmentary character of plant level unions

> contributes significantly to the lack of 'mobilising power' of works councils, their weaker links with the rank-and-file workers, and the limited opportunities for employees to discuss the daily work situation on an equal footing with management. (Poole, 1979, p. 266)

Also in Peru the lack of unions within the worker-managed sector has helped to undermine the effectiveness of participation (Berenbach, 1979).

Instead of maintaining formally separate unions and works councils as in Germany, the Swedish approach has been to combine, via legislation, collective bargaining and employee participation at plant level so as to strengthen union influence.[10] Legislation was introduced since plant-level union organisation in Sweden was relatively underdeveloped in comparison with union 'locals' in the USA and shop steward committees in Britain, and was unable to provide effective counter strategies to deal with management decision-making (Gospel, 1983b). As a result of the 1977 Co-Determination Act every important management decision at the workplace is now open to bargaining, including work reorganisation, expansions and shut-downs, topics which formerly were strictly management prerogatives. Also, if the collective agreement is in dispute, the union is given the prerogative of interpretation.

Although in many countries works councils may function in parallel with strong trade union entrenchment in the undertaking, especially where collective bargaining has traditionally taken place at the regional or industry level, the simultaneous presence of works councils and shop stewards may lead to difficulties. In Holland, for instance, although historically plant-level bargaining was not encouraged by the trade unions because of their weakness on the shopfloor, since the mid-1960s they have been establishing direct representation at plant level, resembling in some respects the British shop steward system. The result has sometimes been the creation of strained relations between works council members and shop stewards since the union may fear that 'the works council weakens the union influence by usurping their functions; or when the works council is [apparently] too much on the side of management' (Andriessen, 1976, p. 52). Similarly, West German unions have in recent years attempted to increase their influence within the firm, particularly in the area of job regulation, by encouraging the election of shop stewards as a countervailing force to the works council. In this respect Herding (1972) has shown in a comparison of the USA and Germany that co-determination has been least effective in providing the equivalent of US shopfloor control, especially since grievance procedures remain underdeveloped, and in humanising immediate job conditions relating to physical effort, heat, safety and health conditions. As a result he concludes that 'on the job itself management's discretion is hardly restricted' (p. 330).

A second important contingency variable affecting the outcomes of participation relates to enterprise characteristics – including size, technology and, especially, hierarchical levels. In West Germany, for instance, there is either minority or parity representation on supervisory boards dependent on the type of industry and size of undertaking.[11] In that country research findings suggest that participation is most effective in representing workers' interests in large organisations in which the management style is professional rather than paternal. Similarly, in Yugoslavia workers in large enterprises were found to experience less sense of powerlessness than those in small organisations, although it is true that opportunities for individual involvement were generally improved in smaller enterprises (IDE, 1981b). The influence of technology on participation, however, is somewhat more problematic. It has usually been assumed that increasing technological complexity will necessarily set limits to the feasibility of participation, at least at shopfloor level. Yet the 12-country IDE study (1981b) finds little evidence of a close relationship between technology and the extent of actual participation – although automation does seem to be a significant obstacle to greater worker involvement.

Of all the enterprise characteristics there is little doubt that the strongest predictor of the distribution of influence – in the sense of capacity to affect decision outcomes – by various enterprise groups under participative arrangements is hierarchical level. Workers have the least amount of influence and top management the greatest (IDE, 1981b). In particular, it would appear that the more strategic the decision, such as capital investment programmes, the greater the concentration of influence in the hands of top management. Obradovic

(1975) and Bertsch and Obradovic (1979) have shown that even with the Yugoslav system of workers' self-management, in which the executive authority (management and staff) are supposed to implement decisions formulated by the policy authority (the workers' council and other organs of self-management), in practice deliberations within these councils are largely dominated by high-level managers and specialist technical experts.[12]

This domination by the firm's 'technocracy' is especially apparent when issues such as sales and financial policy and market planning are debated. Thus workers' control at the top decision-making level does not appear to be a sufficient condition for overcoming inequalities created by a bureaucratic organisational structure and large differences in expertise (IDE, 1981b). Nevertheless, it has been shown that Yugoslav workers can become highly involved in certain issues, such as income distribution, where it involves ideological conflict with another enterprise group, when they consider it is within their interest and competence to do so. At the same time they relinquish the more technical and business policy issues to those whom they see as being most competent to make them (Commisso, 1981). Similar findings have been reported in relation to the more limited and circumscribed participative arrangements in Hungarian factories (Héthy and Makó, 1977).

The importance of the particular subject area itself for the effectiveness of participation has been confirmed by other cross-national research. A three-country study of the Netherlands, Britain and Yugoslavia (DIO, 1979) found that there is a relatively higher level of worker influence with respect to decisions related to personnel problems and working conditions. Danish experience with board-level representation (Westenholz, 1979) also indicates that board members are likely to be more effective when the discussion concerns problems which are of direct interest to workers, such as wage and employment conditions. In West Germany the Biedenkopf Commission in its evaluative study of co-determination in the coal, iron and steel industries found that worker representatives on supervisory boards showed little inclination to want to influence the general business policies of their companies. Rather, they tended to defer to management representatives, particularly on matters such as investment and dividends. Finally, a comparative analysis of some producer-cooperatives in France and Britain set up in the 1970s also confirms that 'worker directors tended to endorse managerial strategies instigated by experts, thus legitimating their control and authority and eradicating any opposition' (Bradley,

1980, p. 165).

A third group of contingency variables concerns managers' and workers' subjective orientations, perceptions and attitudes towards participation. In West Germany available data generally show a rather favourable perception of institutionalised co-determination by those directly concerned, in spite of much criticism of certain aspects of its implementation. Fürstenberg (1980) maintains, however, that its relative success was possible only because the employers' and management side became convinced that such a system provided an efficient sociotechnology for conflict management. Poole (1979) also stresses the importance of perceptions and attitudes and suggests that the view purporting universal effects of participation, such as an assumed link between structural decentralisation and workers' satisfaction regardless of differences in the subjective predispositions of the participants, is not tenable. Where workers regard their jobs in a markedly instrumental way they are unlikely to be concerned with control questions and may not respond positively to participative arrangements. On an inter-country basis although the DIO (1979) research group reported that in all three of its study countries (Britain, Yugoslavia and the Netherlands) workers became more satisfied with participation *per se* the more influence they had – especially because they felt that their capabilities and skills were being better utilised – nevertheless there was found to be a weaker relationship between the extent of their influence and their *general* satisfaction.

An earlier cross-national study (Tannenbaum *et al.*, 1974) compared the attitudes of workers in Yugoslav industry and the Kibbutz in Israel with those of workers in Italy, Austria and the USA. The Yugoslav and Israeli enterprises were seen by their employees as being relatively participative, in that they reported higher levels of involvement than did their counterparts in Italy, Austria and the USA. However, differences in the extent of perceived participation cannot account for expressed differences in employee job satisfaction, trust, sense of responsibility or work motivation. Although Kibbutz employees were found to be typically high in terms of these dimensions, Yugoslav workers were lower than those from less participative enterprises in the USA. The IDE study (1981b) also found that few relationships between participation and attitudes were generally stable across all 12 of its country samples. The type of participation seems to be an important factor since research in Norway and Sweden suggests that while workers are likely to perceive that *direct* participation implies that employees have some degree of control, they are not as likely to see such implications in *representative* participation (Bartölke *et al*., 1982).

A further intervening condition relates to the influence of the external environment upon participation. No enterprise can remain autonomous from the influence of market forces and the effects of economic change. In particular, unemployment may impinge on local processes of decision-making. In Sweden it has been said that co-determination has been affected more by the effects of economic recession, mergers and temporary dismissals of employees than by the new law (IDE, 1981a). In western economies it has been hypothesised by Marxists that the existence of an alien environment – including an economic system dominated by market relationships – inevitably implies inferior performance by producer-cooperative organisations in terms of efficiency, and their ultimate demise (Jones, 1978).[13]

In Eastern European countries since the economic reforms of the mid-1960s the operation of formal, participative machinery via workers' assemblies and the like inevitably reflects the nature of the environment in which it operates since, in practice, highly regulated and directive economic management can encroach upon it. Although the (Communist) Party élite advocates mass participation in management by workers it continually warns that industrial democracy cannot be opposed to state guidance. The consequence for most non-managerial personnel is that participation actually amounts to participation in the implementation of decisions rather than in their prior making (Porket, 1975, 1978).

In some developing economies broader influences relating to an inhospitable environment have been adduced. Thus the failure of government-imposed participation in India has been partly attributed to a cultural and ideological climate of suspicion and distance between organised labour and management, reflected in an underdeveloped industrial relations system (Kannappan and Krishnan, 1977). Similarly, research has shown that the disappointing results of the participative experiment in Peru

> must be examined partly in terms of the Peruvian culture, the evolution of industrial relations, the social structure and the distribution of power that prevailed in the past. Another country where social class lines are not drawn as sharply, where organised labour has been more fully involved in cooperative projects might [have been] able to avoid the negative results of the Peruvian model. (Whyte and Alberti, 1977, p. 112)

Conclusions

The evidence from experience of employees' participation within a variety of countries indicates that the results so far have been limited. In Norway, Belgium and Holland it has been found that workers' representatives on company boards and works councils have had little success in influencing decisions (Wall and Lischeron, 1977), and in the West German iron, steel and coal industries equal employee representation on the boards of companies has not resulted in major changes in the nature and substance of corporate decision-making. In Sweden there is widespread scepticism about the usefulness of the recent co-determination law in ensuring employees' influence over crucial and strategic decisions when their interests are fundamentally at odds with those of their employers, nor evidently has it produced sufficient changes in working conditions on the shopfloor to increase job satisfaction markedly (Haas, 1983). In fact, in all 12 countries investigated by the IDE group (1981b) the degree of democratisation of decision-making processes within work organisations appears to be fairly low, with the one notable exception of Yugoslavia. In that country, despite the discrepancies between formally prescribed participation and its actual practical execution, enterprises seem to provide a more equal distribution of power and individual involvement in decision-making than those elsewhere.

Nevertheless, workers in many countries do appear to have obtained certain benefits from participative arrangements at enterprise level, even though they apparently provide the individual worker with little sense of personal involvement. From the employees' standpoint it has been concluded that the greatest single improvement produced by the Swedish co-determination law is an increase in the flow of information. Similarly, the main achievements of co-determination in the German coal and steel industries have been seen as the growing information potential and advance notice of enterprise change accorded to worker representatives. This has meant that it has been possible to negotiate the substance, pace and conditions of economic reorganisation and technical change with a minimum of labour-management conflict and strikes (Adams and Rummel, 1977).[14] Indeed, the Biedenkopf Commission was apparently more impressed with the pacifying effects which co-determination had on organised labour than by the sense of participation which it imparted to individual workers.

Further evidence that formal participation as a mechanism of conflict resolution does contribute to the reduction of open industrial conflict is also available. In the Mondragon producer-cooperatives, for instance, although conflict does undoubtedly exist there is a 'relative absence of a worker-management gulf' and only one strike has ever occurred within the group (Bradley and Gelb, 1981). Yugoslav enterprises, however, are in this respect something of a paradox. Burdened with contradictions, such as the ambivalent roles and status of workers, management and unions, the self-management system has actually proved to be a source of (mainly unorganised) conflict generation – although actual strikes are not frequent in comparison with western capitalist countries. At the same time these contradictory forces facilitate conflict resolution, particularly since any conflict between managers and works councils can be adversely interpreted by the political élite as an indication of bureaucratic 'usurpation of power' in organisations. As a result strikes which occur are quickly resolved without becoming tests of strength and they do not appear to be very intensive or disintegrative (Rus, 1982).

Cross-national evidence would suggest that the origins and development of participatory institutions are largely context-specific (with the timing of their appearance often being crisis-induced). Yet, as we have noted, there are certain identifiable features for the effectiveness of participation which are common to many countries. Similarly, there are a number of problems which seem bound to arise with representative workers' participation irrespective of the environmental context in which it takes place. These include role-conflict (or 'dual loyalty') with respect to workers' representatives serving on management boards and the difficulties of maintaining effective links with their constituents. In particular

> a key finding in the literature . . . is that committee members' perspectives are substantially modified by the exposure to administrative procedures and that these changes may have the effect of isolating representatives from their constituents . . . and of encouraging attitudes concordant with traditional practices and of sustaining the existing power structure. (Poole, 1979, p. 268)

Regardless of structure and the processes of participation, available experience both in market and centrally-planned economies has also shown the great difficulties which arise in attempting to involve *all* workers. Thus in Germany the practice of holding plant assemblies in working hours has not proved sufficient to neutralise oligarchic tendencies within works councils (Fürstenberg, 1977). For much the same reasons the self-management system in Yugoslavia was restructured in the 1970s towards a strengthening of participation by individual workers. Each enterprise was subdivided into a number of Basic Organisations of Associated Labour, with power being directly accorded to mass meetings of workers along with attempts to limit the influence of supervisory, executive and technical staffs.

Although it is clear that employees' participation in decision-making is not only an evolving, but has also been an expanding, phenomenon it is more doubtful whether this can be interpreted as support for the 'convergence' thesis that as countries under the influence of industrialisation become more alike they develop similar institutions. As we have shown marked divergences exist in the institutional forms of participation adopted by various countries, and although some authorities (Walker, 1977; Lansbury, 1978b) claim to detect a cross-national trend towards greater participation such developments have by no means been uniform. The major innovations in market economies have occurred principally in the continental countries of Western Europe. Thus, as Windmüller (1977) has pointed out, discussion of a trend extending across a broad range of countries may easily create an impression of a universal and inexorable force at work which would be misleading.

Notes

1. The EEC's Fifth Directive, at present under discussion, would require the harmonisation of company law in each member state to provide for workers' participation in the affairs of their companies.

2. Schregle (1976, p. 2) regards the related term, 'industrial democracy' which is often used in the literature as being of 'an emotive and ill-defined nature'. Sometimes the two terms are used interchangeably. Thus, for the IDE (1981b), industrial democracy is 'a deliberate process designed to increase the participation of . . . members of an industrial organisation so that [they] have more "say" ' (p. 16).

3. In Europe workers, or works, councils exist in West Germany, France, Austria, Belgium, Netherlands, Luxembourg, Spain and Norway (in the last country via general union-employer agreement). For a comparison of the councils in these eight countries, see *European Industrial Relations Review*, no. 88, 1981.

4. For a recent discussion of the relative merits of collective bargaining and some other representative forms of participation, see Ogden (1982a).

5. Forms of self-management systems also exist in Algeria, Poland, Peru, Tanzania and Madagascar.

6. Compare Loveridge (1980, p. 297):

> For the Marxian the division of labour in society tends to complement the intensity achieved in the accumulation of capital and both are in turn related

to the effects of technological innovation. Local modifications in managerial controls are therefore mere *placebos* designed to distract attention from wider trends in ownership and technological innovation. Structural strains resolved in one area of employment will recur in another.

7. Similarly with respect to Austrian industrial relations it is claimed that 'conflict avoidance is an attitude, socioculturally based upon still prevailing authoritarian interaction patterns and founded upon a basic consensus of authorities, which thereby stabilises the *status quo*' (Fürstenberg, 1982, p. 363).

8. He attributes the change in union attitudes to the new political background after the establishment of the democratic Weimar Republic. For the German trade unions at that time their

> sudden increase in influence over state legislation can be imagined to have had an effect on ideology, in that working through the legislative machinery seemed a hopeful and rational strategy under the circumstances, which also generated a closer attachment to the prevailing order of society compared to that under imperial rule. (Sorge, 1976, p. 288)

9. At a period of industrial upheaval and 'crisis' following upon the effects of a rapid rate of technical change, rationalisation and major structural problems in the economy. On the basis of more limited Anglo-centric evidence, Ramsay (1977) argues that workers' participation schemes have appeared cyclically rather than evolutionarily over the course of time, as a management-induced method of securing greater labour force compliance during periods of challenge and threats to managerial authority.

10. Under legislation introduced in 1972 provision is also made for two union-appointed employee representatives on company boards.

11. A characteristic of joint stock companies under German law is the two-tier management structure in the form of a policy-making supervisory board together with a management board. In the mining, iron and steel industries parity of representation on the supervisory board between worker and shareholder representatives was introduced from the outset of co-determination. Elsewhere (since 1976) a parity system of workers' representation has applied in companies with more than 2000 employees, whereas in smaller firms workers continue to elect only one-third of the supervisory board members. Even in the large companies, however, in the event of deadlock the chairman – who is generally appointed by the shareholders – has the decisive casting vote.

12. Similar conclusions emerged from an earlier study in Polish enterprises (Kolaja, 1960).

13. In fact, some producer-cooperatives in France and the USA have actually survived for more than 50 years, and a number appear to have outperformed capitalist firms.

14. Other observers have attributed the smooth transition not directly to the co-determination mechanism but rather to the relative ease with which displaced workers could be resettled during a (former) period of high economic activity (ILO, 1981).

Further Reading

A useful and up-to-date, if somewhat factual, account of workers' participation in decision-making in many countries is the general survey produced by the International Labour Office (1981). A less wide-ranging but more analytical study comparing France, Germany and Britain is the monograph by Marsden (1978), and there is an excellent paper on the evolution of plant-level institutions throughout the EEC countries by Sorge (1976). A number of comprehensive single-country studies can be found in Roberts (1979). Many of the issues raised in this chapter are dealt with more extensively in two international symposia on industrial democracy: *Industrial Relations* (1979, Vol. 18), and *Annals* (1977, Vol. 431).

8 INDUSTRIAL RELATIONS IN MULTINATIONAL ENTERPRISES

In the mid-1970s multinational enterprises (MNEs) accounted for one-fifth of the world's output (excluding centrally-planned economies) and their production was growing at the rate of 10–12 per cent per annum – nearly twice that of the growth of world output. Although the relative rate of expansion of new MNE activities may now be slowing in comparison to that achieved over the last two decades it still remains impressive. Equally, the MNEs themselves are the predominant form of business organisation within international economic relations and they are 'among the most powerful economic institutions yet produced by the capitalist system' (Dunning, 1981, p. 3). Within this overall pattern of activity, US-based MNEs continue to dominate international investment with US holdings abroad in 1979 accounting for half the world's total multinational foreign assets (Little, 1982). The relative importance of US-based enterprises has, however, been declining as a result of a recent trend towards greater diversification in the MNEs' countries of origin, including Japan, West Germany and some other European nations.

Although multinational concerns are by no means homogeneous, since they differ in aspects such as their size, type of technology utilised and the extent to which international production facilities are integrated, their key distinguishing features are subsumed in the following definitional characteristics: they produce or operate functionally in more than one country rather than merely selling abroad; their operations cross national boundaries, often on a global scale; and they engage in foreign direct (rather than portfolio) investment. An additional criterion which is sometimes employed is that they have a ratio of foreign to total operations above some arbitrary percentage:

> All of these definitions emphasise the essential ingredient in the mixture of the overall MNE process; namely that the corporation engages in foreign production and is thereby active in the goods and factor markets of many nations, rather than in one, as would be the case with a purely uninational firm or one that engages in free trade to supply foreign markets. (Rugman, 1980, p. 24)

Enderwick (1982) maintains that one essential qualitative difference between national and multinational firms is the internalisation of formally external markets in the latter, and the consequence importance of intra-enterprise transactions within the MNE itself.

Theories of MNEs

A number of theories purporting to explain the primary impetus for the growth and extension of MNEs have been put forward. Two of the most well-known and general explanations relate first to the need to locate subsidiaries in foreign countries in order to overcome tariff barriers and import quotas which prevent competition via more traditional trading relationships. Secondly, there is the 'runaway' companies hypothesis whereby enterprises may invest abroad in order to secure the advantages of cheaper labour costs in the production process together with weaker unionism. Trade unions in the USA would claim that the establishment by US companies of subsidiaries in Latin America, Asia, the Caribbean and Europe has brought about economic loss to US workers. In relation to this explanation, however, one difficulty is to account for the fact that many countries including the United States are both 'source' and 'host' countries to foreign investment at the same time. Also, there is the more obvious point that the level and rate of change of relative labour costs between countries may be misleading in terms of more crucial *unit* labour cost considerations because of differences in productivity and output growth. Flanagan (1974) has suggested that the hypothesis may prove to be valid only for the limited case of some horizontal multinational investments in less-developed countries, such as electronics in Taiwan or the clothing industry in Mexico – on this view, the primary motive for the extension of multinationals relates to economic variables other than labour costs.

In fact, a more sophisticated explanation holds that firms are encouraged to expand abroad and seek world-wide markets in order to exploit profitably some firm-specific advantage which they have managed to aquire. The advantage may take a number of possible forms such as product differentiation, managerial expertise, technological knowledge and marketing skills, or scale economies. Where knowledge is the firm-specific advantage the MNE may exploit this property right by exporting to countries which do not impose substantial barriers to free trade, or by establishing subsidiaries in those which do.

One of the foremost theories of MNE growth within the manufacturing sector is the product-life-cycle model in which firms develop new products at home (growth stage) and then exploit them abroad, first by means of exporting and later by setting up subsidiaries to which the product and, ultimately process, technologies are transferred. Towards the 'maturity' stage of the cycle the product price tends to be driven down and profit margins decline as other firms begin to produce like products and finally exports are displaced by the expanding, and lower-cost, foreign-based production ('decline' stage). In consequence, the firm's competitive strategy moves away from product technology, where its control has been largely superseded, towards new and superior process technology as a defensive measure designed to reduce production costs. At the same time it establishes its own subsidiaries in foreign markets which enables the elimination of non-competitive cost factors such as tariffs and transport charges so that the firm itself becomes 'multinational'. Within its home country base – although employment on the production side has declined – the enterprise then generates managerial capabilities and supporting services to supply world markets which often entails 'the development of large-scale, high technology, conglomerate organisations with superior financial resources' (Kujawa, 1979, p. 17).

A conceptual scheme relating to the behavioural aspects of the evolution of MNEs has been advanced by Perlmutter (1969). He classifies MNEs in terms of their basic operating strategy which may be ethnocentric (home country-oriented), polycentric (host country-oriented), or geocentric (world-oriented):

> an ethnocentric strategy means that the top management . . . attempts to implement the values, policies and sentiments of the parent company regardless of environmental differences that affect foreign operations. A polycentric strategy, on the other hand, emphasises environmental differences and reflects a deliberate choice by the parent company to make foreign operations as local in identity as possible. The geocentric strategy reflects a truly global outlook; it recognises environmental differences but prescribes the interrelationships with the external conditions on a purely functional basis without any preconceived notion of omniscience at home office or the foreign subsidiary. (Schollhammer, 1973, p. 21)

A fundamental premise of this classificatory approach is that an ethnocentric strategy is more liable to give rise to various forms of industrial relations conflict than either a polycentric or geocentric orientation. Other things being equal, the latter strategies help to promote greater organisational effectiveness.

Industrial Relations Implications

Having delineated some of the factors which account for the emergence and expansion of MNEs, we may now consider their specific relationship to, and impact on, industrial relations – in particular the ways in which they may impinge on trade union and worker interests. In this respect the major considerations derive from the perceived strength of the MNE which operates as a transnational decision-making unit with internationally-spread facilities and can thus marshall and mobilise resources across national boundaries. Unlike a national company whose management is an actor within a single industrial relations system, an MNE operates within a number of systems simultaneously. It can therefore be argued that MNEs represent a possible destabilising force within industrial relations, displacing the existing power balance and resulting in asymmetrical relationships between MNE managements, unions and even governments: 'The discretionary powers inherent in [MNEs'] supranational decision-making structure potentially enable them to impose their will upon the local partners in the industrial relations systems in which they operate' (Bomers, 1976, p. 2). It has also been claimed by Crouch (1982a) that the growth of MNEs constitutes the most important challenge to the position which western trade unions have achieved within their own countries.

One particular implication of the product-life-cycle theory is that labour relations in overseas subsidiaries may be subject to a large degree of managerial control by the parent company as a result of transfers abroad of product and process technologies. Managerial staff seconded to the subsidiaries might attempt to carry over industrial relations policies which appertain in the home country, such as those relating to bargaining structures or union recognition. These may, however, be entirely inappropriate to the different customs, practices and institutional framework found in the host country where they may provoke industrial conflict.

In fact, the literature identifies a number of recurrent themes in which it is alleged that the nature and activities of MNEs may impinge adversely upon the interests of organised labour. Unions have typically viewed the multinational location of a firm's operations as an extension of the historical trend towards widening product markets. This development is seen as raising three major potential threats to trade union members and their organisations. The first relates to employment effects and the concern for job security as a result of direct foreign investment displacing exports from the home country by producing abroad what could have been produced at home (as in the product-life cycle model). In the United States it is also claimed that MNEs, as the main vehicle for transferring information, combines US capital and technology with cheap labour abroad and in the process erode US comparative advantage and damage labour interests (Hood and Young, 1979). Furthermore, the possible job loss from long-term production transfers of existing MNE facilities to more favoured locations has also been of paramount concern, and it is believed that MNE subsidiaries are more likely to disinvest and cease production than are home-based companies.

A second consideration is the undermining or weakening of union bargaining power in relation to that of management[1] which arises particularly as a result of the broader financial base of the MNE. In the event, or threat, of a strike, for instance, at any one of its subsidiaries the enterprise may be able to continue to meet its market commitment, maintain cash inflows and thus minimise the costs which the union is able to impose, by means of production-switching between its various locations. The ability to utilise what have been termed 'industrial relations scale economies' (Ulman, 1974b) for strategic advantage and bargaining leverage is especially prevalent where the MNE has adopted a deliberate policy of dual, or multiple, sourcing (alternative supplies) of either products or components in different countries. Some observers would regard this capacity to continue to generate financial inflows in an environment external to a labour-management conflict as one important distinguishing feature between multi- and uninational companies (Kujawa, 1980). The economic pressure which a nationally-based union can exert upon an MNE is certainly less than would be the case if the company's operations were confined to one country. Within the MNE substantial financial resources and cross-subsidisation can be made available to any part of the organisation which is in conflict with a union, thus enhancing its ability to withstand a strike. In effect, the MNE typically has a greater range of options open to it and more staying-power than a national company. Under certain conditions multinational location of production facilities, especially when combined with conglomerate diversification as between industries, may therefore give the employer the capacity to make the institutionalised collective bargaining system an ineffective method of resolving industrial disputes (Craypo, 1975).

A related characteristic of the MNE which is also regarded as a threat to union bargaining power is the alleged remote locus of its decision-making central authority. Unions claim (Levinson, 1972) that they are being kept at arm's length and that local managements do not have the ultimate authority to respond to union initiatives since the crucial industrial relations decisions are being made from outside the country in which a subsidiary is located. Bargaining and union penetration are made more difficult because of the inaccessibility of the decision-makers and the unions' inability to deal directly with those who make the final decisions on major labour issues. It is often difficult to define the point in the management structure at which to target union influence. Within the areas of corporate strategy and financial policy there is said to be a particular elusiveness, obscurity and lack of 'transparency' as to the real source of decision-making.

There is also likely to be a lack of hard financial information relating to the position of MNE subsidiaries which can be used for collective bargaining purposes since, 'when financial data are reported on a corporate-wide basis, unions are wholly dependent on whatever information the local subsidiary chooses to reveal' (Bomers, 1976, p. 20). The financial performance of individual units may be further concealed because of the use of manipulative, intra-corporate 'transfer pricing' of goods and services between component parts of the organisation, at a higher or lower figure than for actual value received.[2] By this means the MNE can allow profits to accrue at whichever national location it selects within the corporate structure thereby distorting their real source of origin. The shifting of income across national boundaries, with a view to the optimal exploitation of international differences, could be used not only as a means of reducing the overall tax liability of the enterprise but also to diminish trade union demands upon corporate revenue (Weinburg, 1978). For all these reasons trade unions have experienced a sense of power loss from the expansion of MNE operations and wish to attempt to re-establish a measure of equilibrium.

Having identified the basic trade union concerns relating to possible job displacement, reduced bargaining power and a more remote locus of decision-making, it is necessary to examine the research findings from empirical studies of the interaction of MNEs with industrial relations, particularly as between countries, in order to ascertain to what extent such claims appear to be substantiated. A careful examination of the evidence is required since the field is typified by much anecdotal evidence together with specific examples which, although they may be valid on an individual basis, may lack more general applicability. Furthermore, as Hawkins (1979, p. x) has emphasised, 'the controversies are whetted by the fact that [MNE] activities involve conflicts of interest' between groups which gain and those which lose, which may colour both the methodology and evidence employed in the analysis. Consequently, it is necessary to exercise some circumspection when assessing the MNE industrial relations literature, particularly where it claims to be objective and neutral (Liebhalberg, 1980).

Empirical Evidence

The question of the employment effects of MNE activity is a complex one. To the extent that exports from the home country become replaced by sales from overseas subsidiaries domestic employment opportunities would initially diminish. Nevertheless, such possible adverse effects from production displacement could be offset by positive employment influences. For instance, the location of production facilities abroad may enable the MNE to penetrate markets which otherwise would not be readily available to it. A net gain in employment may also result from the subsidiaries' demands for exports of capital goods, intermediate products, or materials from the home country or, indirectly, from the expansion of white-collar employment as a result of the centralisation of management services at the parent headquarters. A number of studies have attempted to estimate more specifically the effects of foreign direct investment by US firms on the net number of US jobs thereby created or lost. Ulmer (1980) suggests that the findings are at least consistent with the hypothesis that, on balance, the growth of home-based MNEs has increased US employment. For industrialised market economies in general it has also been concluded that expansion of MNE activities has not been accompanied by a decrease in the volume of employment in home country activities (ILO, 1981a).

An examination of MNE industrial relations in Western Europe (ILO, 1976), however, instanced a number of production and employment shifts in the food products industries which were intended to offset losses accruing from strikes. Also, there are well-known individual instances of company closures by US organisations and repatriation of capital following a prolonged strike, such as the textile engineering firm of Roberts-Arundel in Britain (Arnison, 1970). There have also been a number of cases of precipitate plant or departmental shutdowns in Belgium, the Netherlands and France – but fewer in West Germany where the works council system and worker representation on supervisory boards offer protection against this sort of arbitrary management action (ILO, 1976). However, the evidence suggests that the possible job displacement which could occur from large-scale production-switching to a more favoured location is limited.

Technical-economic considerations, particularly in capital intensive industries, are likely to reduce the propensity of companies to shift their production in this way. Three factors are identified as being significant in this respect. The high sunk costs in existing production facilities, together with the cost of liquidating large investments, provide effective constraints. Once an investment has been made the enterprise may then be locked-in, especially in the short run, although it could gradually disinvest over the longer term and run down its investment. In addition, a relatively low labour intensity restricts the incentive to move production to a lower wage location, whilst at the same time the greater capital intensity may enhance the ability of organised labour effectively to block potential production transfers (Bomers and Peterson, 1977).

Temporary production switching in order to defeat a strike is more feasible, however, and the evidence suggests that this has occurred in the automobile industry (Kujawa, 1971). It requires that the enterprise maintain some form of parallel production policy across a number of its locations as well as the existence of spare productive capacity, since if all plants are fully employed then production switching would prove costly. In the case of MNEs in West Germany and the Netherlands, however, Bomers and Peterson (1977) found that such a practice was rare, partly as a consequence of union attempts to prevent it and because of subsidiary managements' concern for its possible adverse effects upon local labour relations. An additional constraint may derive from the high 'visibility' of MNEs and hence concern for their public image, which makes them sensitive to unfavourable public opinion.

As a further aspect of the conduct of MNEs in labour matters we can examine the evidence concerning the locus of authority issue (parent/subsidiary relationship) and union claims of over-centralisation in decision-making. The propensity of corporate headquarters to intervene in subsidiaries' operations is partly dependent upon technological and organisational considerations. Intervention is more probable, for instance, if the subsidiary is a key plant (such as a single source of supply) within a production system which is both technologically complex and highly integrated (Hamill, 1984). Similarly, where investment in a given plant is very large because of the capital-intensive nature of its operations, the MNE is likely to exercise a greater degree of influence over the activities of a foreign subsidiary, including its industrial relations practices. As a result MNE food companies located in Western Europe seem to have more decentralised policy-making than do automobile companies (ILO, 1976).

A greater degree of local autonomy is also typical of long-established overseas subsidiaries which, with less well-developed international communications at the time of their founding, were encouraged to be more self-sufficient. This would be true in the case of British and Swedish parent companies, whereas with US MNEs established in more recent times high-speed communications were better developed. Thus the US subsidiaries became accustomed to maintaining closer contacts with the home country (Kassalow, 1978a). Additionally, enterprises which are highly diversified in terms of product range and geographical markets served usually incorporate a multi-divisional organisational structure which also encourages the decentralisation of functions such as industrial relations (Enderwick, 1982).[3]

In fact, it is well established that the extent to which MNEs operate a relatively decentralised structure for managing the operations of their subsidiaries varies according to factors such as the structure of ownership (whether a fully integrated or a holding company) and the actual functional specialism involved. The allocation of investment funds, for instance, which has substantial effects on production and employment, is a strategic matter which is invariably controlled by central headquarters in the home country. In contrast, one of the most heavily decentralised operational functions is industrial relations since inter-country, cultural and legal differences make it a much more complex area than, say, production or marketing (Warner and Turner, 1972). It is usually contended that the more marked are the differences between the customs or culture of the host country and those of the home country, the greater the need for decentralisation in industrial relations decision-making.

There is clear evidence, however, that within the industrial relations function itself significant differences also exist in the extent of parent company involvement, depending on the national origin of the MNE. A number of studies (Roberts and May, 1974; Bomers, 1976; Hedlund, 1981; Hamill, 1984) indicate that US MNEs exercise greater centralised control over labour relations, whereas the subsidiaries of British companies are more decentralised. British multinational firms may give general policy advice to their subsidiaries but rarely become directly involved in collective bargaining issues or negotiating processes as such, believing that there should be minimum central interference on these matters. In contrast, Blake (1973) found a much greater readiness for the headquarters of US MNEs to become involved in their affiliates' industrial relations activities and to make them a more integral part of general corporate management. This was especially apparent in those areas of greatest potential conflict, such as collective bargaining negotiations and strike settlement. Studies of MNE operations in Canada, Brazil, Italy and Nigeria (La Palombara and Blank, 1976), and in Malaysia (Sim, 1977) also indicate that US-based MNEs concentrate authority at corporate headquarters, with greater emphasis on formal management controls and a close reporting system. In contrast, for European-based MNEs there was found to be a looser relationship between head office and local subsidiaries as well as a greater willingness to accept the judgement of local managers.

The reasons for this more pronounced emphasis in US MNEs on close and systematic managerial control may be partly related to the organisational structure of US firms. They display a greater tendency than do European firms to operate rigidly hierarchical decision-making systems at the corporate level (Shetty, 1979), particularly within the area of financial control to ensure that profit planning targets are attained.[4] European companies, on the other hand, tend to operate what is termed a 'collegial' decision-making system where there is collective responsibility among a top management team for the affairs of the enterprise – in contrast to the power embodied in the chief executive of a US firm. This European style of decision-making facilitates greater involvement by managements of foreign subsidiaries and therefore a higher degree of decentralisation and autonomy among the affiliates. European MNEs appear to prefer functional divisions, multiple-reporting and more personalised headquarters-subsidiary relationships than do their US-based counterparts.

In addition to these differences in organisational structure and processes European-owned MNEs have dealt mainly with unions at industry (and sometimes plant) level and have had less well-developed *company*-based industrial relations policies and, possibly, less professionalised managements to implement them in comparison with US enterprises. Also, Roberts and May (1974), in a comparison of British and US MNEs, note the greater tendency for US affiliates to be wholly-owned whereas with the more common British practice of joint ownership, by buying into an overseas company, it is usual to leave current, local industrial relations practices undisturbed, so that with this arrangement, 'it is more likely that local patterns of industrial relations will be allowed to determine policy in this area of management responsibilities' (p. 407).

In those MNEs in which headquarters' control of important aspects of labour relations is extensive, a related question concerns the possibility of non-conforming behaviour by subsidiaries with the norms and industrial relations practices of their host countries, thereby provoking possible conflict. Research findings suggest that some MNEs initially attempted to export the policies characteristic of their home country, such as an unwillingness on the part of some US firms to permit their affiliates in Europe to join employers' associations or, in certain cases, to grant union recognition.

In a six-country study of MNE industrial relations in the food and metal industries of Western Europe (ILO, 1976) few alleged problems were found in respect of lack of union recognition by foreign-based MNEs in France or Belgium. This was attributed to the universal practice in those two countries of large firms becoming members of their appropriate trade or industry employers' organisation since union recognition is generally automatically accorded by these associations. Indeed in Belgium, since the national or regional collective agreement can have a binding effect on all employers regardless of whether or not they are association members, some MNEs joined the employers' body in order to secure an influence on the negotiation of agreements which affect them. Also in Germany the extensive legal prescription of the structure and substance of industrial relations is an important constraining influence on the conduct and labour practices of MNEs, leaving them less room for manoeuvre and ensuring closer conformity with national practices in the host country. The greater legal prescription of industrial relations in Germany (and to a lesser extent in France) therefore means that in some ways MNEs may constitute less distinctive problems to unions in those countries than in, say, Britain – despite the fact that their union membership densities are relatively lower. For Sweden the strength of the employer and union federations and the primacy accorded to their joint regulation of industrial relations again makes it difficult for any large enterprise to hold out against employer association membership and conforming practices, which include union recognition.

There have been rather more problems, however, of an initial, and sometimes continuing, refusal by MNEs to grant recognition in Britain and to some extent in the Netherlands. Some US companies such as Kodak and IBM attempted to carry over their home country practices of opposition to union recognition, together with non-membership of employers' organisations in order to retain direct control over their own enterprise negotiations. Enderwick and Buckley (1983) have shown that in British manufacturing industry a major advantage of the preference for single-employer bargaining by foreign-owned firms is the greater discretion which it affords them in labour utilisation, together with enhanced control over labour costs. Foreign-owned establishments show a greater reluctance than indigenous plants to negotiate over recruitment, manning levels and changes in production methods (i.e. on matters of labour utilisation they assert managerial prerogative).

In addition to the importance of employer association membership as an intervening variable affecting the industrial relations conduct of MNEs and their assimilation of host country practices, another important factor would appear to be the influence of the extent of the national product market. Because of the very large size of the US home market, for example, US overseas subsidiaries may represent only a relative minority of the parent MNE's business. Consequently, in proportion to their total sales, 'where the overseas share is relatively small the home office may tend to regard overseas problems, including some labour problems, as a mere extension of home country operations and try to impose home country standards' (ILO, 1976, p. 26). By way of contrast, however, for Dutch, Swedish, Swiss (and some British) MNEs subsidiary operations abroad can represent the major part of their total business. Domestic sales of the two leading Swiss MNEs, for instance, amount in both cases to less than 4 per cent of their output, with the result that adaptation to host country institutions and conditions may more easily be accepted than by US companies.

A related element affecting trade union views of the activities of MNEs is the size of a given host country itself and the proportionate importance of MNE operations within its economy. Trade unionists in Belgium and the Netherlands may have felt particularly threatened by the potential of MNE power partly because of their greater economic role in these countries than elsewhere in Western Europe. In the mid-1970s foreign-owned companies accounted for some 33 per cent of total industrial turnover in Belgium and 19 per cent in Holland as compared with only about 10 per cent in Britain and 9 per cent in Sweden. Furthermore, Belgium and Holland are themselves small countries relative to Germany and France, so that 'even a few multinationals which do not conform well to national labour practices stand out vividly in a small country landscape' (ILO, 1976, p. 65).

Gennard (1974) has pointed out, however, that certain MNE labour practices may be regarded as a positive and sometimes innovating – rather than adverse – influence upon host country industrial relations. Within MNE subsidiaries located in Britain he instanced the development in the 1960s of productivity bargaining and measured day-work schemes of wage payment to promote better labour utilisation. A comparative study by Takamiya (1981) of the operation of two Japanese television set factories located in Britain with similar British and US-owned factories, broadly equivalent in size and technology (although not perfectly matched), found that the superior productivity performance of the Japanese plants could be attributed mainly to organisational factors carried over from the company's home base. Work practices and occupational categories were more flexible than in the British factory and there were fewer hierarchical as well as functional demarcations among workers. Since it was felt that the typical British multi-union structure with its potential for demarcation difficulties would be detrimental to flexible working practices one union (together with its white-collar section) was given organising rights for the entire workforce in the Japanese-owned plants, in contrast to the six unions which existed in the British factory. There was thus a partial introduction of some elements of Japanese-style union structure into the production units, although this factor should not be overrated (White and Trevor, 1983).

Although the empirical evidence for Western European countries is limited and much of it based on general questionnaire survey techniques, Bomers and Peterson (1977) maintain that within the highly integrated and institutionalised industrial relations systems which typify those countries the potential for substantial negative effects from MNE activities is considerably constrained. For these authors the critical, unresolved issue is somewhat different, namely the unilateral and supranational decision-making powers of the MNE itself. They recognise, however, that the discretionary powers of MNEs and their potential for adverse industrial relations consequences could be considerably greater in other locations. This might be the case in those countries with weak trade unions, a buyers' labour market and less well-entrenched industrial relations institutions and regulatory arrangements, as in many Third World developing nations which have been receptive to the inflow of foreign investment.

In support of such a possibility Kassalow (1978a), in his three-country study of MNEs in Asia, finds that in Malaysia there have been problems of resistance to union recognition, aided by restrictive government legislation designed to attract foreign investment (see Chapter 9). Once again this was especially noticeable in the case of certain US companies which do not bargain with unions at home and have implemented a similar policy abroad. Yet equivalent problems do not seem to have arisen in Singapore where the unions' close relationship with the ruling political party helped membership recruitment campaigns. In fact, in both countries – as well as in the Philippines – unions appear on the whole to have found it somewhat easier to organise and bargain with MNEs than with indigenously-owned companies. The latter had less experience of dealing with unions, were more hostile towards them, and had less systematically developed procedures for grievance-handling.

Strike Incidence

We have already noted that foreign-owned MNEs may have a greater potential for labour conflict than indigenous companies. This may occur either from the importing of 'alien' home country practices into a different and unreceptive environment, or because of the remoteness of ultimate decision-taking at too great a distance from the workforce concerned. On the other hand, it is generally conceded that wages and other economic benefits provided by MNEs usually compare very favourably with those of comparable national firms. This could be a direct reflection of the fact that

> for many [multinationals] the cost of a global division of labour is acute sensitivity to production disruption. Avoidance of such disruption may be one factor influencing the high wage policies and the use of financial inducements . . . to regulate labour relations. (Enderwick, 1982, p. 37)

It is, therefore, an empirical question as to whether or not foreign-owned subsidiaries do experience more strike activity (used as a quantitative measure of conflict) than do domestic firms. The results of such comparisons might also influence the relative attractiveness of further MNE investment abroad.

A number of investigations have been carried out concerning the relative strike-proneness of foreign and indigenous firms operating in the UK, but the findings of the early studies have been contradictory.

The first study of comparative strike records (Gennard and Steuer, 1971) found that, contrary to expectations, for two years during the 1960s for which data were available foreign-owned firms had a less than proportionate frequency of strikes and of man-days lost in relation to their contribution to total manufacturing output. This remained true even when the aggregate strike figures were standardised to eliminate any differences arising from the industrial structures of the domestic and foreign-owned sectors (e.g. the possibility that foreign firms might be concentrated more in the less strike-prone industries). However, the conclusion that foreign-owned firms had a better strike record than their domestic counterparts may be queried on the basis of the methodological deficiencies in the study. Not only did the investigation not control for differences in plant size – a major variable affecting strike propensity[5] – but by comparing strike activity ratios with output ratios it possibly biased the results in favour of the foreign-owned sector (i.e. because of the superior labour productivity record of foreign-owned enterprises operating in the UK).

Forsyth (1973) confined his comparative analysis over the 1960s merely to that between US-owned and UK firms located in Scotland. He found that, conversely, the US firms had a worse strike record (some 25 per cent more working-days lost per employee) than had the domestic firms. Such disparity between the results of the two studies is probably to be explained not only by data differences but also, in part, by the size factor – US-owned firms in Scotland are, on average, larger (and therefore more strike-prone) than domestic ones. Therefore, in order to attempt to control systematically for the influence of other possible factors affecting strike-proneness, such as plant size and proportion of labour cost to total cost,[6] Creigh and Makeham (1978) employed multiple regression analysis. Using cross-sectional data on foreign and indigenous enterprises located in Britain for 15 manufacturing industry groups they were then unable to find any statistically significant relationship between the extent of foreign ownership and differences in strike activity, either in terms of frequency or man-days lost. However, more recent and comprehensive evidence on this question (Enderwick and Buckley, 1982) criticises the methodology employed in the former study, since aggregating varying plant sizes across an industry fails to control adequately for the extreme sensitivity of strike incidence to *particular* size ranges, as measured by the number of employees.

Enderwick and Buckley find in fact – as did an earlier study using a similar data base (Millward, 1979) – that foreign-owned plants in

British manufacturing over the period 1971-73 (particularly US-owned ones) did have both comparatively higher strike frequency and man-days lost than domestically-owned plants. However, the adverse strike magnitude of foreign-owned, in relation to domestic, establishments was confined to the smaller bands of plant size. As plant size increased above 1000 employees the overseas affiliates then appeared to have a much better comparative record in relation to indigenous plants within that size range. It may be that large, foreign-owned plants, especially those with greater capital intensity and interrelated production processes, would face higher strike costs and that this encourages them to develop procedures for containing the conflict.

It is necessary, however, to note another important finding of this study that, as regards strike-proneness, foreign-owned firms do not represent a homogeneous set. When strike frequency (after controlling for plant size) is subdivided by country groupings in terms of origins – USA, EEC or 'other' – it is found that MNEs with a home base other than the United States or EEC country seem to experience a rather lower relative strike record at plant sizes below 1000 employees, whereas above that size band their record then rapidly deteriorates. It is suggested that this may be a consequence of their experience in operating plants typically of only a limited size in their home base, particularly where it is a small country such as Switzerland, together with the management difficulties which arise when the location of their (larger) overseas operations is in a markedly different social and cultural context. Yet the fact remains that, despite such qualifications, for most plant size ranges US firms experience a somewhat higher strike rate than non-US firms and, when analysed by strike 'cause' (i.e. the principal reasons given for striking), they also have a proportionately greater number of disputes over trade union questions and labour utilisation – manning levels, work allocation, etc. – especially in larger-sized plants. This 'supports the view that their higher productivity and the demands of operating a global division of labour may well be obtained at the price of proportionately more such disputes' (Enderwick and Buckley, 1982, p. 318).

By distinguishing between US and non-US plants this study also indicates that part of the explanation for the contradictory findings of the earlier analyses by Gennard and Steuer, and Forsyth may be a result of the higher strike propensity of US as opposed to non-US, foreign-owned plants operating in Britain. Yet the level of aggregation used by Enderwick and Buckley in their country groupings for comparative purposes, although necessitated by data limitations, is still too high. Clearly, more work remains to be done on this important question in order to clarify the issues involved in relative strike-proneness as between MNEs of differing national origins.

Trade Union Response to MNEs

Trade unions have initiated a number of responses within their collective bargaining activities in order to countervail the organisational structure and activities of MNEs and redress their own sense of power loss. These may be regarded as preparatory steps towards the ultimate aim of developing bargaining structures which are coextensive with the boundaries of the multinational itself (i.e. transnational, or global, collective bargaining). Such an objective is felt to be necessary since a basic premiss of international trade union strategy in relation to MNEs is that the national trade union is becoming less of a primary actor in industrial relations. The fact is that 'because of its single-state orientation and tradition, the union associated with a subsidiary does not have the legal, political or customary base to bargain with or pressure a foreign headquarters' (Blake, 1972).

As a means of facilitating coordinated action and the provision of mutual assistance the unions have utilised the services of the International Trade Secretariats (ITSs) to which they are affiliated.[7] These represent one possible institutional form through which international collective bargaining structures can develop. The 17 ITSs, mostly Geneva-based, consist of individual unions from around the world grouped into more or less closely related industrial categories such as metals, transport, public services and chemicals (Windmüller, 1980). Thus within any particular ITS the major principle which links the unions is their attachment to a specific industry, or industry groups, and their common problems. The secretariats seek to advance the collective bargaining objectives of their member unions and are 'industrial' rather than 'global' internationals, unlike the World Federation of Trade Unions (WFTU) or the International Confederation of Free Trade Unions (ICFTU). The latter organisations are composed of national trade union *federations* (such as the TUC in Britain) rather than industrial unions, and both their orientation and mandate are primarily political rather than industrial. A further structural innovation on the part of the ITSs in the last two decades has been to establish World Councils for individual MNEs, such as the auto councils for each of the major European, US and Japanese automobile producers

(Treckel, 1972). Their purpose is to coordinate union bargaining for specific MNEs and organise solidarity action where necessary via regular meetings for the exchange of information and agreement on a common bargaining strategy.

Although international collective bargaining with MNEs remains the long-term aim of organised labour there are a number of more limited forms of union reaction which have already taken place, sometimes on a regularised basis. The first is the collection, circulation and exchange of information regarding terms and conditions of employment in the various MNE subsidiaries as an aid to union bargaining strategy and a basis from which to launch its initiatives. Also, as a result of improvements in the flow of information, the unions may then react more quickly and positively to any developing situation affecting industrial relations. A second type of response relates to international assistance given to a single union which becomes in dispute with an MNE subsidiary. Although international sympathy strikes are infrequent, and may be limited in part by legal difficulties, nevertheless a number of instances of the imposition of a union boycott have occurred. Such action might prevent the switching of production between countries during a strike. Similarly, union pressure may be imposed at the parent company's home base to help secure objectives such as union recognition in less well-organised subsidiaries abroad.

A third and more ambitious union response relates to multiple negotiations with an MNE in several different countries simultaneously. This represents a preliminary attempt to create a unified bargaining strategy in that although the sizes of the claims are not yet identical the timing is coordinated so as to put greater pressure upon the MNE. In these cases union coordination can prove effective only if existing collective agreements have common, or close, expiration dates to enable trade union pressure to be deployed on a consolidated basis. The first successful transnational, coordinated bargaining on a significant scale occurred in 1969 with the French-owned St Gobain glass manufacturing company. Favourable settlements were secured at the German and Italian plants – and in the United States after a strike – as a result of joint union action coordinated by the chemical workers' trade secretariat (ICF) to forestall possible production-switching together with agreement not to conclude bargaining in any one country without general concurrence. The communist unions in France, however, were not a party to the ICF's coordination policy and accepted a more modest settlement than had been secured in the United States (Roberts, 1981).

Another well-publicised instance of coordinated union action took place at AKZO, a Dutch chemical firm. When the company decided to close down a number of plants in Holland, Belgium and Switzerland it was met by sit-ins and fierce resistance from Dutch trade unions which also secured the support of unions in Belgium and West Germany. The closure decision was reversed in the face of a lengthy and bitter dispute along with the considerable public, as well as private, pressure. However, doubts have been expressed as to whether in these two cases international union assistance was a *decisive* influence upon the outcome, or whether it was a more peripheral factor (Northrup and Rowan, 1979).[8]

The final stage of union reaction would be fully integrated negotiations around common demands designed to achieve parity and an upward harmonisation of terms and conditions throughout the constituent parts of the MNE.[9] Direct international collective bargaining between the central management of an MNE and a trade union federation representing employees in several countries would then take place. To date, however, the most developed form of international union cooperation has been the international gathering and exchange of information rather than more substantive, strategic action. Similarly, although meetings between ITSs and some MNEs have occurred, for the most part they have centred on consultation and information-exchange rather than bargaining. According to an extensive review of the documented evidence by Northrup and Rowan (1979), the only significant examples of actual international bargaining relate to two industries – ocean transport and entertainment. Because of its strategically-placed dockworkers' affiliates and the threat to boycott vessels the International Transport Workers' Federation has been able to secure direct negotiations with individual shipping companies and associations. Similarly, MNE collective bargaining has become established in the European entertainment industry, setting performers' fees in radio and television, partly because of the international nature of its labour market (Miscmarra, 1981).

In addition to such limited attempts to confront MNEs via the mobilisation of an international union counterforce, indirect pressure has also been employed in the form of a legislative approach. Blanpain (1977) maintains that because of the unions' weakness at international level in collective bargaining they have been forced into lobbying and pressurising national governments to implement protective legislation to contain MNE activities, such as controls on the export of capital. At the international level via inter-governmental agencies they have supported the establishment of guidelines designed to regulate the conduct of MNEs. Recently, both the OECD and the ILO have drawn up codes of conduct for MNEs to observe in their industrial relations practices.[10] Although the observation of these guidelines is voluntary rather than mandatory it is believed that unions might use them as an extra lever in any disputes with MNEs by bringing instances of non-compliance to the attention of signatory governments.

Obstacles to Transnational Bargaining

The slow progress in moving towards the attainment of international bargaining can be attributed to a number of factors, not least of which has been determined management resistance towards efforts to establish union-MNE relations, since generally the benefits of refusing to negotiate with unions on an international basis have far outweighed the costs that unions aie able to impose. In Europe, for instance, most managements oppose multinational bargaining because they see it as a means of proliferating a further layer of bargaining in addition to those which already exist, which would risk escalating the scope of industrial disputes and create another level of power capable of shutting down the entire enterprise. Also, union pressure to align pay and conditions to the highest levels prevailing throughout the MNE could result in significant cost increases (Roberts, 1975; Northrup and Rowan, 1977).

Once again significant differences are found in the reported attitudes of US and British companies towards trade union responses. A much higher proportion of US-owned firms consider that the effects of union strategies to extend bargaining across international frontiers would be far more harmful to their ability to conduct business internationally than do British firms, and are therefore more prepared to resist such developments (Roberts and May, 1974). This difference may be associated with a more basic anti-union attitude in the United States and the fact that US companies have appeared to regard the possibility of the onset of international collective bargaining as being more imminent, that is, they have a shorter time-horizon than do British companies. The greater awareness and concern by US firms probably reflects the tendency of unions to concentrate their overtures in this respect upon the largest and most international of the MNEs as being particularly vulnerable to the application of pressure.

Prospects for an internationalisation of industrial relations processes have also been limited because of difficulties within the labour movement.

Although the ITSs regard themselves as a vehicle through which various national unions representing MNE employees can combine and co-ordinate their actions to present a united front in bargaining, their power and influence have never been as great as their membership size (numbered in millions) would suggest. Rather, they are loosely-knit federations in which the real source of power resides in the affiliated, national unions rather than in the trade secretariats. Officials of member union organisations are reluctant to relinquish decision-making powers and authority to an international bargaining body since their own constituents – whom it is their primary responsibility to represent – are nationally, and not internationally, based. Because of disparities in conditions of production and wage levels across national boundaries there is, in fact, little coincidence of short-term economic interest between workers in different countries. As a result, trade unions seem more willing to commit themselves to long-term relationships with unions in other countries where the potential cost of compliance or the degree of commitment is relatively small, as with routinised information-exchange and consultation (Blake, 1973).

International trade union collaboration is also made more difficult because of the plural and fragmented union structures and the divisions which these create in many European countries, in contrast with the US system of majority union rule and exclusive bargaining rights. Ideological and, to a lesser extent, religious differences both within and between national labour movements in Europe present barriers to effective joint action. Thus the metalworkers' trade secretariat (IMF) refused to admit into its membership the major metalworkers' unions in France and Italy because of their communist affiliations. Not only may there be difficulties in securing full cooperation between union organisations but also in mobilising rank-and-file support in concerted action against the MNEs, particularly where good wages and conditions prevail. In this respect

> it is not easy to convince the average trade unionist that he or she is working for a multinational corporation and that it is in his or her long-term self-interest to support fellow workers abroad who are encountering difficulties with the same employer. (Bomers, 1976, p. 45)

Moreover, there are fundamental environmental disparities among countries as regards varying legal provisions and the extent to which they set the terms and conditions of employment rather than collective bargaining, together with differences in bargaining structures and industrial relations practices. All these present further obstacles to the extension of bargaining across national boundaries. For instance, even the more limited objective of the realisation of common contract termination dates throughout the operations of an MNE is complicated by the variety of existing bargaining arrangements which in a number of countries incorporate not only national or multi-plant systems but also local level bargaining with works councils (as in Germany) or shop steward committees (as in Britain). In fact, for the terms of a negotiated settlement between an international union and an MNE to be similarly implemented on a global basis it seems there would have to be a good deal more commonality in the economic, social and legal environments of the countries concerned than exists at present.

Future Prospects

It is apparent that there are a number of serious impediments to the attainment of transnational collective bargaining and the possibility of deploying an international trade union strategy which is an analogue of the organisational structure of the MNEs. This is particularly true at times of economic recession and rising unemployment which tend to trigger protectionist or nationalist reactions on the part of the union movements. These take the form of demands for the imposition of tariffs and quota restrictions on foreign production and the drive towards concerted, international union action becomes notably diminished. Nevertheless, although the available evidence does not support the view that multinational bargaining is, as yet, either widespread or generally imminent the potential for its development over the longer term is by no means negligible. It can be claimed that regional union groupings such as the European Metalworkers' Federation, a European-based trade union federation within the EEC,[11] are better placed to move towards bargaining with MNEs since they are more unitary in outlook and interest than are the world-wide trade secretariats: 'To involve unions from all over the world, including those both from developed and underdeveloped countries, is more likely to preclude bargaining than to further it' (Northrup and Rowan, 1979, p. 541).

We may conclude with Bomers (1976) that the future emergence of international industrial relations depends largely upon the extent of environmental similarity in which the actors find themselves. To the extent that the economic, social, legal and political similarities between countries increase, as with the intended harmonisation policies within the EEC, the instruments and procedures of industrial relations can become more congruent. So far the existing disparities, together with conflicting interests between trade unions in the main countries in which the MNEs are located, provide a major limitation on effective international collective bargaining.

Notes

1. As the OECD (1977) notes, this could still be the case even if the shift in the balance of power towards the MNE is only a phenomenon present in the minds of employee representatives, because the outcome of negotiations can be significantly influenced by psychological factors.

2. For an analysis of transfer pricing practices, see OECD (1979c). The reaction of one trade union body has been to state, uncompromisingly, that 'transfer pricing is quite simply robbery' (Postal International Trade Secretariat, quoted in Weinburg, 1978, p. 35).

3. It is possible that despite the formal management structure requiring a delegation of organisational responsibilities there could still be quasi-control by group headquarters since 'functional specialists [at head office], whose role was intended to be advisory, could gradually attract to themselves powers of decision-making in their areas' (OECD, 1977, p. 10).

4. Thus one research study found that management of US-owned MNEs in the metal industry claimed the existence of broad, local autonomy on industrial relations but at the same time cautioned that cost-effective decisions or new initiatives had to be cleared at corporate headquarters (ILO, 1977).

5. 'The incidence of strikes is usually expected to increase with the size of plant. In large plants relations between workers and management are less personal than in small plants and thus more disputes can occur. There are also more interactions among work groups in large plants and therefore more bases for stoppages' (Caves, 1980, p. 144); see also Prais (1978, 1982).

6. In labour-intensive industries because total costs will be more sensitive to increases in labour costs a given wage claim is hypothesised to meet with greater employer resistance – possibly precipitating strike action.

7. Most ITSs were established before 1914 in order to promote international trade union understanding and for the exchange of experience at industry level. Until the growth of the MNEs, however, they played only a relatively minor role.

8. Union publicists such as Levinson (1972) may have overstated their case in claiming the importance in specific disputes of the coordinating role of the ITSs across national boundaries. On the other hand, management-oriented interests tend to downgrade the potential for international bargaining capabilities (Weinburg, 1978).

9. A further possible step in the future, once this objective had been attained, could then be to press for international workers' participation in multinational management within such areas as investment planning and production allocation policies.

10. For EEC countries the 'Vredeling' directive aims to ensure that MNEs inform and consult their employees on a wide range of policies.

11. This is an industrial committee of the European Trade Union Confederation (ETUC) formed in 1973 to play a direct role in confronting the multinationals.

Further Reading

A useful symposium is the volume edited by Flanagan and Weber (1974). More theoretical aspects of MNEs are dealt with in Enderwick (1982), and their relative strike incidence in Enderwick and Buckley (1982). The most comprehensive empirical discussion of union collective bargaining attempts with MNEs is Northrup and Rowan (1979).

9 INDUSTRIAL RELATIONS IN DEVELOPING COUNTRIES

Developing or Third World societies – defined in terms of their *per capita* GDP levels together with growing social and political modernisation – are located predominantly in Africa, Asia (excluding Japan and the Middle East) and Latin America. Despite the generic, catch-all category of the term 'developing' countries[1] it is by no means easy to generalise about them with respect to their industrial relations. Within the Latin American region, for instance, Cordova (1980) has distinguished four separate groups of countries. First, there are those such as Mexico and Venezuela whose industrial relations and collective bargaining practices are highly developed; second is a group where the institutional framework of industrial relations, although similarly long-established, has been undergoing profound change (e.g. Argentina,[2] Chile, Uruguay); third, there are those such as Ecuador and Honduras in which collective labour relations are still very much in a formative stage, with workers' and employers' organisations being relatively weak. Fourth, a single-country category is that of Brazil in which collective bargaining is of somewhat less importance, and legal enactment has played a dominant role – partly in order to keep industrial relations under government control and direction.

Likewise, for purposes of comparative analysis, in the African continent the countries of tropical Africa display a greater similarity of features than either North Africa, because of a different cultural development, or the settler countries of South Africa and pre-independence Rhodesia with different forms of industrialisation and political control. Furthermore, in examining African as opposed to Latin American industrial relations a different weight has to be accorded to factors such as the colonial legacy, the associated racial stratification of employment and the post-independence Africanisation programmes. Most of the Latin American republics acquired independence at a much earlier date, and racial problems are less complex than those in Africa (Lucena, 1980). Certainly, trade union development in Latin America was of a different order from that in Africa and Asia for much of its formative period in the late nineteenth century. The most important distinction is the effects of (later) colonial control in the latter two continents and therefore the inevitable overlap between the economic and political activities of the labour movement (Busch, 1983).

Major Characteristics

More generally, as Hyman (1979) has noted, it is often difficult to attempt to translate the perspectives of westernised industrial relations to the developing countries. For instance, the proportion of the population engaged in formal wage-earning employment in some African states is less than 10 per cent of the economically-active population,[3] as in Nigeria, where agriculture still provides nearly two-thirds of all employment. In Kenya and Zambia the proportion is notably higher (yet still less than one-third of the total labour force), probably a consequence of an earlier start as a wage economy under colonial rule. Among East African countries at the time of independence Kenya had a larger industrial sector than either Uganda or Tanganyika due to the market provided by a larger immigrant population, a more developed infrastructure and access to the protected East African market for manufactured goods (Sandbrook, 1975). Even in Kenya, however, in 1972 less than 20 per cent of the labour force was employed in the 'modern' sector, including urban employment, large-scale farming and the public services, whilst the rest were absorbed in small-scale subsistence agriculture together with the rural and informal sectors. As a result 'the wage earners in the modern sector, where wage rates and conditions of employment are subject to collective bargaining, form a small minority of all those actively engaged in productive employment' (Henley, 1978, p. 226). In the African countries, therefore, because of this dual structure the purview of industrial relations in the usual sense of the term is very much a minority interest to the country as a whole, although the wage-earning sectors themselves are of crucial significance to the economy, and wage-earners are a forceful interest group. Similarly, in India the industrial relations framework is relevant principally to wage-earning labour in the urban and modern sector of the economy, covering no more than 3–4 per cent of the total labour force (Krishnan, 1981).

A consequence of the narrowness of the wage-earning base upon which the industrial relations system is typically built is the limited extent of trade unionism for, as Allen has observed in relation to Africa,

> Trade unionism is collective action by people who sell their labour power in order to protect and improve their living standards. The necessary condition for trade unionism, therefore, is the buying and selling of labour power on a significant scale, which in turn is the core element of industrialisation. But this in Africa has proceeded slowly. (Allen, 1969, p. 290)

Arrighi and Saul (1968), in fact, developed a 'labour aristocracy' thesis: that in African countries there is a privileged minority of urbanised, unionised wage-workers whose economic advantages have been secured not at the expense of the ruling élite but from the urban sub-proletariat, the peasant class in that part of the economy geared to subsistence agriculture, small-scale traders and the unemployed. In the ensuing debate which was generated considerable scepticism has been expressed as to the plausibility and implications of this thesis, especially the assumption of a complementarity of economic interest between urbanised workers (particularly the skilled sector) and the professional and managerial groups. It was pointed out that, for wage-workers, relative earnings are not the same as relative standards of living since their differential pay advantage is markedly reduced because of the higher cost of living in urban as compared with rural areas. Also, there is clear evidence of interdependence of the economic interests of wage-earners in the formal sector of the economy via their consumption of the goods produced by craftsmen and petty-traders in the informal sector. In contrast, patterns of managerial consumption mostly favour goods which are factory-produced and often imported.

According to Nicol a background factor also generally missing in Africa has been an underpinning class-conscious proletariat. In this respect he sees one difference between a country such as Uganda and some Western European countries as being that in the latter

> trade unionism grew from the fertile soil of a class-conscious, exploited proletariat, dependent on wage-earning for survival. In Uganda these conditions have not existed and the trade union movement has had itself to foster the lateral class-consciousness previously obscured in the clan and tribal system [uniting workers across tribal, ethnic or caste divisions]. (Nicol, 1979, p. 303)

Again, unlike Europe in the nineteenth and early twentieth centuries, most unions in the newer African states have not been confronted to the same extent with major political deprivations, at least in terms of basic political voting and citizenship rights. Moreover, the major driving-force of economic development in the new countries has been the state rather than a growing bourgeoisie, which may help to explain why in most African (and Asian) countries the unions have become increasingly limited since independence to a more restricted industrial, as opposed to an earlier and broader political, role: 'Where political actions are engaged in, these are usually limited to fairly narrow, industrially-related needs' (Kassalow, 1978b). There are, of course, exceptions such as India until recently, and some Latin American states where politically-oriented unionism is more important. In India, both organisationally and ideologically, the principal wings of the labour movement have been political in nature, part of a broader political movement with an implicit reconciliation of trade union and political goals within one framework (Krishnan, 1981).

As Lipset (1961) has noted, in comparing labour movements as betweeen economically developed and developing countries, one would expect to find the chief explanations for differences in production processes and levels of technology, in the nature of class relationships and in political structures. Undoubtedly a number of factors within developing societies may inhibit the emergence of western-type trade unions and collective bargaining, including a low degree of industrialisation, the high level of illiteracy and lack of basic education, as well as instability of the workforce and a lack of organisational resources. A further prerequisite for the expansion of collective bargaining relates to the organisation of undertakings as production units of a certain size since in medium- and large-scale undertakings 'the higher concentration of the workforce and greater complexity of functions has inevitably resulted in a need to lay down ground-rules best adapted to the circumstances of each undertaking' (Cordova, 1980, p. 23). However, large production units are by no means absent from the modern enclaves of developing economies since the character of late development brings with it the sudden appearance of large-scale industrial enterprises (often MNE subsidiaries) which are conducive to the formation of (enterprise-based) unions (Kassalow, 1978b).

The Role of Government

One of the most distinctive features of developing countries concerns the role of government which has increasingly sought (varying degrees of) control over the trade union movement and its activities in industrial relations – not least, to protect the interests of foreign capital. The governments of these countries play a much more active and interventionist role in industrial relations than was traditionally the case in the USA and some Western European countries. This role is strengthened by the fact that policies are guided by the requirements of national, growth-oriented development plans, and the state itself is much more central to the development process. It may therefore have been largely inevitable in many late-developing countries that the functions of unions 'should be defined and re-defined according to new needs and roles' (Kassalow, 1978b, p. 8). Thus in Zambia since independence, as Gertzel (1979) has shown, there has been a progressive subordination of the trade unions to government along with the extension of governmental regulation of labour–management relations. In French-speaking West Africa 'efforts by governments to control all aspects of national life through single political parties and socio-economic development plans have narrowed the scope of industrial relations' (Martens, 1979, p. 29). In Malaysia government policy has been similarly to subordinate the labour movement and 'guide' trade unionism to broader considerations of national economic development as defined by the ruling élite. In both Singapore and South Korea the primary actor in the industrial relations scene is the government itself.

Nevertheless, it does not follow as a result of these requirements that unions in the new African and Asian countries can be considered simply as 'administrative arms of the state' – although in a country such as Singapore, where since 1968 the assigned role of the labour movement has been to help preserve industrial peace and explain the ruling élite's policies and programmes to its members, they have come close to it. Equally, although they are certainly more restricted in their economic activities than their counterparts in western market economies, they have managed to perform some of the bargaining functions and pressure-group activities usually regarded as essential for the functioning of an independent union role (Sandbrook and Cohen, 1975). Gray (1980) argues that in Ghana, in particular, the bargaining achievements of the labour movement are significant, and collective agreements have produced fundamental changes in the country's national wage structure. Some observers such as Kassalow (1978b) view unions in developing countries as being 'intermediate forms' between the polar types of state-controlled unions on the one hand, and sectional interest group representatives within a pluralist society on the other.

Governments in Third World countries maintain that industrial relations have a direct bearing on the development process since industrial conflict may adversely affect productivity and exports, particularly in fragile economies highly dependent on perhaps a single primary commodity (countries such as Ghana and Zambia), or as in South Korea, reliant upon the production of labour-intensive manufactured goods targeted for export. Also, strikes are not likely to provide a climate which is conducive to the welfare of capital and the attracting of foreign investment, especially in import-substituting manufactures (an important engine of economic development), which have become identified with the 'national' interest. In the case of Ghana it has been stated that

> Before 1957, labour unrest was a valuable tool in the struggle for independence; later it was perceived as a threat to domestic order, productivity and the willingness of foreign governments and companies to invest in Ghana. (Gray, 1980, p. 179)

Similarly, a development plan (such as that in Kenya) which calls for an altered form of income distribution or requires wage restraint in the interests of higher savings and investment, together with the achievement of greater competitiveness in international markets, has a greater probability of success if trade unions are supportive or at least acquiescent (Gladstone, 1978). Therefore, in Kenya strike activity in practice became illegal with disputes being subjected to compulsory arbitration. Also, the process of collective bargaining can be considered trilateral – as opposed to bilateral in the pre-independence period – in that, as regards wage-fixing, it has to satisfy the objectives not only of management and the union but also the government. Indeed, in many Third World countries it has been said that strikes 'were considered a luxury that a developing society could not afford . . . thus industrial action and unfettered collective bargaining as traditional trade union instruments could no longer be countenanced' (Gladstone, 1980, p. 56). In these countries the predominant position of the government as the biggest single employer often employing more than half the total number of wage-earners, in French West Africa for instance, also gave the state an additional interest in regulating industrial relations processes and outcomes.

For all these reasons it has become usual to delineate a certain duality of trade union functions within developing nations – on the one hand defending and promoting the interests of their own members, yet at the same time being required to contribute to the national development effort. However, the role of early trade unionism in these countries during the pre-independence era – particularly in Africa – was markedly different in character and requires some examination.

Colonial Period

Given the very limited industrialisation during the colonial period in the first half of the twentieth century early and indigenous union organisations in British and French African territories tended to emerge mainly among groups of permanent employees (whose bargaining power was greater) including mineworkers, lower grade civil servants and those within major public enterprises such as the docks and railways. Reductions in real wages as a result of rising prices led both to spontaneous protests and the embryonic growth of trade unions which the colonial governments interpreted, especially for their own employees, as being politically subversive activities and rebellion. In consequence, 'the early history of African trade unions . . . became as much a reaction to imperial rule [to which workers attributed their grievances] as a reaction to working conditions' (Damachi *et al.*, 1979, p. 3). In contrast, to the position in, say, nineteenth-century Europe, employers in Africa were both foreign and socially different and the main employer was in fact the government. In Kenya the struggle against the employer necessarily involved the unions in political activities since the employers were also associated with the ruling power (Iwuji, 1979). Ultimately in that country it became increasingly difficult to differentiate between trade union activities and African independence activities, although this was much less true of Ugandan unions whose part in the pre-independence struggle was peripheral rather than central. Similarly, in Singapore, Malaya and India anti-colonialism seems to have been an important motivating factor for certain sectors of the labour movement. (In the absence of a significant number of skilled craftsmen in the early stages of industrialisation it is also not surprising – as Kilby (1967) has noted – that unions were initially organised on the basis of the place of employment, unlike the economically strong craft-protective unionism found in nineteenth-century Britain and USA.)

Although the colonial governments in Africa originally wished to ensure that the labour force lacked leverage and openly opposed the development of a trade union movement – fearing its political potential especially – over the course of time (particularly after World

War II) government policy shifted significantly, towards the fostering of trade unions patterned on the British or French models, albeit within a limited and well-controlled sphere of activity (Muir and Brown, 1978). On the basis of his research in Tanzania, Bienfeld (1979) interprets the rapid expansion of trade unionism under government tutelage as an institutional response to changes which were occurring in the processes of colonial production. To meet world competitive pressures more efficient patterns of employment practices and labour utilisation were required. These included a more skilled, predictable and stable labour force in place of a classic colonial pattern of part-time wage-earning (the migrant labour system having been encouraged by the colonial authorities as the basis of a 'cheap labour' policy), which in turn required new forms of labour control:

> The new order required more regular, more settled, more productive labour compatible with greater degrees of mechanisation, with more complex labour processes, and with a demand for increased security of supply. (Bienfeld, 1979, p. 564)

Also, in India a policy of outright opposition to union recognition was revised to some extent in the modernised sector of the economy because of the growing complexity of business organisation: 'The search for improved productivity led to the modernising of equipment, accentuated the shortage of skills and added to the responsibility for careful handling of costly machines' (Krishnan, 1981, p. 242).

A further and related consideration in the African territories was an increasing appreciation on the part of the colonial authorities of the benefits of institutionalising labour protest along trade union lines as a mechanism of social control.[4] They had come to learn that 'nothing was more inimical to their interests than spontaneous, guerilla-like actions of workers who were beyond their control and out of the hands of their own leaders' (Damachi *et al.*, 1979, p. 6). Hence, the policy became one of encouraging union development whilst at the same time attempting to steer it in the direction of 'economistic' objectives and away from political involvement which could provide a serious threat to the colonial powers (i.e. the requirement was for union development to be narrow, sectional, and therefore basically controllable.)[5] Therefore, unlike the situation in Europe during the early period of industrialisation where workers had a long and difficult struggle for recognition, in most African countries (though not all) the place of unions was more quickly recognised within a more compressed timeframe, to suit the administrative convenience of the colonial powers. Similar considerations appear to have been paramount in some Asian countries as well. In Ceylon and Malaya the objective was to foster 'responsible' unions which would assist the colonial administrators to maintain labour peace without becoming involved in political activities (Fong and Cheng, 1978).

An effort towards containing overt industrial conflict was also apparent in some of the Latin American countries. In Chile and Argentina the labour movement was politicised from the start, partly under the influence of European immigrants, with worker demands for improved wages and hours at the turn of the century escalating into calls for the abolition of capitalism and the establishment of a more egalitarian, socialist regime. In Chile,

> the creation of an institutionalised industrial relations system represented a response by governing élites to the conflict associated with increasing labour activism in the nineteenth and early twentieth centuries in order to preserve the capitalist system by institutionalising the peaceful resolution of industrial conflict. (Loveman, 1981, p. 93)

More generally in the Latin American region, state regulation of industrial relations, as embodied in the labour codes which were promulgated during the inter-war period setting out detailed regulation of conditions of work and labour union activity, was based upon the assumption that labour relations were a manifestation of class struggle which if not controlled would have repercussions on society as a whole. The purpose of the codes was

> to coopt and assimilate labour . . . [which] had become politically dangerous [and] incorporate it into the state structure. It was a means of keeping the unions from launching radical challenges to the system; it helped keep them dependent, and tied to the state. (Wiarda, 1978, p. 14)

According to Cordova (1980), however, the codes are now becoming obsolete and their capacity to set adequate standards has diminished over the course of time. This is one reason why collective bargaining has developed considerably in recent years, enabling changing conditions affecting labour to be dealt with more flexibly. In the Latin American countries, although industry-wide bargaining is common in

Argentina and Brazil, there are nevertheless many enterprise unions. This in itself is a reflection not only of economic structure, in terms of the fragmentation and concentration of the labour force in a few large enterprises, but also, in part, of employer and state action. There was mistrust of national union organisations because of their potential for extensive politicisation and the possibility of their calling general strikes (Cella and Treu, 1982).

Post-Independence Period

Once the African and Asian territories had achieved independence from colonial rule a change took place in the attitude of government towards trade unions which were soon accorded a new and more closely-prescribed role. In a comparative study of industrial relations in Kenya and Malaysia, Henley (1980) discerns three parallel trends within the two countries. There has been continuity in labour policies from the colonial period in assigning a major role to the registrar of trade unions (who would regulate their formation and supervise their activities with a view to ensuring a compliant union movement), together with an industrial court as a form of compulsory or semi-compulsory arbitration to settle disputes. Secondly, there is a notable willingness on the part of government to subordinate the interests of labour to national economic development plans. Finally, he notes a weakening of the labour movements in both countries as a result of 'communalism' (segmentation into socially-isolated population groupings within an ethnically heterogeneous society).[6] Yet despite these similarities there is one important difference: in Kenya there were close links between the labour movement and a faction of the political leadership. These links facilitated a government policy of collaboration and incorporation of labour leaders into a web of state patronage (which was also to occur in Zambia), channelling the labour movement towards economistic objectives. In return for union agreement to limitations on the right to strike, for instance, the unions secured legislative institutional support in the form of a compulsory check-off system (deduction of union dues at source). The check-off was to prove very important for their stability and growth since one of the most serious problems faced by unions in a developing country is inadequate financing. By contrast, in Malaysia a government-union link never developed to the same extent, mainly as a result of the labour movement's early association with the Malayan Communist Party. In the consequent absence of state patronage and incorporation of the labour movement the legal framework is much more elaborate and detailed.

In many of the ex-colonial states a restructuring and consolidation of trade union organisations was also entailed. In Zambia the government actively promoted a policy of one union for each industry. Kenya, however, is unusual in this respect in that the labour movement was remodelled towards industrial unionism[7] prior to independence. This was primarily a consequence of the accelerated development of the union movement and its early recognition by employers as a result of the important and influential role which it had played during the State of Emergency at the time of the Mau Mau uprising in the 1950s. Elsewhere, changes in trade union structure and a greater measure of centralisation took place during the post-colonial period. In Ghana in the immediate post-independence phase the government wished to enlist the cooperation of the unions in accelerating the process of economic development and modernisation. But the fragmented and enterprise-oriented nature of existing trade unions was not conducive to the attainment of a high degree of governmental regulation and influence and might also have threatened the development effort by exacerbating labour unrest via inter-union disputes. As a result 24 industrial-type unions (later reduced to 10) were created by legislation from the existing 85 small and fragmented ones (Kraus, 1979). Similarly, although at a later date, the labour movement in the Sudan – which had also been characterised by a preponderance of small, amorphous and unstable enterprise unions – was reconstructed in order to create bigger, and therefore more viable, unions. Between 1971 and 1974 the proportion of large unions (with more than 10,000 members) increased from 1 to 30 per cent and small unions (with below 200 members), which had accounted for three-quarters of the total number of unions in 1971, had been eliminated three years later (Ali Taha, 1982).

A contrasting development, however, to such consolidated structures is again the case of Malaysia. So anxious was the government to prevent a resurgence of communist influence and the use of unions for political action[8] that the Trade Union Ordinance 1959 limited the growth of widely-drawn industrial unions (and horizontally-based federations) by restricting union organisation to that of 'similar occupations or trades'. One consequence of limiting union size has been the development of a multiplicity of 'peanut' unions, confined to organising the workers of a single employer (Henley, 1980). Also, in India where the ideological base of the labour movement is still strong a multiplicity of unions continues to exist (more than 5000 in 1975) and little attempt has been made to integrate and consolidate them.

As well as reducing trade union multiplicity in the newer African countries, a further government restructuring measure has been the creation of a strong and unified central union organisation – most recently in Nigeria in 1978 – which would have extensive powers over its affiliates as well as close relations with the government or ruling party. The Ghana TUC was established by law as the single central organisation to which all unions had to affiliate, and in post-independence Zambia trade union power was centralised through the newly constituted Zambia Congress of Trade Unions (ZCTU). In Kenya the Central Organisation of Trade Unions (COTU) has the appointment of its leaders subjected to government ratification and a state official sits on its governing council. All these government measures (designed to unify, reorganise and rationalise trade unions) have had important implications for the collective bargaining process which will now be considered.

Collective Bargaining

The creation of more effective unions as a result of the reduction in their multiplicity, clearer lines of industrial and sectoral demarcation, along with associated measures such as check-off arrangements (and in some countries an obligation upon employers to negotiate) have aided and promoted collective bargaining. In Ghana the guaranteed check-off also helped promote less conflictual union-management relations since the control which the government maintained over certification of unions for bargaining purposes relieved employers of the obligation to deal with rival organisations claiming to represent their workers (Gray, 1980). At the same time it has to be recognised that the constraints placed on trade union activities necessarily affect and restrict the free exercise of bargaining rights. In Kenya wage agreements made by independent collective bargaining – highly centralised at national level with little scope for workplace bargaining – have required the approval of the government-appointed Industrial Court. But one important difference in relation to wage determination as between the Anglophone and Francophone countries in Africa, reflecting their colonial heritage and transplantation of the metropolitan framework, is that in the latter countries (Senegal, Guinea, Benin, etc.) government-established minima set the bench-mark for wages throughout the country and are of considerable importance. In consequence 'the unions' role becomes not that of a bargaining adversary, but an institution trying to influence government action [and] wage-setting is usually a process subject to political pressures and considerations' (Damachi *et al.*, 1979, p. 12). By contrast, in the former British colonies such as Ghana there has been more extensive reliance upon voluntary collective bargaining for workers in the private sector. Exceptions exist, however, such as Nigeria where government-appointed commissions have been a major mechanism for fixing wages in the unionised sector, partly because of the actions of government itself which, by failing to fix the wages of its own employees by collective bargaining, undermined the bargaining potential within the private sector.[9]

Restrictions on strike activity, where – as in Zambia and Tanzania – the mandatory conciliation procedure makes legal strike action difficult if not impossible, also weaken the unions in their dealings with employers. Similar limitations on strikes apply in Singapore and, as an additional measure designed to attract foreign investment, the rights and prerogatives of management have been clearly asserted by means of legislation. These include the setting of ceilings on fringe benefits and restricting the number of negotiable issues to exclude items such as employee transfer, dismissal, lay-off and work assignments.

The role of employers in industrial relations within African and Asian countries has been variable and may be differentiated partly on the basis of company size together with the relative importance of either indigenous or foreign-owned firms. In both Nigeria and Ghana prior to independence small firms were reluctant to recognise unions and engage in collective bargaining whereas the larger, expatriate firms (and more latterly MNEs) were more willing to do so. Not only could these firms afford to pay relatively high wages but they also found the process of collective bargaining the easiest and most efficient way of dealing with the complexities of their industrial relations (Kilby, 1967). In Ghana a more recent study found that although indigenous private employers were generally hostile to unions, preferring to deal with their own employees on a paternalist basis, most foreign private employers considered trade unionism to be an advantage since it was easier to deal with workers as an organised body than as individuals, that is to say, the union functioned as 'the transmission belt between the employers and the workers' (Damachi, 1976, p. 31).

Nevertheless, foreign-owned firms were not always prepared to form employers' organisations – in Nigeria, for example, the evidence suggests that they preferred to retain maximum individual autonomy in labour matters. Rather, in many of these countries employers' organisations developed primarily in response to the growth of trade unions (or in Nigeria as a result of government request). At the present time in Kenya, unions in their bargaining relationships confront well-organised employers combined into an association for industrial relations purposes, with a central national employers' federation (FKE) coordinating employer relations with unions and government. This body conducts negotiations on behalf of many of its members and represents them in almost all cases which come before the Industrial Court. It also provides general advice for its membership on labour relations matters and encourages collective bargaining to be conducted on an industry-wide basis. Finally, on the Asian continent in India, in those industries where employers are relatively well organised for industrial relations purposes (such as textiles which employs the bulk of the industrial labour force) three distinct sub-categories of employers' associations may be distinguished: first, those which provide legal and other services and function as a common forum for discussion of mutual interests; secondly, associations which in addition to supplying advice and expertise for their members also provide a pool of personnel officers who act as trouble-shooters; and third, associations which actually negotiate with unions (Krishnan, 1981).

Summary

In this chapter we have shown that because industrial relations is presumed to have a direct bearing on the development process, the role of the state has become notably obtrusive and pervading. In a number of developing countries governments have sought to influence both the role and structure of unions often by means of trade-offs whereby, in return for conforming to the requirements of the development effort and limiting their independence of action, benefits such as a mandatory union shop and/or check-off arrangement would be granted. One result of this has been that in African and most Asian countries the labour movement is no longer committed to politics and political parties to the extent that was evident at the time of independence. Indeed, in many of the newly-independent states an important requirement has been that the trade union movement should not contribute a possible source of political opposition to the ruling élite and that 'its orientation be supportive of official policies of economic growth and national development (rather than defence and promotion of the immediate interests of the wage-earning membership)' (Gladstone, 1980, p. 58).

In Kenya the labour movement would appear to correspond most closely to a variant of 'business unionism' (emphasising economically/industrially-oriented objectives) since this was all that remained feasible given the nature of the environment which it confronts. Even within this more limited area of operations further restrictions in the form of incomes policy requirements on union activities have also been introduced, that is to say, government control was extended from the political to the economic sphere. At the same time the efficacy of these government measures remains open to question. Initial governmental efforts to reorganise, incorporate and limit the scope of union actions were challenged in Tanzania and to some extent in Ghana, and in French-speaking West Africa led to general strikes in Benin and the Upper Volta. Although the extent of union independence and autonomy differs considerably within the African continent, even in those countries where government control is maximal and national union federations and individual union leaders[10] have been responsive to government requirements, the rank and file at local level have not always been so accommodating. Grass-roots militancy has persisted, and strikes, although often technically illegal and therefore frequently of short duration, have still taken place to draw attention to sectional grievances.

A further consequence of extensive government influence and regulation relates to a certain reorientation of trade union functions in some of these countries. Where its collective bargaining role has been considerably diminished the union movement has sought to broaden its range of interests and define new functions. As an adjunct to their more usual activities, trade unions in Ghana and Kenya operate their own business enterprises such as consumer cooperatives and banking services. The objective was partly to become more directly involved in their countries' development efforts but also to retain membership and subscriptions by continuing to provide a range of services. Probably the most notable example is Singapore where the central trade union body has created an extensive range of insurance, transport, dental and consumer cooperatives.

From a comparative perspective some observers such as Gray (1980) see certain similarities between the institutional development of organised labour and industrial relations in a Third World nation like Ghana and that in the United States. In both countries unions have become increasingly bureaucratic, they have come to agree with employers on general areas of conflict resolution in industrial relations and government legislation has been vital for union recognition and development. No doubt formal recognition of, and government support for, union organisation in African countries has strengthened the process of bureaucratisation both within unions and in the entire system of industrial relations (Damachi *et al.*, 1979). But, more generally, we have shown that there are important and overriding differences between newly developing and western countries in their industrial relations practices, not least in the attempts of the trade unions in the former to remain viable, independent organisations – and sometimes even to survive.

Also, although there are many parallels between developing countries themselves in their industrial relations, consequent upon the drive towards industrialisation, it is important not to overstate the degree of homogeneity among them since there are also significant differences. These reflect not only differential levels of attained development but also appear to be rooted in the particular and specific historical circumstances of the various countries. Certainly, organisational forms cannot be separated from the total environment in which they operate and an examination of developing countries highlights, even more clearly than in industrialised western countries, the vital importance of the nature of the political economy and wider societal influences in shaping the salient features of industrial relations systems.

Notes

1. In fact, there is marked dispersion in *per capita* income and other characteristics as between Third World countries themselves.

2. After the military *coup* of 1976 the main unions were placed under military control, strikes banned and hundreds of trade unionists were imprisoned or 'disappeared'.

3. However, because of a high rate of labour turnover as a result of the links with the peasant economy (especially marked during the colonial period to the end of the 1950s) whereby many employees were migrant or 'target' workers who would subsequently return to village life, many more workers than the average number in employment at a particular time would have experience of wage-earning.

4. The Chief Inspector of Labour in the Gold Coast (later Ghana) observed:

> It is much better to recognise a reputable and responsible organisation through whom workers can voice their grievances than to allow those grievances to remain unventilated. If such recognition is made there will be less danger from the agitators and secret societies. (Quoted in Kraus, 1979, p. 113)

5. As well as legitimising trade unions, legislation could be an important instrument of control – for instance, by way of registration and de-registration provisions for particular unions.

6. In Zambia, in contrast, the organised labour movement – founded upon perceptions of common interest as industrial labour – appears to have been characterised for the most part by an absence of ethnic cleavages (Gertzel, 1979).

7. Thereby also forestalling the possible growth of politicised general unions.

8. In the post-World War II period strikes had been used not 'to wrest economic concessions from employers but to demonstrate the power and supremacy of the Malayan Communist Party' (Fong and Cheng, 1978, p. 34).

9. Kilby (1967) interprets the causes of the failure of collective bargaining in the public sector as including union leadership rivalries, status-conscious employer representatives and disagreements over the scope of bargaining.

10. Sandbrook (1975) maintains that where union leaders are dependent on financial and personal support from the rank and file they have pressed workers' demands on a militant basis.

Further Reading

A useful general survey on unions, growth and development (particularly in relation to the African continent) is Gladstone (1980); the earlier studies on Africa by Allen (1971) are also well worth reading. There is a very readable short symposium on unions in developing economies, including Asian countries, edited by Kassalow and Damachi (1978). A good case-study of the post-independence union movement in Kenya and its relations with the state is Sandbrook (1975); and a recent study of Nigeria is Ubeku (1983).

10 AN OVERVIEW OF COMPARATIVE INDUSTRIAL RELATIONS

In the preceding nine chapters we have considered industrial relations from the standpoint of cross-national comparisons within a number of mainstream areas. For the most part there has been a concentration upon advanced market-type economies since, although the institutions and arrangements differ across a wide amplitude in the various countries, nevertheless there are sufficient common elements of importance (in terms of a basic similarity of political and economic backgrounds, as well as a comparable state of economic development) to permit a meaningful comparative examination of the structures, procedures and problems involved. Thus, for example, as 'between France and the United States the differences are enough to make the studies intriguing, yet the similarities enough to make the comparisons valid and significant' (Lorwin, 1957, p. 26). In contrast to western countries, in communist systems a different conceptualisation of the trade union role is required, and in African nations there has been an overriding influence on the employment relationship of a different cultural context and traditions.

From a methodological viewpoint the reason for comparing countries which are similar, but not identical, in economic and social structure is to reduce and control for the number of possible influencing conditions in order to make the investigation more manageable. A basic distinction is between conditions to be treated as parameters (assumed not to vary) and conditions treated as operative variables. (By making variables into parameters and thereby holding constant many of the potential determinants, the influence of a few conditions can be isolated and examined.) If two or more countries which are chosen for comparison differ in almost every respect then the researcher has to consider all sources of difference as being operative variables. Whereas if the countries have some important conditions in common, these common elements can be treated as parameters and attention focused on the operation of the other variables.

> The more similar two or more societies are with respect to crucial variables, in short, the better able is the investigator to isolate and

> analyse the influence of the variables that might account for the differences he wishes to explain. (Smelser, 1967, p. 18)

However, even within the more restricted ambit of a comparable set of countries there may be a danger of over-generalisation from comparative investigation and the temptation to accord the conclusions from a limited number of cases the status of universal propositions. One critic has characterised comparative industrial relations as being 'an area abounding with pretensions and superficial generalisations' (Worm, 1982, p. 273). Thus, although broad European-USA comparisons, for instance, are often adduced, Europe itself is by no means a homogeneous entity. Not only are there important differences between France and Germany, for example, but also the similarities implied in the familiar Franco-Italian grouping ignore the (increasingly significant) contrasts between employer attitudes, the strategies of the Communist Party and the patterns of industrial conflict in these two countries. The emphasis may therefore need to be directed towards more closely-focused comparisons – although it is of course true that, despite the importance of exceptions and qualifications, 'if comparison is to be essayed, some crudity and seeming dogmatism must be the ransom of synthesis and brevity' (Lorwin, 1957, p. 27).

Comparative analysis, according to Shalev (1981), is most successful when carried out on the basis of a close familiarity with the national characteristics of industrial relations systems and their historical role since misinterpretations can abound in the absence of an understanding of the economic, political and social context of industrial relations within a given country. It can be argued, therefore, that much of the debate concerning co-determination in Germany is unintelligible when viewed from the perspectives of British or US industrial relations and abstracted from the historical context of the German labour movement or contemporary neo-corporatist thought in that country. Similarly, in the case of Japan it has been said that many of the views expressed in the English-language literature lack balance since they tend to be over-dominated by a preoccupation with social traditions and the unique cultural heritages of pre-industrial Japanese society (Shirai and Shimada, 1978). For France outside observers have tended to consider trade unions (and industrial relations) as some sort of aberration – 'weak, ineffective, chaotic and even tragic' (Hough, 1981, p. 43). The emphasis placed upon the 'uniqueness' of French industrial relations according to Reynaud – and despite the developments which have been taking place in recent years – has also meant that too little attention has been paid to a comparative orientation, which he considers to be the most useful direction in which future research in that country can proceed:

> The political shift of the Catholic Church and its organizations should be studied comparatively in Quebec, Italy and France. The new patterns and the new results of conflict deserve a general review, but special comparison should be made between Italy and France. The emphasis on procedural instead of substantive content in the agreements should induce French scholars to scrutinize British experience closely. For the role played by 'working conditions' as an issue in industrial relations, attention should be given to Norway and Sweden. (Reynaud, 1981, p. 265)

At the same time, however, not all observers would subscribe to the view that elements of cultural bias in comparative studies can best be reduced if the investigator is himself a national of the particular country under examination. Marsden (1978) has pointed to a possible danger in relying on research done by nationals in various countries that the resulting comparisons may reflect differences in conceptual approaches as much as actual empirical differences in the industrial relations systems of the various countries themselves. By way of illustration he cites the different conceptions of the nature of collective bargaining which exist among industrial relations researchers from diverse backgrounds. In Germany and France collective bargaining tends to be contrasted with unilateral employer regulation, whereas in Britain it has often been conceived as a collective form of individual bargaining.

In surveying the literature of comparative industrial relations it is apparent that a number of conceptual frameworks may be utilised in order to aid systematic analysis and identify the core elements of complex processes. Littler (1983) relates the patterns of industrial relations to the phases of capitalistic development, a basic distinction being that between competitive and monopoly capitalism. Under competitive capitalism collective bargaining tends to be conducted at national or regional level whereas monopoly capitalism is associated with bureaucratic work organisation, firm-specific internal labour markets and the conduct of collective bargaining at the enterprise level. He shows that for Japan, the USA, Germany and Britain from the 1880s to the 1930s there were certain historical commonalities in the form of a 'transition from a period of small family-based enterprises within highly competitive product markets to one of large, bureaucratised corporations with varying degrees of monopoly power' (p. 180). Nevertheless, because the transition in the various countries occurred under differing economic and social conditions, with differences in the timing of the industrialisation process as well as other historical particularities – all of which exerted a powerful influence – no simple, invariable relationship between phases of capitalism and industrial relations arrangements in any given country can be discerned.

As we saw in Chapter 1, an earlier perspective maintained that the common technological and market features of societies consequent upon the drive towards industrialisation would gradually tend to bring industrial relations systems closer to each other. Moreover, it was implied that the systems would attain a certain autonomy and coherence, becoming largely independent of their broader social milieux (Rose, 1979). Empirical evidence would suggest that certainly in the case of the important metalworking industry across a sample of five countries (Derber, 1976) there are a number of characteristics shared by all the industrial relations systems, including both substantive and procedural rules, which can be attributed to the common technological-economic character of the metalworking industry itself. At the same time, however, significant inter-country differences within this industry can also be discerned – especially in the distribution of power – which seem to be primarily a function of differences in national environments. Thus

> the balance of power in the industrial relations systems of Australia, Britain and the United States would appear to be consistent with the power distribution in the greater society. Labour's dominant role in Israeli metalworking is matched and most probably produced by the economic and political dominance of organised labour in the nation. Similarly employer dominance in Japan's enterprise system seems compatible with their economic and political dominance in the nation. (Derber, 1976, p. 26)

Clearly, the influence of the national environment is deeply embedded within a country's industrial relations methods and practices, its institutions and procedures. Indeed, not only are the contours of industrial relations systems shaped to an important degree by contextual variables but, as has been shown, changes and adaptations have occurred within the systems so as to accommodate the shifts in market and social forces, as well as in political circumstances which have taken place.

In conclusion, our objective in this book has been not merely to locate the similarities and differences which exist as between various countries but, as Blanpain puts it, to

> transcend the descriptive approach to foreign industrial relations systems and concentrate upon . . . explanation . . . in order to identify the role, importance and interaction of the different factors shaping and influencing industrial relations . . . in a variety of national contexts. (Blanpain, 1982b, p. 23)

Comparative examination can have an important heuristic benefit for the student of industrial relations in helping to correct any insularity of orientation, putting the arrangements in one's own country into perspective, and promoting an awareness that an industrial relations system (in the sense of a set of institutions and practices expressing one aspect of the interrelations between employers, employees and the state) is closely related to the social, political and economic environment in which it operates. Moreover, from the standpoint of research, systematic studies which produce similar findings in different settings further the generalisability of such findings, even if they cannot be considered as universally applicable, and can thereby help to promote the further development of the industrial relations discipline itself.

BIBLIOGRAPHY

Aaron, B. (ed.) (1971) *Labour Courts and Grievance Settlement in Western Europe*, University of California Press, Berkeley.

Adams, R.J. (1974) 'White-collar union growth: The case of Sweden', *Industrial Relations, 13.*

Adams, R.J. (1975) *The Growth of White-Collar Unionism in Britain and Sweden: A Comparative Investigation*, University of Wisconsin Press, Madison.

Adams, R.J. (1981) 'A theory of employer attitudes and behavior towards trade unions in Western Europe and North America', in G. Dlugos and K. Weirermair (eds), *Management Under Differing Value Systems*, de Gruyter, New York.

Adams, R.J. (1983) Review, *Industrial and Labor Relations Review, 36.*

Adams, R.J. and Rummel, C.H. (1977) 'Workers' participation in management in West Germany: Impact on the worker, the enterprise and the trade union', *Industrial Relations Journal, 8.*

Ahiauzu, A. (1982) 'Cross-cultural study of job regulation at the workplace: A framework for analysis', University of Aston Management Centre, Working Paper No. 234.

Albeda, W. (1971) 'Recent trends in collective bargaining in the Netherlands', *International Labour Review, 103.*

Albeda, W. (1977) 'Changing industrial relations in the Netherlands', *Industrial Relations, 16.*

Ali Taha, A.R.E. (1982) 'Industrial relations in the Sudan', *Labour and Society, 7.*

Allen, G.C. (1981) 'Japan', in E. Owen Smith (ed.), *Trade Unions in the Developed Economies*, Croom Helm, London.

Allen, V.L. (1969) 'The study of African trade unionism', *Journal of Modern African Studies, 7.*

Allen, V.L. (1971) *The Sociology of Industrial Relations*, Longman, London.

Andriessen, J.H.T.H. (1976) 'Developments in the Dutch industrial relations system', *Industrial Relations Journal, 7.*

Arnison, J. (1970) *The Million Pound Strike*, Lawrence & Wishart, London.

Arrighi, G. and Saul, J.S. (1968) 'Socialism and economic development in tropical Africa', *Journal of Modern African Studies, 6.*

Ashenfelter, O. and Johnson, G.E. (1969) 'Bargaining theory, trade unions and industrial strike activity', *American Economic Review, 59.*

Bain, G.S. and Clegg, H.A. (1974) 'A strategy for industrial relations research in Great Britain', *British Journal of Industrial Relations, XII.*

Bain, G.S. and Elsheikh, F. (1976) *Union Growth and the Business Cycle: An Econometric Analysis*, Basil Blackwell, Oxford.

Balfour, C. (1972) 'Industrial relations in Norway', *Industrial Relations Journal, 3.*

Banks, J.A. (1974) *Trade Unionism*, Collier-Macmillan, London.

Barbash, J. (1977) 'Price and power in collective bargaining', *Journal of Economic Issues, XI.*

Barbash, J. (1979) 'Collective bargaining and the theory of conflict', *Relations Industrielles, 34*.

Barkin, S. (1980) 'European industrial relations: A resource for the reconstruction of the American system', *Relations Industrielles, 35*.

Bartölke, K., Eschweiler, W., Flechsenberger, D. and Tannenbaum, A.S., (1982) 'Workers participation and the distribution of control as perceived by members of ten German companies', *Administrative Science Quarterly, 27*.

Beaumont, P.B., Thomson, A.W.J. and Gregory, M.B. (1980) 'Bargaining structure', *Management Decision, 18*.

Berenbach, S. (1979) 'Peru's social property: Limits to participation', *Industrial Relations, 18*.

Bertsch, G.K. and Obradovic, J. (1979) 'Participation and influence in Yugoslav self-management', *Industrial Relations, 18*.

Bienfeld, D.A. (1979) 'Trade unions, the labour process and the Tanzanian state', *Journal of Modern African Studies, 17*.

Blake, D.H. (1972) 'Trade unions and the challenge of the multinational corporation', *Annals of the American Academy of Political and Social Science, 403*.

Blake, D.H. (1973) 'Cross-national cooperative strategies: Union response to the MNCs', in K.P. Tudyka (ed.), *Multinational Corporations and Labour Unions*, Sun, Nijmegen.

Blanpain, R. (1974) 'The influence of labour on management decision-making. A comparative legal survey', *Industrial Law Journal, 3*.

Blanpain, R. (1977) 'The OECD guidelines for multinational enterprises', *Journal of the Royal Society of Arts, 126*.

Blanpain, R. (ed.) (1978ff) *International Encyclopaedia for Labour Law and Industrial Relations*, Kluwer, Deventer.

Blanpain, R. (1982a) 'Belgium', in R. Blanpain (ed.), *International Encyclopaedia for Labour Law and Industrial Relations*, Kluwer, Deventer.

Blanpain, R. (ed.) (1982b) *Comparative Labour Law and Industrial Relations*, Kluwer, Deventer.

Blum, A.A. (ed.) (1981) *International Handbook of Industrial Relations: Contemporary Developments and Research*, Aldwych, London.

Bok, D.C. and Dunlop, J.T. (1970) *Labor and the American Community*, Simon & Schuster, New York.

Bomers, G.B.J. (1976) *Multinational Corporations and Industrial Relations: A Comparative Study of West Germany and the Netherlands*, Van Gorcum, Amsterdam.

Bomers, G.B.J. and Peterson, R.B. (1977) 'Multinational corporations and industrial relations: The case of West Germany and the Netherlands', *British Journal of Industrial Relations, XV*.

Bomers, G.B.J. and Peterson, R.B. (eds.) (1982) *Conflict Management and Industrial Relations*, Kluwer, Boston.

Bradley, K. (1980) 'A comparative analysis of producer cooperatives: Some theoretical and empirical implications', *British Journal of Industrial Relations, XVIII*.

Bradley, K. and Gelb, A. (1981) 'Motivation and control in the Mondragon experiment', *British Journal of Industrial Relations, XIX*.

Bradley, K. and Gelb, A. (1982) 'The replication and sustainability of the Mondragon experiment', *British Journal of Industrial Relations, XX*.

Brandini, P.M. (1975) 'Italy: Creating a new industrial relations system from the bottom', in S. Barkin (ed.), *Worker Militancy and its Consequences, 1965-75: New Directions in Western Industrial Relations*, Praeger, New York.

Brody, D. (1980) *Workers in Industrial America: Essays on the Twentieth-Century Struggle*, Oxford University Press, New York.

Bronstein, A.S. (1978) 'Collective bargaining in Latin America: Problems and trends', *International Labour Review, 117.*

Brown, W. (ed.), (1981) *The Changing Contours of British Industrial Relations*, Basil Blackwell, Oxford.

Burrage, M. (1972) 'Democracy and the mystery of the crafts: Observations on work relationships in America and Britain', *Daedalus, 101.*

Busch, G.K. (1983) *The Political Role of International Trades Unions*, Macmillan, London.

Caloia, A. (1979) 'Industrial relations in Italy: Problems and perspectives', *British Journal of Industrial Relations, 17.*

Caves, R.E. (1980) 'Productivity differences among industries', in R.E. Caves and L.B. Krause (eds), *Britain's Economic Performance*, Brookings Institution, Washington, D.C.

Cella, G. and Treu, T. (1982) 'National trade union movements', in R. Blanpain (ed.), *Comparative Labour Law and Industrial Relations*, Kluwer, Deventer.

Chamberlain, N.W. (1961) 'Determinants of collective bargaining structures' in A.R. Weber (ed.), *The Structure of Collective Bargaining: Problems and Perspectives*, Free Press of Glencoe Inc., Illinois.

Clark, G.deN. (1971) 'Remedies for unfair dismissal: A European comparison', *International and Comparative Law Quarterly, 20.*

Clarke, R.O. (1980a) 'The development of industrial relations in European market economies', Industrial Relations Research Association: *Proceedings*, 33rd Annual Meeting.

Clarke, R.O. (1980b) 'Labour-management disputes: A perspective', *British Journal of Industrial Relations, XVIII.*

Clarke, R.O., Fatchett, D.J. and Roberts, B.C. (1972) *Workers' Participation in Management in Britain*, Heinemann, London.

Clegg, H.A. (1976) *Trade Unionism Under Collective Bargaining: A Theory Based on Comparisons of Six Countries*, Basil Blackwell, Oxford.

Clegg, H.A. (1979) *The Changing System of Industrial Relations in Great Britain*, Basil Blackwell, Oxford.

Cohen, S. (1975) *Labor in the United States*, Merrill, Columbia.

Commission of the European Communities (1979) *Problems and Prospects of Collective Bargaining in the EEC Member States*, Brussels.

Comisso, E.T. (1981) 'The logic of worker (non-) participation in Yugoslav self-management', *Review of Radical Political Economics, 13.*

Cordova, E. (1978) 'A comparative view of collective bargaining in industrialised countries', *International Labour Review, 117.*

Cordova, E. (1980) 'Collective labour relations in Latin America. A reappraisal', *Labour and Society, 5.*

Craypo, C. (1975) 'Collective bargaining in the conglomerate multinational firm: Litton's shutdown of Royal Typewriter', *Industrial and Labor Relations Review, 29.*

Creigh, S.W. (1982) 'Strikes in OECD countries: A research note', *Industrial*

Relations Journal, 13.

Creigh, S.W. and Makeham, P. (1978) 'Foreign ownership and strike-proneness: A research note', *British Journal of Industrial Relations, XVI.*

Creigh, S.W., Donaldson, N. and Hawthorn, E. (1980) 'Stoppage activity in OECD countries', *Department of Employment Gazette, LXXXVIII.*

Crouch, C. (1978) 'The changing role of the state in industrial relations in Western Europe', in C. Crouch and A. Pizzorno (eds), *The Resurgence of Class Conflict in Western Europe Since 1968, 2* (Comparative Analyses), Holmes & Meir, New York.

Crouch, C. (1979) *The Politics of Industrial Relations*, Fontana, London.

Crouch, C. (1982a) Review, *Industrial Relations Journal, 13.*

Crouch, C. (1982b) *Trade Unions: The Logic of Collective Action*, Fontana, London.

Cupper, L. and Hearn, J.M. (1981) 'Australia', in E. Owen Smith (ed.), *Trade Unions in Developed Economies*, Croom Helm, London.

Dahrendorf, R. (1968) *Society and Democracy in Germany*, Weidenfeld & Nicolson, London.

Damachi, U.G. (1976) 'Government, employers and workers in Ghana: A study of the mutual perception of roles', *British Journal of Industrial Relations, XIV.*

Damachi, U.G., Seibel, H.D. and Trachman, L. (eds) (1979) *Industrial Relations in Africa*, Macmillan, London.

Daniel, W.W. and Millward, N. (1983) *Workplace Industrial Relations Survey*, Heinemann, London.

Davis, H.B. (1941) 'The theory of union growth', *Quarterly Journal of Economics, LV.*

Deaton, D.R. and Beaumont, P.B. (1980) 'The determinants of bargaining structure: Some large-scale survey evidence for Britain', *British Journal of Industrial Relations, XVIII.*

Decisions in Organizations (DIO) (1979) 'Participative decision-making: A comparative study', *Industrial Relations, 18.*

Delamotte, Y. (1982) 'Conflict management in French industrial relations: Recent developments and trends', in G.B.J. Bomers and R.B. Peterson (eds), *Conflict Management and Industrial Relations*, Kluwer, Boston.

Derber, M. (1976) 'Strategic factors in industrial relations systems: The metalworking industry', *Labour and Society, 1.*

Despax, M. and Rojot, J. (1979) 'France', in R. Blanpain (ed.), *International Encyclopaedia for Labour Law and Industrial Relations*, Kluwer, Deventer.

Doeringer, P.B. (1981) 'Industrial relations research in international perspective', in P.B. Doeringer (ed.), *Industrial Relations in International Perspective: Essays on Research and Policy*, Macmillan, London.

Donovan, (1968) Royal Commission on Trade Unions and Employers' Associations, *Report*, Cmnd. 3623, HMSO, London.

Dore, R. (1973) *British Factory Japanese Factory: The Origins of National Diversity in Industrial Relations*, University of California Press, Berkeley.

Dubois, P. (1978) 'New forms of industrial conflict 1960–1974', in C. Crouch and A. Pizzorno (eds), *The Resurgence of Class Conflict in Western Europe since 1968, 2* (Comparative Analyses), Holmes & Meir, New York.

Dunlop, J.T. (1958) *Industrial Relations Systems*, Holt, New York.

Dunlop, J.T. (1972) 'Political systems and industrial relations', *Bulletin of the*

International Institute for Labour Studies, No. 9.

Dunlop, T.J. (1976) 'Structural changes in the American labor movement and industrial relations system', in R.L. Rowan (ed.), *Readings in Labor Economics and Labor Relations*, Irwin, Homewood, Illinois.

Dunlop, J.T. (1978) 'Introduction', in J.T. Dunlop and W. Galenson (eds), *Labor in the Twentieth Century*, Academic Press, New York.

Dunning, J.H. (1981) *International Production and the Multinational Enterprise*, Allen & Unwin, London.

Edelstein, J.D. and Warner, M. (1975) *Comparative Union Democracy*, Allen & Unwin, London.

Edwards, P.K. (1977) 'A critique of the Kerr–Segal hypothesis of strikes and the isolated mass', *Sociological Review, 25.*

Edwards, P.K. (1978) 'Time-series regression models of strike activity: A reconsideration with American data', *British Journal of Industrial Relations, XVI.*

Edwards, P.K. (1981) *Strikes in the United States 1881–1974*, Basil Blackwell, Oxford.

Edwards, R. (1979) *Contested Terrain: The Transformation of the Workplace in the Twentieth Century*, Heinemann, London.

Elbaum, B. and Wilkinson, F. (1979) 'Industrial relations and uneven development: A comparative study of the American and British steel industries', *Cambridge Journal, 3.*

Eldridge, J.E.T. (1975) 'Panaceas and pragmatism in industrial relations', *Industrial Relations Journal, 6.*

Elvander, N. (1974) 'The role of the state in the settlement of labor disputes in the Nordic countries: A comparative analysis', *European Journal of Political Research, 2.*

Enderwick, P. (1982) 'Labour and the theory of the multinational corporation', *Industrial Relations Journal, 13.*

Enderwick, P. and Buckley, P.J. (1982) 'Strike activity and foreign ownership: An analysis of British manufacturing 1971–73', *British Journal of Industrial Relations, XX.*

Enderwick, P. and Buckley, P.J. (1983) 'Industrial relations practices in Britain: A comparative analysis of foreign and domestically-owned firms', *Labour and Society, 8.*

Espinosa, J. and Zimbalist, A.S. (1978) *Economic Democracy: Workers' Participation in Chilean Industry, 1970–73*, Academic Press, New York.

Evans, E. (1976) 'On some recent econometric models of strike frequency', *Industrial Relations Journal, 7.*

Fina, L. and Hawkesworth, R.I. (1984) 'Trade unions and collective bargaining in post-Franco Spain', *Labour and Society, 9.*

Fisher, M. (1973) *Measurement of Labor Disputes and their Economic Effects*, OECD, Paris.

Flanagan, R.J. (1974) 'Introduction', in R.J. Flanagan and A.R. Weber (eds), *Bargaining Without Boundaries: The Multinational Corporation and International Labor Relations*, University of Chicago Press, Chicago.

Flanagan, R.J., Soskice, D.W. and Ulman, L. (1983) *Unionism, Economic Stabilization and Incomes Policies: European Experience*, Brookings Institution, Washington, D.C.

Flanders, A. (1974) 'The tradition of voluntarism', *British Journal of Industrial Relations, XII.*

Fong, P.E. and Cheng, L. (1978) 'Changing patterns of industrial relations in Singapore', in E.M. Kassalow and U.G. Damachi (eds), *The Role of Trade Unions in Developing Societies*, International Institute for Labour Studies, Geneva.

Ford, G.W. (1980) 'Employers' associations: An introduction' in G.W. Ford, J.M. Hearn and R.D. Lansbury (eds), *Austrialian Labour Relations: Readings*, Macmillan, Melbourne.

Form, W.H. (1973) 'Job vs. political unionism: A cross-national comparison', *Industrial Relations, 12.*

Forsebäck, L. (1980) *Industrial Relations and Employment in Sweden*, Swedish Institute, Uppsala.

Forsyth, D.J.C. (1973) 'Foreign-owned firms and labour relations: A regional perspective', *British Journal of Industrial Relations, XI.*

Fox, A. (1978) 'Corporatism and industrial democracy: The social origins of present forms and methods in Britain and Germany', in SSRC Industrial Relations Research Unit, Industrial Democracy: International Views, University of Warwick (mimeo).

Fulcher, J. (1975) 'Industrial conflict in Britain and Sweden', *Sociology, 9.*

Fürstenberg, F. (1977) 'West German experience with industrial democracy', *Annals of the American Academy of Political and Social Science, 431.*

Fürstenberg, F. (1980) 'Co-determination and its contribution to industrial democracy: A critical evaluation', Industrial Relations Research Association: *Proceedings*, 33rd Annual Meeting.

Fürstenberg, F. (1982) 'Conflict management in the Austrian system of social partnership', in G.B.J. Bomers and R.B. Peterson (eds), *Conflict Management and Industrial Relations*, Kluwer, Boston.

Galenson, W. (ed.) (1952) *Comparative Labor Movements*, Prentice-Hall, New York.

Gallie, D. (1975) Review, *British Journal of Industrial Relations, XIII.*

Gallie, D. (1978) *In Search of the New Working Class: Automation and Social Integration Within the Capitalist Enterprise*, Cambridge University Press, Cambridge.

Garson, G.D. (1977) *Worker Self-Management in Industry: The West European Experience*, Praeger, New York.

Geary, D. (1981) *European Labour Protest 1848-1939*, Croom Helm, London.

Gennard, J. (1974) 'The impact of foreign-owned subsidiaries on host country labor relations: The case of the United Kingdom', in R.J. Flanagan and A.R. Weber (eds), *Bargaining Without Boundaries: The Multinational Corporation and International Labor Relations*, University of Chicago Press, Chicago.

Gennard, J. and Steuer, M.D. (1971) 'The industrial relations of foreign-owned subsidiaries in the United Kingdom', *British Journal of Industrial Relations, IX.*

Gertzel, G. (1979) 'Industrial relations in Zambia to 1975', in U.G. Damachi, H.D. Seibel and L. Trachman (eds), *Industrial Relations in Africa*, Macmillan, London.

Gifford, A. (1974) 'The impact of socialism on work stoppages', *Industrial Relations, 13.*

Gill, C. (1969) 'One approach to the teaching of industrial relations', *British Journal of Industrial Relations, VII.*

Gill, C. (1984) 'Industrial relations in Denmark: Problems and perspectives', *Industrial Relations Journal, 15*.
Gladstone, A. (1978) 'Preface', in E.M. Kassalow and U.G. Damachi (eds), *The Role of Trade Unions in Developing Societies*, International Institute for Labour Studies, Geneva.
Gladstone, A. (1980) 'Trade unions, growth and development', *Labour and Society, 5*.
Gladstone, A. (1984) 'Employers' associations in comparative perspective: Functions and activities', in J.P. Windmüller and A. Gladstone (eds), *Employers' Associations and Industrial Relations. A Comparative Study*, Clarendon, Oxford.
Goetschy, J. (1983) 'A new future for industrial democracy in France?', *Economic and Industrial Democracy, 4*.
Goldthorpe, J. (1974) 'Industrial relations in Great Britain: A critique of reformism', *Politics and Society, 4*.
Goodman, J.F.B. (1978) 'Trade unions and collective bargaining systems', in D. Torrington (ed.), *Comparative Industrial Relations in Europe*, Associated Business Programmes, London.
Goodman, J.F.B. (1981) 'United Kingdom', in A.A. Blum (ed.), *International Handbook of Industrial Relations*, Aldwych, London.
Gospel, H.F. (1978) 'European managerial unions: An early assessment', *Industrial Relations, XVII*.
Gospel, H.F. (1983a) 'Managerial structures and strategies: An introduction', in H.F. Gospel and C.R.Littler (eds), *Managerial Strategies and Industrial Relations: An Historical and Comparative Study*, Heinemann, London.
Gospel, H.F. (1983b) 'Trade unions and the legal obligation to bargain: An American, Swedish and British comparison', *British Journal of Industrial Relations, XXI*.
Gray, P.S. (1980) 'Collective bargaining in Ghana', *Industrial Relations, 19*.
Guigni, G. (1981) 'The Italian system of industrial relations', in P. Doeringer (ed.), *Industrial Relations in International Perspective: Essays on Research and Policy*, Macmillan, London.
Günter, H. and Leminsky, G. (1978) 'The Federal Republic of Germany', in J.T. Dunlop and W. Galenson (eds), *Labor in the Twentieth Century*, Academic Press, New York.
Haas, A. (1983) 'The aftermath of Sweden's co-determination law: Workers' experiences in Gothenburg 1977–80', *Economic and Industrial Democracy, 4*.
Hamill, J. (1984) 'Labour relations decision-making within multinational corporations', *Industrial Relations Journal, 15*.
Hanami, T. (1979) *Labor Relations in Japan Today*, John Martin, London.
Hannah, L. (1976) *The Rise of the Corporate Economy*; Methuen, London.
Hare, A.E.C. (1946) *Report on Industrial Relations in New Zealand*, Victoria University College, Wellington.
Hartman, H. (1975) 'Co-determination today and tomorrow', *British Journal of Industrial Relations, XIII*.
Hartman, H. and Lau, C.F. (1980) 'Trade union confederations: A comparative study of identity and strategy', *International Studies Quarterly, 24*.
Hawkins, R.G. (1979) 'The economic effects of multinational corporations',

Research in International Business and Finance, 1, Jai Press, Greenwich, Connecticut.

Hedlund, G. (1981) 'Autonomy of subsidiaries and formalisation of Headquarters-Subsidiary Relationships in Swedish MNCs', in L. Otterbeck (ed.), *The Management of Headquarters-Subsidiary Relationships in Multinational Corporations*, Gower, London.

Hendricks, W.E. and Kahn, L.M. (1982) 'The determinants of bargaining structure in U.S. manufacturing industries', *Industrial and Labor Relations Review, 35.*

Henley, J.S. (1978) 'Pluralism, underdevelopment and trade union power: Evidence from Kenya', *British Journal of Industrial Relations, XVI.*

Henley, J.S. (1980) 'The management of labour relations in industrialising market economies', *Industrial Relations Journal, 10.*

Herding, R. (1972) *Job Control and Union Structure*, Rotterdam University Press, Rotterdam.

Herman, E.E. (1966) *Determination of the Appropriate Bargaining Unit By Labour Relations Boards in Canada*, Queen's Printer, Ottawa.

Héthy, L. and Makó, Cs. (1977) 'Workers' direct participation in decisions in Hungarian factories', *International Labour Review, 116.*

Hibbs, D.A. (1976) 'Industrial conflict in advanced industrial societies', *American Political Science Review, 70.*

Hibbs, D.A. (1978) 'On the political economy of long-run trends in strike activity', *British Journal of Political Science, 8.*

Hildebrand, G.H. (1979) *American Unionism: An Historical and Analytical Survey*, Addison-Wesley, Reading, Mass.

Hill, S. and Thurley, K. (1974) 'Sociology and industrial relations', *British Journal of Industrial Relations, XII.*

Hoffman, C. (1981) 'People's Republic of China', in A.A. Blum (ed.), *International Handbook of Industrial Relations*, Aldwych, London.

Holt, J. (1977) 'Trade unionism in the British and US steel industries, 1888-1912. A comparative study', *Labor History, 18.*

Homburg, H. (1983) 'Scientific management and personnel policy in modern German enterprise, 1918-1939: The case of Siemens', in H.F. Gospel and C.R.Littler(eds), *Managerial Strategies and Industrial Relations*, Heinemann, London.

Hong, Ng Sek (1984) 'One brand of workplace democracy: The workers' congress in the Chinese enterprise', *Journal of Industrial Relations, 26.*

Hood, N. and Young, S. (1979) *The Economics of Multinational Enterprise*, Longman, London.

Hough, J.R. (1981) 'France', in E. Owen Smith (ed.), *Trade Unions in the Developed Economies*, Croom Helm, London.

Howard, W.A. (1980) 'Australian trade unions in the context of union theory', in G.W. Ford, J.M. Hearn and R.D. Lansbury (eds), *Australian Labour Relations: Readings*, Macmillan, Melbourne.

Hoxie, R.F. (1920) *Trade Unionism in the United States*, D. Appleton, New York.

Huxley, C. (1979) 'The state, collective bargaining and the shape of strikes in Canada', *Canadian Journal of Sociology, 4.*

Hyman, R. (1975) *Industrial Relations: A Marxist Introduction*, Macmillan, London.

Hyman, R. (1979) 'Third World strikes in perspective', *Development and Change, 10*.

Hyman, R. (1982a) 'The concept of the public interest in industrial relations', in Lord Wedderburn and W.T. Murphy (eds), *Labour Law and the Community: Perspectives for the 1980s*, Institute of Advanced Legal Studies, London.

Hyman, R. (1982b) Review Symposium, *Industrial Relations, 21*.

Hyman, R. (1983) 'Trade unions: Structure, policies and politics', in G.S. Bain (ed.), *Industrial Relations in Britain*, Basil Blackwell, Oxford.

IDE Research Group (1981a) *European Industrial Relations*, Clarendon, Oxford.

IDE Research Group (1981b) *Industrial Democracy in Europe*, Clarendon, Oxford.

Ingham, G. (1974) *Strikes and Industrial Conflict: Britain and Scandinavia*, Macmillan, London.

International Institute for Labour Studies (IILS) (1969) 'Strategic factors in industrial relations systems – a programme of international comparative industry studies', *Bulletin of the International Institute for Labour Studies*, No. 6.

International Labour Office (ILO) (1973) *Multinational Enterprises and Social Policy*, Geneva.

International Labour Office (1974) *Collective Bargaining in Industrialised Market Economies*, Geneva.

International Labour Office (1976) *Multinationals in Western Europe: The Industrial Relations Experience*, Geneva.

International Labour Office (1977) *Social and Labour Practices of Some US-Based Multinationals in the Metal Trades*, Geneva.

International Labour Office (1978) *Collective Bargaining in Industrialised Countries. Recent Trends and Problems*, Geneva.

International Labour Office (1980) *Conciliation and Arbitration Procedures in Labour Disputes: A Comparative Study*, Geneva.

International Labour Office (1981a) *Employment Effects of Multinational Enterprises in Industrialised Countries*, Geneva.

International Labour Office (1981b) *Workers' Participation in Decisions Within Undertakings*, Geneva.

Isaac, J.E. (1973) 'Industrial relations', in R.I. Downing (ed.), *The Australian Economy: A Manual of Applied Economics*, Weidenfeld & Nicolson, London.

Iwuji, E. (1979) 'Industrial relations in Kenya', in U.G. Damachi, H.D. Siebel and L. Trachman (eds), *Industrial Relations in Africa*, Macmillan, London.

Jackson, M.P. (1982) *Trade Unions*, Longman, London.

Jackson, P. and Sisson, K. (1976) 'Employers' confederations in Sweden and the UK and the significance of industrial infrastructure', *British Journal of Industrial Relations, XIV*.

Jacobs, E., Orwell, S., Paterson, P. and Weitz, F. (1978) *The Approach to Industrial Change in Britain and Germany: A Comparative Study of Workplace Industrial Relations and Manpower Policies in British and West German Enterprises*, Anglo-German Foundation for the Study of Industrial Society, London.

Jacoby, S. (1979) 'Origins of internal labour markets in Japan', *Industrial Relations, 18*.

Johnston, T.L. (1962) *Collective Bargaining in Sweden*, Allen & Unwin, London.

Jones, D.C. (1978) 'Producer-cooperatives in industrialised western economies: An overview', *Annals of Public and Co-operative Economy, 49.*

Kahn-Freund, O. (1972) *Labour and the Law*, Stevens, London.

Kahn-Freund, O. (1974) 'Uses and misuses of comparative law', *Modern Law Review, 37.*

Kahn-Freund, O. (1979) *Labour Relations: Heritage and Adjustment*, Oxford University Press, Oxford.

Kahn-Freund, O. (1981) *Labour Law and Politics in the Weimar Republic*, Basil Blackwell, Oxford.

Kahn-Freund, O. and Hepple, B. (1972) *Laws Against Strikes*, Fabian Research Series, London.

Kannappan, S. and Krishnan, V.N. (1977) 'Participative management in India: Utopia or snare?', *Annals of the American Academy of Political and Social Science, 431.*

Kassalow, E.M. (1968) 'The comparative labour field', *Bulletin of the International Institute for Labour Studies*, No. 5.

Kassalow, E.M. (1969) *Trade Unions and Industrial Relations: An International Comparison*, Random House, New York.

Kassalow, E.M. (1977) 'Industrial conflict and consensus in the United States and Western Europe: A comparative approach', Industrial Relations Research Association: *Proceedings* 30th Annual Meeting.

Kassalow, E.M. (1978a) 'Aspects of labour relations in multinational companies: An overview of three Asian countries', *International Labour Review, 117.*

Kassalow, E.M. (1978b) 'Introduction', in E.M. Kassalow and U.G. Damachi (eds), *The Role of Trade Unions in Developing Societies*, International Institute for Labour Studies, Geneva.

Kassalow, E.M. (1982) 'Industrial democracy and collective bargaining: A comparative view', *Labour and Society, 7.*

Kassalow, E.M. (1983) 'Japan as an industrial relations model', *Journal of Industrial Relations, 25.*

Kaufman, B.E. (1982) 'The determinants of strikes in the United States, 1900–1977', *Industrial and Labor Relations Review, 35.*

Kendall, W. (1975) *The Labour Movement in Europe*, Allen Lane, London.

Kerr, C., Dunlop, J.T., Harbison, F.H. and Myers, C.A. (1962) *Industrialism and Industrial Man*, Heinemann, London.

Kerr, C., Dunlop, J.T., Harbison, F.H. and Myers, C.A. (1971) 'Postscript to Industrialism and Industrial Man', *International Labour Review, 103.*

Kilby, P. (1967) 'Industrial relations and wage determination: Failure of the Anglo-Saxon model', *Journal of Developing Areas, 1.*

Kilby, P. (1973) 'Trade unionism in Nigeria 1938–66', in A. Sturmthal and J.G. Scoville (eds), *The International Labor Movement in Transition*, University of Illinois Press, Urbana.

Kobrin, S.J. (1976) 'Industrialisation and variation in social structure: An empirical test of the convergence hypothesis', Industrial Relations Research Association: *Proceedings*, 29th Annual Meeting.

Kolaja, I. (1960) *A Polish Factory. A Case-Study of Workers' Participation*, University of Kentucky Press.

Korpi, W. (1978a) *The Working Class in Welfare Capitalism: Work, Unions and*

Politics in Sweden, Routledge & Kegan Paul, London.

Korpi, W. (1978b) 'Workplace bargaining, the law and unofficial strikes: The case of Sweden', *British Journal of Industrial Relations, XVI.*

Korpi, W. (1980) 'Industrial relations and industrial conflict: The case of Sweden', in B. Martin and E.M. Kassalow (eds), *Labor Relations in Advanced Industrial Societies: Issues and Problems*, Carnegie Endowment, Washington, D.C.

Korpi, W. (1981) 'Sweden: Conflict, power and politics in industrial relations', in P. Doeringer (ed.), *Industrial Relations in International Perspective: Essays on Research and Policy*, Macmillan, London.

Korpi, W. and Shalev, M. (1979) 'Strikes, industrial relations and class conflict in capitalist society', *British Journal of Sociology, 30.*

Kraus, J. (1979) 'The political economy of industrial relations in Ghana', in U.G. Damachi, H.D. Siebel and L. Trachman (eds), *Industrial Relations in Africa*, Macmillan, London.

Krishnan, V.N. (1981) 'India', in A.A. Blum (ed.), *International Handbook of Industrial Relations*, Aldwych, London.

Kuisel, R.F. (1981) *Capitalism and the State in Modern France*, Cambridge University Press, Cambridge.

Kujawa, D. (1971) *International Labor Relations Management in the Automobile Industry: A Comparative Study of Chrysler, Ford and General Motors*, Praeger, New York.

Kujawa, D. (1979) 'The labor relations of United States multinationals abroad: Comparative and prospective views', *Labor and Society, 4.*

Kujawa, D. (1980) 'Labour relations of US multinationals abroad', in B. Martin and E.M. Kassalow (eds), *Labor Relations in Advanced Industrial Societies: Issues and Problems*, Carnegie Endowment, Washington, D.C.

Lange, P., Ross, G. and Vannicelli, M. (1982) *Unions, Change and Crisis: French and Italian Union Strategy and the Political Economy, 1945–80*, Allen & Unwin, London.

Lansbury, R.D. (1978a) 'The return to arbitration: Recent trends in dispute settlement and wages policy in Australia', *International Labour Review, 117.*

Lansbury, R.D. (1978b) 'Industrial democracy under liberal capitalism: A comparison of trends in Australia, France and the USA', *Journal of Industrial Relations, 20.*

La Palombara, J. and Blank, S. (1976) *Multinational Corporations and National Élites: A Study of Tensions*, The Conference Board, New York.

Lazonick, W.H. (1983) 'Technological change and the control of work: The development of capital–labour relations in US manufacturing industry', in H.F. Gospel and C.R. Littler (eds), *Managerial Strategies and Industrial Relations*, Heinemann, London.

Leminsky, G. (1980) 'Worker participation: The German experience', in B. Martin and E.M. Kassalow (eds), *Labor Relations in Advanced Industrial Societies: Issues and Problems*, Carnegie Endowment, Washington, D.C.

Levine, S.B. (1958) *Industrial Relations in Postwar Japan*, University of Illinois Press, Urbana.

Levine, S.B. (1980) 'Changing strategies of unions and management: Evaluation of four industrialised countries', *British Journal of Industrial Relations, XVIII.*

Levine, S.B. (1981) 'Japan', in A.A. Blum (ed.), *International Handbook of Industrial Relations*, Aldwych, London.

Levine, S.B. and Taira, K. (1980) 'Interpreting industrial conflict: The case of Japan', in B. Martin and E.M. Kassalow (eds), *Labor Relations in Advanced Industrial Societies: Issues and Problems*, Carnegie Endowment, Washington, D.C.

Levinson, C. (1972) *International Trade Unionism*, Allen & Unwin, London.

Lewchuk, W. (1983) 'Fordism and British motor car employers, 1896-1932', in H.F. Gospel and C.R. Littler (eds), *Managerial Strategies in Industrial Relations*, Heinemann, London.

Lewin, D. (1978) 'The impact of unions on American business: Evidence for an assessment', *Columbia Journal of World Business, 13.*

Lewis, R. (1976) 'The historical development of labour law', *British Journal of Industrial Relations, XIV.*

Liebhaberg, B. (1980) *Industrial Relations and Multinational Corporations in Europe*, Gower, London.

Lipset, S.M. (1961) 'Trade unions and social structure', *Industrial Relations, 1.*

Lipset, S.M. (1977) 'Socialism in America', *Dialogue, 10.*

Little, J.S. (1982) 'Multinational corporations and foreign investment, current trends and issues', *Annals of the American Academy of Political and Social Science, 460.*

Littler, C.R. (1983) 'A comparative analysis of managerial structures and strategies', in H.F. Gospel and C.R. Littler (eds), *Managerial Strategies and Industrial Relations*, Heinemann, London.

Littler, C.R. and Lockett, M. (1983) 'The significance of trade unions in China', *Industrial Relations Journal, 14.*

Litvak, I.A. and Maule, C.J. (1972) 'The union response to international corporations', *Industrial Relations, 11.*

Livernash, E.R. (1963) 'The relation of power to the structure and process of collective bargaining', *Journal of Law and Economics, 6.*

Lorwin, V.R. (1957) 'Reflections on the history of the French and American labor movements', *Journal of Economic History, 17.*

Loveman, B. (1981) 'Chile', in A.A. Blum (ed.), *International Handbook of Industrial Relations*, Aldwych, London.

Loveridge, R. (1980) 'What is participation? A review of the literature and some methodological problems', *British Journal of Industrial Relations, XVIII.*

Lucena, H. (1980) 'Industrial relations in an enclave economy: The case of Venezuela', *Labour and Society, 5.*

Lukes, S. (1974) *Power: A Radical View*, Macmillan, London.

Marsden, D. (1978) *Industrial Democracy and Industrial Control in West Germany, France and Britain*, Department of Employment, London.

Marsden, R. (1982) 'Industrial relations: A critique of empiricism', *Sociology, 16.*

Marsh, A., Hackman, M. and Miller, D. (1981) *Workplace Relations in the Engineering Industry in the UK and the Federal Republic of Germany*, Anglo-German Foundation for the Study of Industrial Society, London.

Marsh, R.M. and Mannari, H. (1981) 'Divergence and convergence in industrial organisations: The Japanese case', in G. Dlugos and H. Weiermair (eds), *Management Under Differing Value Systems*, de Gruyter, New York.

Martens, G.R. (1979) 'Industrial relations and trade unionism in French-speaking West Africa', in U.G. Damachi, H.D. Seibel and L. Trachman (eds), *Industrial Relations in Africa*, Macmillan, London.

Martin, R.M. (1975) *Trade Unions in Australia*, Penguin, Melbourne.

Maurice, M. and Sellier, F. (1979) 'Societal analysis of industrial relations: A comparison between France and West Germany', *British Journal of Industrial Relations, XVII.*

Meyers, F. (1967) 'The study of foreign labor and industrial relations', in S. Barkin (ed.), *International Labor*, Harper & Row, New York.

Meyers, F. (1981) 'France', in A.A. Blum (ed.), *International Handbook of Industrial Relations*, Aldwych, London.

Miliband, R. (1969) *The State in Capitalist Society*, Weidenfeld and Nicolson, London.

Miller, R.F. (1978) 'Worker self-management in Yugoslavia: The current state of play', *Journal of Industrial Relations, 20.*

Millward, N. (1979) 'Research note: The strike record of foreign-owned manufacturing plants in Great Britain', *British Journal of Industrial Relations, XVII.*

Miscmarra, P.A. (1981) 'The entertainment industry: Inroads in multinational collective bargaining', *British Journal of Industrial Relations, XIX.*

Muir, J.D. and Brown, J.L. (1978) 'The changing role of government in collective bargaining', in E.M. Kassalow and U.G. Damachi (eds), *The Role of Trade Unions in Developing Societies*, International Institute for Labour Studies, Geneva.

Nicol, B. (1979) 'Industrial relations in Uganda', in U.G. Damachi, H.D. Seibel and L. Trachman (eds), *Industrial Relations in Africa*, Macmillan, London.

Niland, J. (1978) *Collective Bargaining and Compulsory Arbitration in Australia*, University of New South Wales, Sydney.

Northrup, H.R. and Rowan, R.L. (1976) 'Multinational bargaining approaches in the Western European flat glass industry', *Industrial and Labor Relations Review, 30.*

Northrup, H.R. and Rowan, R.L. (1979) *Multinational Collective Bargaining Attempts: The Record, the Cases and the Prospects*, University of Pennsylvania, Philadelphia.

Obradovic, J. (1975) 'Workers' participation: Who participates?', *Industrial Relations, 14.*

OECD (1977) *The Industrial Relations and Employment Impacts of Multinational Enterprises: An Inquiry into the Issues*, Paris.

OECD (1979a) *Collective Bargaining and Government Policies*, Paris.

OECD (1979b) *Wage Policies and Collective Bargaining Developments in Finland, Ireland and Norway*, Paris.

OECD (1979c) *Transfer Pricing and Multinational Enterprises*, Paris.

Oechslin, J.J. (1972) 'Employers' organisations in France', *International Labour Review, 106.*

Ogden, S.G. (1982a) 'Trade unions, industrial democracy and collective bargaining', *Sociology, 16.*

Ogden, S.G. (1982b) 'Bargaining structure and the control of industrial relations', *British Journal of Industrial Relations, XX.*

Okamoto, H. (1979) 'Japan', in B.C. Roberts (ed.), *Towards Industrial Democracy: Europe, Japan and the United States*, Croom Helm, London.

Okayama, R. (1983) 'Japanese employer labour policy: The heavy engineering industry 1900–1930', in H.F. Gospel and C.R. Littler (eds), *Managerial Strategies and Industrial Relations*, Heinemann, London.

Okochi, K., Karsh, B. and Levine, S.B. (1973) *Workers and Employers in Japan: The Japanese Employment Relations System*, University of Tokyo Press.

Owen Smith, E. (ed.) (1981) *Trade Unions in the Developed Economies*, Croom Helm, London.

Padlam, M. and Pederson, P.J. (1982) 'The macroeconomic strike model: A study of seventeen countries, 1948-1975', *Industrial and Labor Relations Review, 35*.

Panitch, L. (1977) 'The development of corporatism in liberal democracies', *Comparative Political Studies, 10*.

Panitch, L. (1980) 'Recent theorizations of corporatism', *British Journal of Sociology, XXXI*.

Panitch, L. (1981) 'Trade unions and the capitalist state', *New Left Review*, No. 125.

Pankert, A. (1980) 'Settlement of labour disputes in essential services', *International Labour Review, 119*.

Perlmutter, H.V. (1969) 'The tortuous evolution of the multinational corporation', *Columbia Journal of World Business, 4*.

Phelps Brown, E.H. (1959) *The Growth of British Industrial Relations: A Study from the Standpoint of 1906-14*, Macmillan, London.

Phelps Brown, E.H. (1983) *The Origins of Trade Union Power*, Clarendon, Oxford.

Pizzorno, A. (1978) 'Political exchange and collective identity in industrial conflict', in C. Crouch and A. Pizzorno (eds), *The Resurgence of Class Conflict in Western Europe Since 1969, 2* (Comparative Analyses), Holmes & Meir, New York.

Plowman, D. (1980) 'Employer associations: Challenges and responses', in G.W. Ford, J.M. Hearn and R.D. Lansbury (eds), *Australian Labour Relations: Readings*, Macmillan, Melbourne.

Poole, M. (1979) 'Industrial democracy: A comparative analysis', *Industrial Relations, 18*.

Poole, M. (1980) 'Managerial strategies and industrial relations', in M. Poole and R. Mansfield (eds), *Managerial Roles in Industrial Relations*, Gower, London.

Poole, M. (1982) 'Theories of industrial democracy', *Sociological Review, 30*.

Poole, M., Mansfield, R., Frost, P. and Blyton, P. (1983) 'Why managers join unions: Evidence from Britain', *Industrial Relations, 22*.

Porket, J.L. (1975) 'Participation in management in communist systems in the 1970s', *British Journal of Industrial Relations, XIII*.

Porket, J.L. (1978) 'Industrial relations and participation in management in the Soviet-type communist system', *British Journal of Industrial Relations, XVI*.

Porter, J. (1967) 'Some observations on comparative studies', *Bulletin of the International Institute for Labour Studies*, No. 3.

Prais, S.J. (1978) 'The strike-proneness of large plants in Britain', *Journal of the Royal Statistical Society, 141*.

Prais, S.J. (1982) 'Strike frequencies and plant size: A comment on Swedish and UK experience', *British Journal of Industrial Relations, XX*.

Pratten, C.F. (1976) *A Comparison of the Performance of Swedish and UK Companies*, Cambridge University Press, Cambridge.

Pravda, A. (1983) 'Trade unions in East European communist systems: Towards corporatism', *International Political Science Review, 4*.

Puységur, S.J. (1951) 'Employers' associations in Europe and North America', *International Labour Review, 63.*

Ramsay, H. (1977) 'Cycles of control: Worker participation and historical perspectives', *Sociology, 11.*

Rees, A. (1952) 'Industrial conflict and business fluctuations', *Journal of Political Economy, 60.*

Reynaud, J.D. (1975) 'Trade unions and political parties in France: Some recent trends', *Industrial and Labor Relations Review, 28.*

Reynaud, J.D. (1980) 'Industrial relations and political systems: Some reflections on the crisis in industrial relations in Western Europe', *British Journal of Industrial Relations, XVIII.*

Reynaud, J.D. (1981) 'Industrial relations research in France 1960–75: A review', in P.B. Doeringer (ed.), *Industrial Relations in International Perspective*, Macmillan, London.

Reynolds, L.G. (1978) *Labor Economics and Labor Relations*, Prentice-Hall, Englewood Cliffs, New Jersey.

Riddell, D.S. (1968) 'Social self-government: The background of theory and practice in Yugoslav socialism', *British Journal of Sociology, 19.*

Rimlinger, G. (1977) 'Labor and the government: A comparative historical perspective', *Journal of Economic History, XXXVII.*

Roberts, B.C. (1979) *Towards Industrial Democracy: Europe, Japan and the United States*, Croom Helm, London.

Roberts, B.C. (1981) 'Multinational enterprise and labour', in P. Doeringer (ed.), *Industrial Relations in International Perspective: Essays on Research and Policy*, Macmillan, London.

Roberts, B.C. and May, J. (1974) 'The response of multinational enterprises to international trade union pressure', *British Journal of Industrial Relations, XII.*

Roberts, I.L. (1975) 'Industrial relations and the European community', *Industrial Relations Journal, 6.*

Rose, M. (1979) *Servants of Post-Industrial Power?*, Macmillan, London.

Rose, M. (1983) Review, *British Journal of Industrial Relations, XXI.*

Rosen, S. (1975) 'The United States', in S. Barkin (ed.), *Worker Militancy and Its Consequences, 1965–75*, Praeger, New York.

Ross, A.M. and Hartman, P.T. (1960) *Changing Patterns of Industrial Conflict*, John Wiley, New York.

Roth, H. (1974) 'Trade unions', in J.M. Howells, N.S. Woods and F.J.L. Young (eds), *Labour and Industrial Relations in New Zealand*, Pitman, Carlton, Victoria.

Ruble, B.A. (1979) 'Dual functioning trade unions in the U.S.S.R.', *British Journal of Industrial Relations, XVII.*

Ruble, B.A. (1981) *Soviet Trade Unions: Their Development in the 1970s*, Cambridge University Press, Cambridge.

Rugman, A. (1980) 'A new theory of the multinational enterprise: Internationalization versus Internalization', *Columbia Journal of World Business, XVI.*

Rus, V. (1982) 'Conflict regulation in self-managed Yugoslav enterprises', in G.B.J. Bomers and R.B. Peterson (eds), *Conflict Management and Industrial Relations*, Kluwer, Boston.

Sandbrook, R. (1975) *Proletarians and African Capitalism: The Kenyan Case 1962–70*, Cambridge University Press, Cambridge.

Sandbrook, R. and Cohen, R. (1975) *The Development of An African Working Class*, Longman, London.

Schmidt, F. (1972) 'Industrial action, the role of trade unions and employers' associations', in B. Aaron and K.W. Wedderburn (eds), *Industrial Conflict: A Comparative Legal Survey*, Longman, London.

Schollhammer, H. (1973) 'Strategies and methodologies in international business and comparative management research', *Management International Review, 13.*

Schregle, J. (1976) 'Workers' participation in decisions within undertakings', *International Labour Review, 113.*

Schregle, J. (1978) 'Co-determination in the Federal Republic of Germany: A comparative view', *International Labour Review, 117.*

Schregle, J. (1981) 'Comparative industrial relations: Pitfalls and potential', *International Labour Review, 120.*

Sciarra, S. (1977) 'The rise of the Italian shop steward', *Industrial Law Journal, 6.*

Seglow, P., Streeck, W. and Wallace, P. (1982) *Rail Unions in Britain and West Germany: A Study of their Structure and Policies*, Policy Studies Institute, London.

Sellier, F. (1973) 'The French workers' movement and political unionism', in A. Sturmthal and J.G. Scoville (eds), *The International Labor Movement in Transition*, University of Illinois Press, Urbana.

Sellier, F. (1978) 'France', in J.T. Dunlop and W. Galenson (eds), *Labor in the Twentieth Century*, Academic Press, New York.

Sewell, W.H. (1977) 'Comment', *Journal of Economic History, XXXVII.*

Shalev, M. (1978a) 'Lies, damned lies and strike statistics: The measurement of trends in industrial conflict', in C. Crouch and A. Pizzorno (eds), *The Resurgence of Class Conflict in Western Europe since 1968, 1* (National Studies), Holmes & Meir, New York.

Shalev, M. (1978b) 'Strikers and the state: A comment', *British Journal of Political Science, 8.*

Shalev, M. (1980a) 'Industrial relations theory and the comparative study of industrial relations and industrial conflict', *British Journal of Industrial Relations, XVIII.*

Shalev, M. (1980b) 'Trade unions and economic analysis: The case of industrial conflict', *Journal of Labor Research, 1.*

Shalev, M. (1981) 'Theoretical dilemmas and value analysis in comparative industrial relations', in G. Dlugos and K. Weiermair (eds), *Management Under Differing Value Systems*, de Gruyter, New York.

Shalev, M. (1983) 'Strikes and the crisis: Industrial conflict and unemployment in the western nations', *Economic and Industrial Democracy, 4.*

Shalev, M. and Korpi, W. (1980) 'Working-class mobilization and American exceptionalism', *Economic and Industrial Democracy, 1.*

Shetty, Y. (1979) 'European and American styles of managing the multinational corporation', *Management International Review, 19.*

Shirai, T. and Shimada, H. (1978) 'Japan', in J.T. Dunlop and W. Galenson (eds), *Labor in the Twentieth Century*, Academic Press, New York.

Shirom, A. and Jacobson, D. (1975) 'The structure and function of Israeli employers' associations', *Relations Industrielles, 30.*

Shorter, E. and Tilly, C. (1974) *Strikes in France 1830–1968*, Cambridge University Press, Cambridge.

Sim, A.B. (1977) 'Decentralized management of subsidiaries and their performance', *Management International Review, 17.*

Sisson, K.F. (1984) *The Management of Collective Bargaining: An International Comparison*, Basil Blackwell, Oxford.

Skeels, J.W. (1982) 'The economic and organizational basis of early United States strikes, 1900–48', *Industrial and Labor Relations Review, 35.*

Slack, E. (1980) 'Plant-level bargaining in France', *Industrial Relations Journal, 11.*

Smelser, N.J. (1967) 'Notes on the methodology of comparative analysis of economic activity', *Social Science Information, 6.*

Smith, D.C. (1980) 'Trade union growth and industrial disputes', in R.E. Caves and L.B. Krause (eds), *Britain's Economic Performance*, Brookings Institution, Washington, D.C.

Smith, D.F. and Turkington, D.J. (1981) 'Testing a behavioural theory of bargaining: An international comparative study', *British Journal of Industrial Relation, 19.*

Snyder, D. (1975) 'Institutional setting and industrial conflict: Comparative analyses of France, Italy and the United States', *American Sociological Review, 40.*

Sorge, A. (1976) 'The evolution of industrial democracy in the countries of the European Community', *British Journal of Industrial Relations, XIV.*

Sorge, A. and Warner, M. (1980) 'The context of industrial relations in Great Britain and West Germany', *Industrial Relations Journal, 11.*

Soskice, D. (1978) 'Strike waves and wage explosions, 1968–1970: An economic interpretation', in C. Crouch and A. Pizzorno (eds), *The Resurgence of Class Conflict in Western Europe Since 1968, 2* (Comparative Studies), Macmillan, London.

Stephens, E.H. (1980) *The Politics of Workers' Participation: The Peruvian Approach in Comparative Perspective*, Academic Press, New York.

Stephens, J.D. (1979) *The Transition from Capitalism to Socialism*, Macmillan, London.

Stern, R.N. (1975) 'Towards an empirical merger: Sociological and economic conceptions of strike activity', Industrial Relations Research Association: *Proceedings*, 28th Annual Meeting.

Stern, R.N. (1978) 'Methodological issues in quantitative strike analysis', *Industrial Relations, 17.*

Stone, K. (1974) 'The origins of job structures in the steel industry', *Review of Radical Political Economics, 6.*

Strauss, G. (1979) 'Workers' participation: Symposium introduction', *Industrial Relations, 18.*

Strauss, G. (1982) 'Bridging the gap between industrial relations and conflict management', in G.B.J. Bomers and R.B. Peterson (eds), *Conflict Management and Industrial Relations*, Kluwer, Boston.

Streeck, W. (1981) 'Qualitative demands and the neo-corporatist manageability of industrial relations', *British Journal of Industrial Relations, 19.*

Strinati, D. (1982) *Capitalism, the State and Industrial Relations*, Croom Helm, London.

Sturmthal, A. (1958) 'The labor movement abroad', in N.W. Chamberlain (ed.), *A Decade of Industrial Relations Research 1946–1956*, Harper, New York.

Taft, P. and Ross, P. (1979) 'American labor violence: Its causes, character and outcome', in H.D. Graham and T.R. Gurr (eds), *Violence in America: Historical and Comparative Perspectives*, Sage, Beverly Hills.

Taira, K. (1973) 'Labor markets, unions and employers in inter-war Japan', in A. Sturmthal and J.G. Scoville (eds). *The international Labor Movement in Transition*, University of Illinois Press, Urbana.

Takamiya, M. (1981) 'Japanese multinationals in Europe: Internal operations and their public policy implications', *Columbia Journal of World Business, XVI.*

Tannenbaum, A.S. Kavić, B., Rosner, M., Vianello, M. and Wesier, G. (1974) *Hierarchy in Organizations*, Jossey-bass, San Francisco.

Thomas, H. and Logan, C. (1982) *Mondragon: An Economic Analysis*, Allen & Unwin, London.

Thompson, M. and Moore, L.F. (1975) 'Managerial attitudes towards industrial relations: A US–Canadian comparison', *Relations Industrielles, 30.*

Thompson, M. and Roxborough, I. (1982) 'Union elections and democracy in Mexico: A comparative perspective', *British Journal of Industrial Relations, XX.*

Thomson, A.W.J. (1981) 'The United States of America' in E. Owen Smith (ed.), *Trade Unions in the Developed Economies*, Croom Helm, London.

Thurley, K. and Wood, S. (eds) (1983) *Industrial Relations and Management Strategy*, Cambridge University Press, Cambridge.

Treckel, K.F. (1972) 'The world auto councils and collective bargaining', *Industrial Relations, 11.*

Treu, T. (1981) 'Italy', in R. Blanpain (ed.), *International Encyclopaedia for Labour Law and Industrial Relations*, Kluwer, Deventer.

Ubeku, A.K. (1983) *Industrial Relations in Developing Countries. The Case of Nigeria*, Macmillan, London.

Ulman, L. (1974a) 'Connective and competitive bargaining', *Scottish Journal of Political Economy, XXI.*

Ulman, L. (1974b) 'The rise of the international union', in R.J. Flanagan and A.R. Weber (eds), *Bargaining Without Boundaries: The Multinational Corporation and International Labor Relations*, University of Chicago Press, Chicago.

Ulmer, M.J. (1980) 'Multinational corporations and Third World capitalism', *Journal of Economic Issues, XIV.*

van de Vall, M. (1970) *Labor Organization. A Macro- and Micro-Sociological Analysis on a Comparative Basis*, Cambridge University Press, Cambridge.

von Beyme, K. (1980) *Challenge to Power: Trade Unions and Industrial Relations in Capitalist Countries*, Sage, London.

Walker, K.F. (1967) 'The comparative study of industrial relations', *Bulletin of the International Institute for Labour Studies*, No. 3.

Walker, K.F. (1970) *Australian Industrial Relations Systems*, Harvard University Press, Cambridge, Mass.

Walker, K.F. (1974) 'Workers' participation in management: Problems, practice and prospects', *Bulletin of the International Institute for Labour Studies*, No. 12.

Walker, K.F. (1976) 'Compulsory arbitration in Australia', in J. Loewenberg, *Compulsory Arbitration. An International Comparison*, Lexington Books, Lexington, Mass.

Walker, K.F. (1977) 'Towards the participatory enterprise: A European trend', *Annals of the American Academy of Political and Social Science, 431.*

Wall, T.D. and Lischeron, J.A. (1977) *Worker Participation: A critique of the Literature and Some Fresh Evidence*, McGraw Hill, London.

Walsh, K. (1983) *Strikes in Europe and the United States: Measurement and Incidence*, Frances Pinter, London.

Warner, M. and Turner, L. (1972) 'Trade unions and the multi-national firm', *Journal of Industrial Relations, 14.*

Waters, M. (1982) *Strikes in Australia*, Allen & Unwin, Sydney.

Weber, A.R. (1963) 'The structure of collective bargaining and bargaining power: Foreign experiences', *Journal of Law and Economics, 6.*

Weber, A.R. (1974) 'Bargaining without boundaries: Industrial relations and the multinational firm', in R.J. Flanagan and A.R. Weber (eds), *Bargaining Without Boundaries: The Multinational Corporation and International Labour Relations*, University of Chicago Press, Chicago.

Wedderburn, D. (1974) 'Perspectives on Sweden', *Personnel Management, 6.*

Wedderburn, Lord (1972) 'Labour law and labour relations in Britain', *British Journal of Industrial Relations, X.*

Wedderburn, Lord. (1982) 'Introduction: A 1912 Overture', in Lord Wedderburn and W.T. Murphy (eds), *Labour Law and the Community: Perspectives for the 1980s*, Institute of Advanced Legal Studies, London.

Wedderburn, Lord (1983) 'Otto Kahn-Freund and British labour law', in Lord Wedderburn, R. Lewis and J. Clark (eds), *Labour Law and Industrial Relations: Building on Kahn-Freund*, Clarendon, Oxford.

Weinburg, P.J. (1978) *European Labor and Multinationals*, Praeger, New York.

Westenholz, A. (1979) 'Workers' participation in Denmark', *Industrial Relations, 18.*

White, M. and Trevor, M. (1983) *Under Japanese Management: The Experience of British Workers*, Heinemann, London.

Whyte, W.F. and Alberti, G. (1977) 'The industrial community in Peru', *Annals of the American Academy of Political and Social Science, 431.*

Wiarda, H.J. (1978) 'Corporative origins of the Iberian and Latin American labor relations systems', *Studies in Comparative International Development, XIII.*

Wilkinson, R. and Burkitt, B. (1973) 'Wage determination and trade unions', *Scottish Journal of Political Economy, XX.*

Willman, P. (1983) *Bargaining for Change: A Comparison of the UK and USA*, University of Durham, Industrial Relations Group, Occasional Paper No. 2.

Windmüller, J.P. (1967) 'Employers and employers' associations in the Netherlands industrial relations system', *Relations Industrielles, 22.*

Windmüller, J.P. (1974) 'European labor and politics: A symposium, II', *Industrial and Labor Relations Review, 28.*

Windmüller, J.P. (1977) 'Industrial democracy and industrial relations', *Annals of the American Academy of Political and Social Science, 431.*

Windmüller, J.P. (1980) *The International Trade Union Movement*, Kluwer, Deventer.

Windmüller, J.P. (1981) 'Concentration trends in union structure: An international comparison', *Industrial and Labor Relations Review, 35.*

Windmüller, J.P. (1984) 'Employers' associations in comparative perspective: Organisation, structure, administration', in J.P. Windmüller and A. Gladstone (eds), *Employers' Associations and Industrial Relations. A Comparative Study*, Clarendon, Oxford.

Worm, P. (1982) Review, *British Journal of Industrial Relations, XX.*

Yarmie, A.H. (1980) 'Employers' organisations in mid-Victorian England', *International Review of Social History, XXV.*

Zeitlin, J. (1983) 'The labour strategies of British engineering employers, 1890–1922', in H.F. Gospel and C.R. Littler (eds), *Managerial Strategies and Industrial Relations*, Heinemann, London.

GENERAL INDEX

The following abbreviations have been used: bargaining for collective bargaining; IR for industrial relations; MNE for multinational enterprise; unions for trade unions.

AUTHOR INDEX